Kristeva's Fiction

SUNY series, Insinuations: Philosophy, Psychoanalysis, Literature

Charles Shepherdson, editor

Kristeva's Fiction

Edited by

BENIGNO TRIGO

SUNY PRESS

On the cover a photographic reproduction of *Judith with the Head of Holofernes* by Luchas Cranach the Elder (1472–1553) courtesy of Vanderbilt University.

Published by State University of New York Press, Albany

Printed in the United States of America

For information, contact State University of New York Press, Albany, NY
www.sunypress.edu

Production by Ryan Morris
Marketing by Kate McDonnell

Library of Congress Cataloging-in-Publication Data

Kristeva's Fiction / edited by Benigno Trigo.
pages cm. — (SUNY series, Insinuations: Philosophy, Psychoanalysis, Literature)
Includes bibliographical references and index.
Summary: "Psychoanalytic perspectives on Kristeva's fiction"—Provided by publisher.
ISBN 978-1-4384-4827-5 (hc : alk. paper) 978-1-4384-4826-8 (pb : alk. paper)
1. Kristeva, Julia, 1941—Criticism and interpretation. 2. Psychoanalysis and literature.
I. Trigo, Benigno, editor of compilation.

PQ2671.R547Z73 2013
843'.914 2012045677

10 9 8 7 6 5 4 3 2 1

Contents

Acknowledgments vii

Introduction 1
Benigno Trigo

PART I

Chapter 1
Whodunit? Reading Kristeva with the Help of Detective Fiction 31
S. K. Keltner

Chapter 2
Revolution Has Italian Roots: Kristeva's Fiction and Theory 45
Carol Mastrangelo Bové

Chapter 3
Not a Country for Old Men: Scapegoats and Sacrifice in Santa Varvara 57
Martha Reineke

Chapter 4
Sebastian's Skull: Establishing the "Society of the Icon" 79
Frances L. Restuccia

Chapter 5
From the Agency of the Letter to the Agency of the Icon: Femininity and Bulgaria in Julia Kristeva's *Murder in Byzantium* 95
Ewa Plonowska Ziarek

PART II

Chapter 6
Noir Analysis: How Kristeva's Detective Novels Renew Psychoanalysis 113
Benigno Trigo

Chapter 7
Fiction, Analysis, Possession, and Violence in Kristeva's Mirror of Writing 125
John Lechte

Chapter 8
Byzantium, or Fiction as Inverted Theory 143
Miglena Nikolchina

Chapter 9
The *Vital* Legacy of the Novel and Julia Kristeva's Fictional Revolt 155
Maria Margaroni

Works Cited 175

Contributors 187

Index 189

Acknowledgments

This book would not have been possible without the love and support of my sweet Kelly.

Thank you to Camille Sutton for her work on the production of the book. Thank you to Charles Shepherdson for his initial interest in the project and for his support and help in the revision process. Thank you to the Museo de Arte de Ponce for permission to use a reproduction of *Judith with the Head of Holofernes* by Lucas Cranach the Elder for the cover of the book.

An earlier version of chapter 6 was originally published in *Cultural Critique* 80 (Winter 2012): 27–55; an earlier version of chapter 8 was originally published in *Lost Unicorns of the Velvet Revolution: Heterotopias of the Seminar* (New York: Fordham University Press, 2012).

Introduction

Kristeva's Fiction is a response to the fact that the doors of the so-called literary temple appear to be opening for Julia Kristeva after the publication of her latest detective novel, *Murder in Byzantium*, in 2004—doors that had been closed for many years (Kristeva 2010, 283). It is a collection of ten original and previously unpublished essays by scholars of Kristeva's work at a time when the critical commentary on Kristeva's novels appears to be increasing. And it is an attempt to fill a gap in the bibliography about her work. Out of thirteen books published in English over the past thirty-four years on the subject of Kristeva's work, only one is dedicated to her fiction (Chen). Of seven anthologies on Kristeva's theoretical work published since 1990, not one has been dedicated to her fiction (see Fletcher and Benjamin; Oliver [1993]; Lechte and Zournazi [1998, 2003]; Crownfield; Oliver and Keltner; and Ziarek and Chanter).

This relative dearth doesn't mean that Kristeva's novels have received no attention at all. In fact, much of Kristeva's fiction has received a negative reception in the popular press; and yet despite this reception, a surprising number of critical articles are dedicated to her fiction. Many of these essays have focused on particular novels, and recently some have evaluated Kristeva's fiction as a whole. *Kristeva's Fiction* attends to this ongoing interest in Kristeva's novels, and to this difference in the reception of her turn to fiction. One might go so far as to say that this collection of essays on Kristeva's fiction is written in the spirit of the strange and paradoxical act of forgiveness that has been the focus of Kristeva's work in recent years: it is an act of encouragement for Kristeva to press on despite the negative judgment of the literary world.

Kristeva's Turn to Fiction

Twenty-two years ago, Julia Kristeva, a renowned linguist and psychoanalyst, published her first novel, *The Samurai*, in 1990. The publication of the novel marked a second important turn in Kristeva's work, this time toward fiction writing. She was initially known for her work in the field of linguistics, particularly after the publication of her thesis *Revolution in Poetic Language* in

1974, where she first developed the influential idea of a "semiotic mode of signification."[1] After undergoing psychoanalytic training between 1974 and 1979, Kristeva changed her theoretical focus and published a series of works including the influential *Powers of Horror* in 1982.[2] Kristeva's turn away from the discipline of linguistics, and toward psychoanalysis, resulted in her development of the concept of "the abject," which also helped her work to cross over into the disciplines of literature and philosophy.[3] Arguably, the concepts of "the semiotic" and "the abject" remain to this day Kristeva's most important contributions to the humanities, and to the social sciences.

Kristeva was a late bloomer to fiction. She published her first novel twenty-one years, and nine books, after her first book: *Séméiotiké: Research Toward a Semanalysis* (1969).[4] Kristeva, the novelist, was forty-nine years old, and characteristically prolific. One year after her first novel appeared, she published *The Old Man and the Wolves* (1991), and five years later she published *Possessions* (1996). And in what seems like an uncharacteristic hiatus in her otherwise constant writing career, Kristeva's next novel appeared eight years later: *Murder in Byzantium* was published in 2004. Although Kristeva has promised another detective novel, as of the writing of this volume, she has not published it yet.

Chronologically (and perhaps conceptually as well), Kristeva's decision to write novels in the 1990s followed from her focus on melancholia in the '80s. In 1985, Ina Lipkowitz and Andrea Loselle ask Kristeva, "are you thinking of writing a novel?" and Kristeva answers, "Maybe someday. For the moment, though, I do not see it happening. I am currently doing research on melancholia . . ." (Kristeva 1996, 34). Notably, after her first novel comes out, many of her interviewers repeatedly ask her, "why a novel?" During an interview with Josyane Savigneau published in the French daily *Le Monde* in 1990, Kristeva gives two answers to that question. Her first answer seems perfunctory. She says she writes her novel in response to a request for an essay on her intellectual generation. But after a rather mechanical explanation justifying her decision to write a novel rather than an essay, Kristeva adds a more personal reason, almost as an afterthought: "And, to write fiction is a more genuine integration to the French language than any theoretical writing," she says (Savigneau, 19; all translations are my own, unless otherwise specified). At the end of the interview, Kristeva is quoted again as saying that by writing a novel she has accomplished "a long attempt to become French where integration and 'estrangement' coexist" (Savigneau, 20).

Over the years, Kristeva has given many interviews, where she has been asked the same question, "why a novel?" Curiously, Kristeva has not returned to her first answers to this question, focusing instead on the relation between her fiction and her psychoanalytic practice and theory. These later answers can be summarized into three related groups that eventually take us back to her initial response. The first group of answers brings Kristeva's novels back to her work with melancholy patients rather than to her research on melancholia. Kristeva answers that her fiction is a response to the psychoanalytic session. More specifically, fiction acts for her as an antidote to the depressing effect of encountering the disillusioned knowledge of her patients. It gives her the energy, renewal, and revitalization necessary to continue her psychoanalytic work as an analyst: "When I wrote *The Samurai* I believed that working on the novel would allow me to continue listening to my patients in a way that was attentive, inventive, and receptive to them and to their symptoms," she says in a 1990 interview with Elisabeth Bélorgey (Kristeva 1996g, 251). The second group of answers to the question "why a novel?" suggests that writing fiction is an advanced, progressive, and perhaps speedier way into the unconscious, for Kristeva: "In comparison, the ability of theoretical discourse to take on *métaphore* and intrigue seemed to be far behind the form of the novel," she says in a 1992 interview with Bernard Sichère, suggesting that by giving form and enacting the essence of the unconscious, fiction takes her further in her thinking than theory (Kristeva 1996c, 164).

But it is only in a later interview with Pierre-Louis Fort, conducted in 2005, and only in an oblique way, that Kristeva returns to her first answer to the question "why a novel?" In that interview, Kristeva again suggests that her fiction is an effect of the psychoanalytic session; but rather than an antidote against the depressive effects of therapy on the analyst, or a more progressive way to the unconscious, Kristeva instead suggests that fiction is a "propitious place" generated by the transference and countertransference with her patients (2010, 297). In keeping with her latest work on forgiveness, Kristeva describes her fiction as an oneiric and safe place that is not judgmental, and that is a necessary complement both to her own ambivalent relationship to her origins and to her violation of a certain trust.[5] Suggesting that her "integration" to both France and to the European Union, as well as the fact that she rarely speaks Bulgarian (a language that she no longer knows how to write) is a "betrayal," Kristeva describes her fiction as a liberation from the daily discipline that ensures her assimilation.[6] She says, "I am made of this Orthodox sensibility, and if I discipline it in the daytime, I am submerged in it at night: my unconscious is an Orthodox land enveloped by a French atmosphere" (2010, 301).

In this sense, Kristeva's decision to write novels becomes the obverse of the so-called betrayal of her Orthodox past and opens a space for the paradoxical return of a mother tongue that she no longer writes. Describing the language of Stephanie Delacour (the narrator of her novels and her alter ego), Kristeva says, "she does not inhabit the phonemes and syntax of the French language . . . but she writes the melody of the sensory that flows beneath her sentences" (2010, 301). Fiction writing then becomes for Kristeva a complement to the "integration to the French language" that she had sought fifteen years earlier. In other words, Kristeva's decision to write fiction becomes an act that neither fights, nor submits to, her "betrayal," that is, to her integration and assimilation into another culture. From this perspective, Kristeva's decision to write novels is an act of psychoanalytic forgiveness, or what Kristeva calls a pardon (*par*, through; *don*, a gift), that interprets, or elaborates in writing, her "betrayal," an unconscious hate that makes Kristeva betray her origins.

It is reasonable to say that Kristeva's turn to fiction has not been well received, particularly when it is compared to the reception of her turn to psychoanalysis. When Fort points out in 2005 that after three novels, "the doors to the literary temple . . . opened for *Murder in Byzantium*," Kristeva answers, "The 'literary world' disgusts me, and I hear the bluntness of that remark, but why retract it? I will never be part of that world, and it doesn't want me either" (2010, 283). Kristeva's rejection of the "literary world" makes it clear that she is sensitive to the way her novels have been read despite her claim in an interview from 1992 that she is not concerned with whether her novels attract readers, and in spite of her remark that "it is enough [for her] that the novel is disturbing" (Kristeva 1996c, 166). Given Kristeva's description of her fiction as a forgiving response to her choice to make a life in the culture and language of France, it is perhaps understandable that she replies with anger to her exclusion from the "literary world" of that country.

But Kristeva's response also contains a number of interesting refusals that take her comments beyond the expression of a defensive anger. First of all, Kristeva refuses to accept Fort's characterization of her reception by the "literary world." She is aware that she has not been well received, and she is prepared to face this fact. Kristeva also refuses to heed the judgment of the "literary world" about her novels. Indeed, it is a credit to Kristeva that she has continued to write novels despite the sometimes virulent nature of the reaction of the popular press to her fiction, and to *The Samurai* in particular (more on this later). And Kristeva also aims the refusal at herself. She says that she will not stop herself from expressing her "disgust" for the "literary world" despite her contradictory feelings about her own words. "I hear the bluntness of that remark, but why retract it?" she asks herself. Hatred, like forgiveness, should also have its say, she seems to say. And the anger she now aims at herself further suggests that Kristeva might be referring here not only to the French "literary world," but also to the world of her words, to the world of her fiction, and perhaps even to the ambivalence she clearly feels toward the mother tongue at the origin of her fiction writing. From this perspective, one wonders whether Kristeva's refusal to silence an anger that is aimed both at the judgment by the other, and at her own words, also requires an act of forgiveness: to forgive a disturbance, a hatred, and a feeling of disgust, all of which seems to give rise to her singular voice.

Kristeva's Novels

Kristeva publishes her first two novels *The Samurai*, in 1990, and *The Old Man and the Wolves*, in 1991. *The Samurai* narrates the interconnected lives, adventures, and transformations of three women (Olga Morena, Carole Benedetti, and Joëlle Cabarus) living in Paris, over a period of twenty years, from the student revolts of 1968 to the beginning of the AIDS epidemic at the end of the eighties. It describes their active participation in the intellectual debates, social and cultural turmoil of the times, and traces some of the implications of the latter for their lives and loves with changing partners, which comprise a varied roster of men including a novelist, a professor, a painter, and a psychiatrist, among others. Most importantly, it follows the development of two of these women into writers: Joëlle, a psychoanalyst, and Olga, a graduate student in linguistics and literature.

The Samurai engages with contemporary political events and finds their origins in "an unknown force that causes us to act" (Kristeva 1992, 43). Published in 1990, three years after the end of a period of "Cohabitation" (1986–1988) between the Socialist president François Mitterand and the right-wing prime minister Jacques Chirac, the novel reinscribes the events of 1968 into the political landscape of France at a time when (Kristeva tells us) political leaders "didn't want people to link the disruption of France in 1968 and the socialist victory of 1981" (2002c, 14). From this angle, the novel also reads as a reevaluation of the legacy of 1968 for the steady move of the country to the political center, together with the marginalization of the Communist Party, implicitly arguing against the opinion that "attributes to '68 the economic crisis and unemployment which ravaged families, especially the least well-off ones" (2002c, 28). It is a personal and a critical account, written as a *roman à clef*, of events that contain for Kristeva the complex message of 1968 that "We aren't done with deciphering" (2002c, 28).[7] In fact, the anamnesic exercise results in a meditation about writing as a means to access a force, an energy, and a rhythm that is described as a "seizure" in the novel and that seems to drive both the private struggles and the public duels of French intellectuals like Olga Morena, and perhaps Julia Kristeva. But the novel can be also read as a summary of the past, a settling of accounts in an effort to prepare for what is to come. From this perspective, the pessimistic tone and abrupt ending of the novel is also an expression of skepticism regarding the ability of sublime forms of utopian and masterful forms of engagement with this force (perhaps exemplified by the events of 1968), as well as an implicit call to write, act, and analyze in a different way.[8]

Kristeva changes the direction of her writing in *The Old Man and the Wolves*, away from the *roman à clef* and toward the genre of detective fiction. Juliana de Nooy emphasizes the search for truth in Freudian psychoanalysis and detective fiction as developed first by Edgar Allan Poe: "Both psychoanalysis and detective fiction promote an interpretative practice that is attentive to clues, to the uncanny, and to the pathological. Both seek truth through the rehearsal of past events" (1998, 47–48). But Stephanie's theory of crime is slightly different from this practice. She says it is "something like 'The Murders in the Rue Morgue'" (1994, 177). And indeed, Kristeva through Stephanie will criticize a disembodied view of language and truth, and the mode of analysis leading to it. Stephanie's reference to "The Murders in the Rue Morgue" signals Kristeva's account of language and truth as embodied still, as still troubled by contradictory passions and disturbing sensations, as well as Kristeva's own development of a mode of analysis (or detection) informed and sustained by the passions and sensations of the body.[9]

Similar to *The Samurai*, *The Old Man* has implications for historical events. Published in 1991 after the death of her father in a Bulgarian hospital shortly before the fall of the Berlin Wall in 1989, *The Old Man* picks up where her first novel (published only a year earlier) leaves off. As allegory, the novel can be interpreted to demystify a turning point in the history of the Cold War, and to bear witness to an increase in violence that paradoxically results from the historical fall of the wall (see Bové, 123). *The Old Man* represents the reach of the unleashed violence, which kills the symbolic father, the master analyst of Freudian psychoanalysis represented by Septicius Clarus, and makes it necessary to think again about the sources and origins of the violence, as well as about the best way to approach it. The novel also dramatizes the birth of a phoenix from these ashes, the emergence of the first-person narrative voice and character of Stephanie, a different kind of investigator and analyst who does not shy away from crime, evil, and violence, but rather finds her own origins as a detective in Dupin's animal thinking, and in the Ourang-Outang's sadomasochistic repetition of an earlier scene with his master. Moreover, Stephanie becomes a detective who is prepared to talk about a mother tongue that she traces back to the sadomasochistic embrace and flagellation at the center of Poe's story.

As the title of Kristeva's next detective novel suggests, *Possessions* (1996) continues the investigation of the widespread "killer instinct" that drives the dueling characters of *The Samurai*, and the haunting passion at the center of *The Old Man*. This second installment of the adventures of the journalist-cum-detective, Stephanie, transforms the earlier instinct and sordid passion into a "spirit" or "demon" that possesses the inhabitants of the fictional Santa Varvara and drives them first to murder, and then to decapitate, Stephanie's friend, Gloria Harrison (not unlike the Ourang-Outang disposes of the mother in Poe's story, Madame L'Espanaye). In later works, Kristeva suggests that this spirit is also an image of decapitation that possesses her as well as her mother. She states that she wrote the novel after being possessed by a decapitated woman (1998d, 45), that she is the headless woman in the novel (2002c, 70), and that the fantasy goes back to a drawing by her mother that she often remembers (1998d, 13). Kristeva goes on to suggest that the novel works through this possession by coming closer to its disturbing image, by becoming more familiar with it, by studying and analyzing it like a detective in a *roman noir*.[10]

Similar to the two previous novels, *Possessions* is also inflected by contemporary history and politics, even as the novel interrogates the sources of both. Kristeva writes the novel during a decade of consolidation by the extreme right in France. It is published in 1996, one year after the National Front, presided by Jean-Marie Le Pen, "sets a new record for the far right in a French national election," rising to prominence on a wave of anti-immigration sentiment by garnering 15 percent of the vote in the first round of the 1995 presidential election (Shields, 251). Significantly, the political platform of the National Front included reinstating capital punishment after its abolition in 1981, and it influenced the focus of the eventual winner, conservative Jacques Chirac, who turned his attention to "immigration, crime, and national identity" (Shields, 252, 258). Stephanie's investigation of the decapitation of her foreigner friend Gloria can be interpreted as an investigation not only of this growing anti-immigration sentiment, but most importantly of the widespread turn "to crime," and of the wish to return to capital punishment by French society. In an essay on the visual representations of the guillotine during the French Revolution, Kristeva states that the death penalty is synonymous with decapitation in France, and that both "sinister events" are examples of what she calls "works in *noir*": prehistoric acting-out rituals that include the totemic feast (1998d, 102). For Kristeva, the erasure of the guillotine from the national consciousness has paradoxically prepared its return in full force, and a novel like *Possessions* reads partly as an attempt to analyze the origin and the fantasies of a "killer instinct" that leads a majority of the population in 1972, and then again in 1993, to express support for the death penalty (1998d, 107).[11] From this perspective, the novel is an investigation into the way to control or cope with this insistent desire, not by disavowing it, but by representing it, by learning to speak its sinister language. Such investigations into what Stephanie calls the language of the mother's womb, can (paradoxically) set the conditions of possibility for a different social, cultural, and political beginning, one unlike the rudimentary and impoverished state that follows orgies of violence such as the guillotine or the death penalty. This beginning would be based instead on both Stephanie's linguistic analysis, and on the representation of a dark possession that leads to the matricide and decapitation of an innocent foreigner.

More so than in her earlier novels, narrators and readers alike of *Murder in Byzantium* (2004) repeatedly find themselves asking the question "Where am I?" (2006b, 234). Maria Margaroni answers by claiming that we are in melancholy contemplation of death in the form of widespread crime, which paradoxically succeeds in animating redemptive hope in us (2009, 117).[12] But if the novel places us at a crossing that produces hope, this hope depends on something other than crime or death. There is something alive (if strangely so) at this crossroads for Kristeva. There is a trace of life, a miasma-like remainder, the *ignis fatuus* from a dead sensation, the revolting material of the lost mother tongue, that Stephanie's "gruesome" (2006b, 118) form of detection reveals as a "*feu follet*" (a will-o-the-wisp) (2005c, 129). In *Murder* Kristeva tells the reader of the growing need to spin out fantasies from this seemingly intractable and expanding darkness. And analysis in the novel is both a police investigation, and a form that this fantasy can take: a turbulent (rhythmic) voyage or journey through the landscape of the psyche in an effort to rewrite meaning back into it. From this perspective, both Santa Varvara and Byzantium become versions of Freud's Eternal City (1989, 726), and inversions of his infamous "dark continent" (Kristeva 2004b, 27). (Indeed, Kristeva's "mother tongue" can be interpreted as an inversion of Freud's unintelligible "Minoan-Mycenaean," an inversion that turns on the signifying point of darkness.) In short, *Murder* shows the way in which the unconscious processes screened by the obscure spaces of *noir* detective fiction can return meaning to the depleted life of Santa Varvara's inhabitants.

Murder (2004) is published three years after the attacks by Al Qaeda in 2001, which destroyed the World Trade Center in New York City, and one year after the 2003 invasion of Iraq by the United States and a "coalition of the willing," which caused much damage to that Middle Eastern country and fractured the former alliance between the United States and the European community. As such, *Murder* broadens Kristeva's analysis in *Possessions* of what she calls the "national depression" and its "manic manifestation in [French] nationalism" (2004b, 22) to include an analysis of the symptoms of what she calls "our dark times," and in particular of the underlying causes of the so-called "clash of religions" (2006c, 16) or the "clash between fundamentalisms" represented by these geopolitical events (2004b, 32). Again, Kristeva's literary work takes us back to the meaning of the "killer instinct," the "dark passions," or the "demons" in the earlier novels. Here it is imagined as a question of place, the question of the point of negativity, instability, and reversibility that I study in chapter 6 of this collection and that is at the origins of characters like Sebastian Chrest-Jones and Xiao Chang (a bastard and a foreigner, respectively).

The Book Reviews

All of Kristeva's novels have been translated into English within a short period of their publication in French, and they have all received a fair amount of attention in the popular press, both in French and in English.[13] Most of the attention by the international media has been extended (so far) on Kristeva's first novel, with reviews and interviews in Paris's *Le Monde*, London's *Times Literary Supplement* and *The Independent*, as well as New York's *The Village Voice* (see Savigneau; Showalter; Hughes-Hallet; and Gehr). Notably, her later novels have not received the same kind, or the same amount, of attention. Perhaps this relative lack of interest in her later novels is explained by the fact that the reception that the international media gave Kristeva's first novel was not positive. Indeed, it would be generous to characterize it as mixed, abounding as it was in left-handed compliments like Lucy Hughes-Hallet's remark, "Philip Roth (who has a walk-on part in *The Samurai*) has called Sollers 'an intellectual clown,' and Kristeva too, combines a formidable brain with a certain playfulness" (26). More characteristic of the scathing tone of the majority of the reviews of Kristeva's novels is the opening sentence of Richard Gehr's review of novels by Kristeva and Sollers: "What a couple of remarkable sellouts" (S31). In fact, much of the negativity directed at Kristeva's first novel seemed to be the result of her association with Philippe Sollers (her husband) and with the intellectual group that she portrayed in that first book, as suggested by Elaine Showalter's ironic description of Kristeva as "one of the most versatile stars of the international post-structuralist circuit" (1038).[14]

There have been fewer reviews of Kristeva's later novels, but they have been somewhat less critical than those of *The Samurai*. In fact, both *Possessions* and *Murder in Byzantium* have received some positive reviews (Irvine 1998; Hooper; Gleize; and Thorne). And as we have seen, Fort has even suggested that "the doors to the literary temple" opened for Kristeva's latest novel, referring to its reception in *Le Monde*, *La Vie*, *La Croix*, *Le Point*, and *Metropolis*. However, a broader look at the reviews of Kristeva's novels still reveals a mixed reception at best, and one that tends to describe them as reactionary, difficult to read, and boring.

Politically, many reviewers consider Kristeva's novels to be conservative on several counts. These include a suspicion of the autobiographical nature of much of her fiction, which is interpreted as a turn away from social and political concerns (see Judt; Steinberg). Both Hughes-Hallet and Gehr consider Kristeva to have sold out to Western European bourgeois values and implicitly appear to criticize her turn away from her Eastern European upbringing under Communism. Others, more "feminist" in their approach, find a nostalgic, if not reactionary, return to the family, motherhood, and the patriarchy in her novels (see Donadey; Hite). From a stylistic point of view, some reviewers complain that her novels do not satisfy the reader's desire for succinct and direct prose, referring to Kristeva's forays into history or philosophy as boring digressions that one reviewer describes as "breathless blather" (Zipp). Others describe her novels as poorly crafted, either because they breach the strict conventions of a literary genre, or because they do not meet the reviewers' expectations of verisimilitude. Declaring herself to be a lover "of realist novels like Balzac's, Stendhal's and Flaubert's," Kaylie Jones of the *Los Angeles Times* lets out a "yawn of boredom" after reading *The Samurai* (Jones; see also Irvine 1994; Enjolras; and Rubin).

Perhaps the negative reception by the popular press of Kristeva's novels can be explained, in part, as the shortcomings of a book market driven by economic forces that put a premium on so-called liberal ideas, simple pleasures, and clarity, the latter understood as a transparency achieved by staying close to familiar conventions. But the truth is that Kristeva's *theory* is also often criticized by feminist and post-feminist critics of being politically conservative, and it is also the target of a broader cultural impatience with the substance and style of so-called high theory in general, and of psychoanalysis in particular—including, by the way, the theoretical approach of those who criticize Kristeva's theoretical work.[15] In his book review, Michael Wood points out the "tragic sense of life" that runs through Kristeva's *Old Man and the Wolves* as well as through two books by her on Marcel Proust. Wood calls their harshness both "cozy" and "unadventurous" and states that "Lukács spoke of modern philosophers as living comfortably in the Grand Hotel of the abyss; the Freudian story can look like setting up house in a rat-trap" (18).

It might be accurate to say that Kristeva's poor reception by the popular media is a reaction to the theoretical and psychoanalytic content of Kristeva's novels. Most reviewers don't see, or comment on, the connection between the novels and the theory, but nevertheless it seems to influence their descriptions of her novels as obscure, ponderous, and boring. Many reviewers have instead focused on putting Kristeva's novels in a literary context. Despite some minor disagreement, they place the first novel within the genre of the *roman à clef* and the rest within detective fiction. Characteristically, most reviewers have negatively compared Kristeva's novels to two successful examples of both genres: Simone de Beauvoir's award-winning *The Mandarins*, 1954, and Umberto Eco's bestseller *The Name of the Rose*, 1984.[16]

Despite the generally unfavorable reception by the popular press of Kristeva's novels, it seems to have had a generally positive effect on the academic community, which has rushed in to fill the gap opened by the reviews and has responded by sometimes elaborating and sometimes defending the novels from the objections raised by the reviewers. As we will see further on, much critical commentary on Kristeva's fiction has focused on establishing the connections between her theory and her fiction. Often the critics have sought to explain the so-called reactionary turn inward, her interest in the psychology of patriarchy, and her turn away from direct political commentary by reading her fiction from the perspective of her psychoanalytic theory. They have also elaborated on the literary context of Kristeva's novels, sometimes placing the novels in surprising literary fields. In short, one could argue that the overall negative reception of Kristeva's fiction in the popular press might have had the unlikely effect of stimulating a different and perhaps more thoughtful engagement by the academic community.

The Academic Critics

Twenty years after Kristeva published *The Samurai*, academic critics are beginning to take stock of the reception of her fiction, and their assessment is twofold. They claim that critics have neglected Kristeva's fiction for the most part and that those that have paid attention are confused by it (see Chen, 19; Greaney, 294). Some, like Bianca Rus, have gone so far as to make the more extreme claim that Kristeva's "fiction has been conspicuously neglected, if not completely ignored" (2010a, 16). Noting the "perplexity" of the few critics who read her novels, Rus also describes their reactions as marked by "confusion and frustration" (16). My study of more than twenty-five book reviews could be said to contradict both claims, since Kristeva's fiction has received substantial attention from the media and from the international press, and rather than express confusion or frustration, the attention has been straightforwardly negative for the most part. What is to be made, however, of the reception by the academic community? Is the assessment of neglect and confusion an accurate description of how critics in academic journals have read Kristeva's fiction?

On the subject of strict quantity, the more than twenty academic articles I examined in preparation for this introduction appear to contradict the assessment of the critics. There is some truth to their claim, however, if by "confusion" the critics mean that the reviewers in the popular press mostly give a negative assessment of the novels (some going so far as to caricaturize them), while the studies by the critics in the academic journals tend toward a more serious, sustained, and forgiving approach to the novels, one that suggests a more positive reception. Contrary to the way Kristeva's novels have been read in the popular press, most of the readings of Kristeva's novels from academic journals insist on their link with her theory in general, and with her psychoanalytic theory in particular. One could even describe some of these academic readings of Kristeva's novels as oblique apologias of her theory, defending Kristeva against the accusation (both in the popular press and in academic journals) that her theory is amoral and even reactionary, an accusation perhaps best represented by Wood, who writes in the *London Review of Books* "Stephanie Delacour . . . believes that . . . We need not good and evil but the difference between them. This isn't 'essentially amoral,' it's just alarmingly reactionary" (18).

Much of the critical commentary about Kristeva's novels is more informed about (and more sympathetic to) her overall psychoanalytic project than the reviews. And much of it also appears to be written in answer to the similar critiques of Kristeva's theory that appeared in academic journals between 1989 and 1990, by Judith Butler, Teresa de Lauretis, and Nancy Fraser, all of them written before the publication of Kristeva's first novel (see Brooksbank, 2; Kolocotroni, 149; Kirkby, 109; and Rus 2010a, 15–16). For these academic readers familiar with Kristeva's psychoanalytic theory, the practice of writing fiction is therapeutic at a personal level, but more significantly, it is also loaded (some might say fraught) with social and political implications.[17] Thus, Colin Davis suggests that Kristeva's fiction is a "gift of meaning" that helps us to confront, displace, and forgive our individual and social criminal desires, and her novels represent Kristeva's encouragement of individuals to heal their communities one story at a time. Davis also interprets the novels as a call for a broader social commitment to encourage and support the act of storytelling: "The profusion of narratives and the effects of transference whereby each story becomes the story of another correspond to the analyst's gift of meaning. Through this gift, something like the understanding of the other can be achieved," Davis concludes (2002, 304).

From this perspective the writing of fiction in general, and of Kristeva's analytical or psychoanalytic mode of fiction writing in particular, can be a gift, a cure, a return to the act of imagination, fantasy, and representation, though, for some it can also be a *pharmakon* delivering us to our self-destructive drives and to an illusion of clarity and revelation. But for the most part, academic critics see a certain antidote in Kristeva's writing. They see Kristeva's novels as a mode of treatment for an individual (and for a collectivity) that suffers from a psychosocial melancholy, which stems in part from a depressive economy at the foundation of subjectivity (itself imbued with what Freud called the death instinct), but also in part from the pulverizing catastrophes of the twentieth century (e.g., Hiroshima, Auschwitz, the Gulag, and 9/11). Following Kristevan psychoanalysis, most of these critics believe that these traumatic and catastrophic experiences have carbonized the imaginary. That is, they have shut down our ability to imagine, to elaborate our constitutive traumatic experiences, threatening instead to destroy the antidote necessary to overcome the trauma of being in general, but also the particular nature of the trauma that the speaking subject suffers due to sexual difference, and thanks to the effect of this difference on our relations to the maternal body.[18] Both for Kristeva, and for these academic critics, the act of writing and reading (and of writing and reading what Kristeva calls "poetical detective novels") becomes the origin of (and the necessary condition for) all other ethical and political acts (Kristeva 2004, 119). By putting us in contact with an other (who is also in ourselves), the act of writing and reading offers the promise of renewal, and psychoanalytic forgiveness, necessary to overcome the trauma of our death instinct and the catastrophes of the twentieth century.[19] As Davis suggests, Kristeva's novels are proof of the fact that "the desire to kill is not the last word," at least not yet (304).

For many of these critics, Kristeva's novels are laboratories for personal therapy where the writer gets in touch (so to speak) with her death drive, or at least keeps open the border to the bodily drives (Kolocotroni; Tidmarsh; de Nooy; and Greaney). They are critiques of, and antidotes for, the society of the spectacle, critiques and antidotes based on self-analysis (Brooksbank). From their perspective, Kristeva's novels can restore to health the social "paternal function"[20] by insisting on a retelling of our myths (Margaroni 2008); they can change the view of Europe by generating new allegorical illusions (Kirkby; Margaroni 2009); they can remap our cultural memory by displacing and translating the unconscious (Rus 2010a); they can restructure and repair our relationship with our fundamental separations, breaks, and splits, including those from the mother tongue (de Nooy; Raoul); they can be acts of forgiveness beyond the death instinct—and beyond the violence that is at the origins of our selves and of our social bonds according to psychoanalysis (Davis), and as such they can move us toward an ethics based on compassion, or a humanism based on forgiveness, an ethics and a humanism that accommodates the exiled nature of the human experience (Smith 1997).

While this overall positive assessment puts the academic critics at odds with the reviewers of Kristeva's fiction, there are important points of agreement between them as well. Not surprisingly, and given the psychoanalytic approach of many of these critics, they agree with the reviewers that the nature of Kristeva's novels is profoundly autobiographical. But the critical commentary has also developed an aspect of Kristeva's autobiographical fiction that is absent from the reviews. These critics focus on the references in Kristeva's novels to her vexed identity, to her separation from her country of origin, and to her disturbing mother tongue, calling attention to the political problems of assimilation and exile that these references suggest (de Nooy; Agoston-Nikolova; and Raoul). Some of these critics put Kristeva's fiction in the literary context of exile novels by Nancy Huston and Ilija Trojanow (Raoul; Agoston-Nikolova). Others apply Kristeva's theoretical notion of the semiotic to the linguistic experience of bilingual code-switching in the United States (Kraver). Not surprisingly, this critical assessment of Kristeva's fiction appears after border studies and bilingualism became legitimate fields of study in the United States, and after the publication of *Possessions* in 1996, a novel about the beheading of a translator.[21]

Similarly, Juliana de Nooy writes about Kristeva's novels in the context of Kristeva's theory of translation of bodily drives, comparing the vexed experience of moving from one language to another to the similarly disturbing movement between semiotic and symbolic modes of signification. E. Agoston-Nikolova interprets Kristeva's novel in the context of a nomadic experience caused by political and economic upheavals like the rise and fall of Communism under the Soviet Union. She points to the healing power of the novels that dramatize the suffering of the émigré, as well as the construction of an identity based on something other than the mother tongue. Also Valerie Raoul similarly puts Kristeva's novel in the context of bilingualism, and suggests that there might be a relation of identity between Kristeva's concept of matricide and her acquisition of another language.

All of these academic critics echo Kristeva's own account of her novels in her interviews, as well as Kristeva's account of writing in the detective mode, as an investigation of the genesis of writing (Kristeva 2004, 119). From Kristeva's perspective, the writer is a melancholy analyst who investigates the genesis of her own writing, which is nothing short of an investigation into the origins of our selves, and of our social bonds. Like Freud in the story of the primal horde in *Totem and Taboo*, Kristeva finds a crime at the center of her stories of investigation. However, Kristeva also suggests in her interviews that the crime might not be so much the murder of the Father as the betrayal of the mother tongue, and that the writer forgives this betrayal even as she repeats it in her fiction. In this way, fiction writing for Kristeva has the potential of turning betrayal into renewal in a foreign language. Kristeva has referred to this process as a necessary translation but also as a graft and a transfusion of the remains of the mother tongue onto the foreign language: "It is this double of language . . . that I have tried to translate . . . through the detective story," she says (Kristeva 2010, 301).

The critical commentary on Kristeva's novels also reveals some persistent gaps in the commentary about her fiction. Perhaps one of the most intriguing of these *lacunae* concerns the theme of matricide in Kristeva's practice of fiction writing, and particularly in relation to her first novel. While *The Samurai* has elicited the most (and the most negative) responses from the international and popular press, it has received little critical attention in academic journals.[22] Most of the critical commentary has focused instead on Kristeva's later detective fiction, and while the assessment of these novels has been favorable for the most part, the criticism surrounding *The Samurai* is not only sparse, but it is also negative. In fact, the negative assessment of Kristeva's first novel is one of the few points in which there is agreement between the reviewers in the popular press and the critics in the academic journals.

In her essay, Davis refers to her preference for Kristeva's detective novels. She explains her relative lack of interest in *The Samurai* by pointing to the nature of the *roman à clef* as a genre based on facts (2002, 299). She suggests that as a critic interested in psychoanalysis she is less interested in facts than in the fantasies that we weave around the facts, and also in our ability to continue to produce such fantasies. But this explanation of her preference fails to convince mainly because it is based on a strict difference between the factual and the fantastic elaboration of those facts in literature that should be suspect to a psychoanalytic critic. Indeed, from the perspective of the psychoanalytic critic, a meaningful gray area separates fact from fiction, and the *roman à clef* should be just as interesting to her as the detective novel, if not more so, given the conventional disavowal of the porosity of this border by the autobiographical genre.

Perhaps a more convincing explanation of Davis's preference (and of the similar preference of many academic critics) might be that *The Samurai* resists the reading that academic critics rehearse and repeat. In other words, *The Samurai* is not as willing an object of what Kelly Oliver has called a psychoanalytic social theory as her later detective novels seem to be (see 2003, *passim*). That is, Kristeva's first novel appears to be resistant to a psychoanalytic social theory that defines fiction writing as an act that has a political effect on both the individual and society; or as a laboratory of writing, where the writer puts herself at risk; or as a journey to the dark continent of the unconscious as Kristeva might put it, where the antidote to our maladies might be found. Instead, *The Samurai* might read more like an example of a novel rigorously orchestrated to defend the self from such inquiries into the unconscious. It is, after all, a novel that looks back to a lost time, with more nostalgia than irony, with more regret and bitterness than self-awareness and self-criticism.

More to the point, *The Samurai* can be interpreted as a novel that performs a foundational matricide that the scanty criticism about it has seen, and described, but whose function has yet to be fully understood. Like the reviews before them, much of the criticism about the novel centers on the fact that *The Samurai* is Kristeva's reply to de Beauvoir's novel *The Mandarins*. And much of the criticism has argued that Kristeva's novel (sometimes described as if it were a copy) falls short of the accomplishments of the "original." But from the perspective of Kristeva's theory of matricide, and from her comments about the poetical detective novel, *The Samurai* should also be fertile ground for a study of the novel that searches for a symbolic matricide within it, that is necessary for the beginning of Kristeva's writing. From this perspective, *The Samurai* could be the novel that not only hides the "true crime" behind the mask of the *roman à clef*, but it also would be the foundational act that the subsequent detective novels both hide and reveal. That is, the first novel might best represent the matricide that the later novels elaborate, filled as they are with repeating references to symbolic parricides and castrations. Moreover, if *The Samurai* were understood as a foundational symbolic matricide giving birth to Kristeva's fiction writing, it also could be interpreted as the similarly abject pretext to Kristeva's writing in a social-psychoanalytic mode. Perhaps this symbolic matricide at the center of *The Samurai*, Kristeva's betrayal of the original novel by de Beauvoir, but also her matricide in writing of her predecessor as an author, makes the novel universally unpalatable, mocked as it is, by the reviewers, and ignored as it is, by most of the academic critics. Kristevan psychoanalysis suggests that it is difficult if not impossible to face the matricide at the center of our speaking subjectivity, and that we resort to all kinds of perversions to work through it. And it is a credit to Kristeva's focus, self-determination, and understanding of the vexed nature of our matricidal selves that she continues to write fiction even after the universally negative reaction to her first novel.

There are other points of agreement between the book reviews and the academic criticism, including a general consensus regarding the literary genres to which Kristeva's novels belong (i.e., the *roman à clef* and the detective novel), although the criticism has developed subtle differences within the genres. Regarding the *roman à clef*, for example, the most compelling critical readings place the novel within the more specific and limited frame of the French intellectual novel, which includes not only *The Mandarins*, but also *The Uprooted* by Maurice Barrès, *The Order* by Marcel Arland, *The Conspiracy* by Paul Nizan, and *The Side of the Angels* by Jean Louis Curtis (see Renard; Atack). Regarding the detective genre, Davis places the novels in the context of modernist and postmodern writers such as Alain Robbe-Grillet, Michel Butor, Patrick Modiano, Daniel Pennac, and Marguerite Duras, all of whom were similarly attracted to the genre of detective fiction but only to confound its promise of meaning-making. Nilsson's comparison of Kristeva's novels to similar Byzantine murder mysteries, including Umberto Eco's *Baudolino* (2001) and Panagiotis Agapitos's *The Ebony Lute* (2003), is both compelling and convincing. Finally, there is a group of critics that places Kristeva's novels in altogether different genres and traditions including the allegorical novel and the patristic tradition (see Kirkby; O'Grady; Margaroni 2009; and West).

Should we conclude, then, that Kristeva's fiction has been neglected or ignored, as some academic critics have noted? The fact is that Kristeva's fiction has received some attention by academic critics, though not as much as the attention it has received from reviewers in the popular press, and less attention by far than the academic critics have devoted to Kristeva's *theory*.[23] Still, the respectable quantity of academic criticism devoted to her novels (one book and more than twenty essays over nineteen years), and the sophisticated nature of the analysis, would seem to suggest that academic critics have neither neglected nor ignored Kristeva's novels. The so-called confusion might be the result of mixing together the readings of two very different audiences publishing in two different venues: the popular press and the academic journal. Indeed, it seems that while most book reviewers are frustrated by the presence of theory in Kristeva's novels, many academic critics are instead frustrated by novels that are not "Kristevan enough." For example, Levenson asks, "where is the shock to father's law?" (22).[24] Because of a resistance to theory in general and to psychoanalytic theory in particular, book reviewers have tended to read Kristeva's fiction as narcissistic and self-celebratory, as apolitical at best and reactionary at worst. Academic critics, who are more receptive to both, have tended to see an attempt to explore and critique the self in Kristeva's fiction. And following the implications for our civilization and its discontents, psychoanalytic critics insist that Kristeva's fiction has political implications for the larger society because it helps us to confront the vexed desires at the origins of our social bonds, and because it helps us to tend to their potentially deadly effects, both on the individual and on the social collective.

Most book reviews have pointed to the autobiographical nature of the novels as evidence of Kristeva's ideological shortcomings, whether she is described as apolitical, antifeminist, or bourgeois. Most academic critics, on the other hand, have offered a more positive interpretation of Kristeva's novels, interpretations that also address the characterization of her theory as both apolitical and antifeminist. Many have focused on their autobiographical character in order to argue that the novels are relevant to debates ranging from immigration to exile and nationalism, as well as to the related issues of assimilation, integration, and transculturation and their often ambiguous effects.

Academic critics have expanded on the literary context of Kristeva's novels, making useful distinctions and establishing helpful differences between the genres. However, they have not offered a comprehensive account of her fiction writing, one that transcends the generic differences that seem to split Kristeva's works into two moments, the moment of the *roman à clef* exemplified by *The Samurai* and the moment of detective fiction that seems to extend through the rest of her novels. But the work of the academic critics has gone some distance in echoing Kristeva's account of detective novels as an investigation of the genesis of writing—though more work can be done in this direction, particularly on the affects of betrayal and forgiveness that seem to accompany these troubled origins and their relevance to the society at large. The essays in *Kristeva's Fiction* follow the lead set by these academic critics, even as they fill in some of the gaps left by the existing scholarship on Kristeva's novels.

Among the academic studies of Kristeva's fiction, Szu-Chin Hestia Chen's *French Feminist Theory Exemplified Through the Novels of Julia Kristeva* (2008) deserves special mention as the only book so far dedicated to Kristeva's fiction, and as a predecessor of this collection. Chen gives a chronological account of Kristeva's thoughts on the novel, from her earliest writings influenced by formalist linguistics to her later writings influenced by Lacanian psychoanalysis. In her account, she also suggests that the object of analysis of Kristeva's theory and fiction remains the same, although Kristeva gives different names to this object: to wit the semiotic mode of signification and poetic language.[25] Chen claims that the distinction between theory and fiction proves problematic for Kristeva, and she states that her novels may "simply be a different form of her theoretical work" (17). Drawing from Kristeva's early writings, Chen points to the Bakhtinian nature of the complex interaction of theory and fiction in Kristeva's work. She rightly states that they are in a "dialogical" relationship; and it is the precise nature of this dialogue that the writers in our collection try to describe.

"Yes, but is Kristeva any good as a novelist?"

So far, I have tried to make the argument that there are two relatively discrete readerships for Kristeva's fiction, and that each group has a different opinion as to the worth of Kristeva's fiction depending on whether they assign value to her psychoanalytic theory or not. The book reviews eschew theory in general, and psychoanalysis in particular, and are negative by and large. The academic critics, on the other hand, are open to theory and positive for the most part. But it is also true that the question of the value of Kristeva's fiction (closely followed by the related question, "Would we read these books if they weren't by Kristeva?") is also asked by a wide array of readers who straddle these two groups: readers who are both theoretically informed and are interested in literature, whatever the criteria used to assign literary value to it. For these readers, it is not enough to answer these questions by simply bracketing-out aesthetic value, based on universal categories such as beauty and perfect form. They also ask whether Kristeva's novels are more than "scholarship," more than "theoretical indirection or exploration." For example, if her novels are indeed a form of embodied detective fiction (as I suggest here), then does the corporeal supplement of her novels satisfy as fiction? Simply put, does Kristeva's fiction "deserve a read"?

These repeating questions, and others like them ("Is it really any good as fiction?"; "Is it great literature?") are symptoms of what Kristeva and the writers of the collection are in fact trying to address, which is the reason why the writers of this volume, instead of answering these questions of literary quality, urge Kristeva's readers to go beyond them and to experience writing that puts ideas at the same level as character, pacing, plot, suspense, form, and style. What is at stake for Kristeva, and for the writers of this volume, is precisely the ability first to read, and then to enjoy, such work. It is indeed a question of reading and enjoyment, and, more specifically, it is a question for Kristeva of the inability of the modern reader to enjoy the kind of experimental fiction that escapes easy definition and classification and that has a reputation for being difficult to read. This fiction includes the so-called French intellectual novel, the *nouveau roman*, but also novels of contemporary writers like the Chilean Roberto Bolaño, whose works, for example, Michael Schaub describes as "flawless, majestic" but also as "hard to read." What makes such novels so hard to read?

In her book *New Maladies of the Soul* (1993), Kristeva goes some distance in answering this question, which I believe applies to her own novels. In that book, Kristeva describes the effects of contemporary events like the Shoah, the deployment of the atom bomb, but also the collapse of Communism and the fall of the Berlin Wall (1989) on our internal defenses, or on what she calls the psyche or the soul. I believe that Kristeva refers obliquely to Europeans victims of the Cold War in that book, by referring to the analysis of a patient whose dreams and speech are like an "iceberg." Didier's dreams are monumental, cold, and they lie hidden just below the surface. His speech is visible but reduced, shrunk, hard and brittle, like the top of an iceberg. Didier's artwork is a set of monstrous collages, and each one represents a similarly frozen object that stands for his sense of self, his soul, or his psyche. Indeed, Didier is a figure for European man after the Cold War. He is unable to feel and transform something that is both inside and outside of him, something that is familiar but that is nevertheless so disturbing that it freezes him, something as catastrophic as the mythical severed head of the Medusa. Paradoxically, the sudden loss of his defenses, like the sudden loss of the Berlin Wall, threatens to compound the catastrophe. The fall of the Berlin Wall is both a liberation and also a threat to this man, who abruptly loses a reduced space, or a wall, that both separated and also connected (albeit thinly) the two sides of his split self, and his feelings from his language.

Although *New Maladies* is essentially a commentary on the effects of the Cold War on Europeans, it has broader implications that also affect readers outside the European community. Didier also could be a figure for Kristeva herself and for the contemporary reader in more general terms, insofar as they all uncomfortably and imperfectly straddle binaries that are at odds with each other: binaries such as feeling and language, theory and fiction, Eastern and Western civilizations. The Berlin Wall could similarly be a figure for Kristeva's novels and for contemporary writing, insofar as they are similar defenses that both separate and connect the different sides of a split subject: a person split between Bulgaria and France, or a novel split between ideas and plot, for example. Could modern readers of Kristeva's novels be cold to them because these novels mirror their frozen and split selves? Is this the reason why they are unable to interpret, transform, and then enjoy her novels, and why these novels are so hard to read? This seems to me to be the case. Sadly, the fact is that when these novels are simply dismissed as imperfect and boring, the defenses they enact and represent don't disappear, instead they go underground and hide from our view; like the bottom half of an iceberg they can become more treacherous.

From this perspective, modern readers suffer from a malady that makes them ask the same questions over and again; questions that presuppose the failure of such novels for not being literary enough, for being too philosophical and boring. These questions remind us that Kristeva is not an ideal author devoted to the craft of writing novels, and they are a symptom of our devotion to this ideal. In other words, these questions express our need and our desire to imagine ourselves in relation to an ideal object and to remain stuck, frozen, in front of that freezing object. Kristeva, instead, asks us to move beyond this paralyzing ideal, and to do it for our own good.

Kristeva's novels urge us to stop idealizing and to start finding pleasure and enjoyment in objects that are represented in a different way, in a way that is more enabling, more forgiving. They suggest that we model our reading after a different, docile, object. What is at stake for Kristeva is not to forgive a novelist for writing imperfectly, but to forgive the reader for being a perfectionist. Better yet, what is at stake is to continue to read imperfectly, with full knowledge of the fact that the reader cannot see something in himself: the very imperfection that the reader denies through what Kristeva calls idealization, the other side of abjection. By continuing to ask, "Is Kristeva any good as a novelist?" we continue to tell ourselves that it is not possible that there is no ideal object. By describing her novels as boring, hard to read "blather," we display the pleasure we feel when we protect the existence of an ideal object. Instead, we should try to ask different questions, such as whether Kristeva's novels liberate us from our tendency to idealize. How does Kristeva's blend of fiction and theory free us from our ideals? Does it allow us to overcome this punishing need? The authors in this collection help us to ask such questions by moving through and beyond the question of literary value.

Our Collection

Kristeva's Fiction is a collection that includes essays by academic critics who have dedicated much of their attention to the theoretical work of Julia Kristeva, scholars who now turn their focus to her novels. It includes an essay by John Lechte, whose *Julia Kristeva* (published in 1990) was one of the first monographs dedicated to the work of Kristeva, as well as an essay by Stacy Keltner, whose *Kristeva: Thresholds* (published in 2011) is one of the latest books published on the subject. It also incorporates essays by other academic critics who have similarly published books on Kristeva, including Carol Bové, the author of *Language and Politics in Julia Kristeva* (2006), and Martha Reineke, the author of *Sacrificed Lives: Kristeva on Women and Violence* (1997), as well as essays by scholars who have published numerous essays on the subject. The collection is also unique in the international composition of its contributors and in the eclectic character of their disciplines, which range from philosophy to literature, from sociology to women's and religious studies.

The collection is representative of the general trend in the academic criticism discussed in this introduction insofar as all of the essays can be said to be open to theory in general and to psychoanalytic theory in particular. In fact, most of them can be described as examples of psychoanalytic social theory. In other words, the essays included in this collection, like the academic commentary discussed earlier, repeat the Freudian exchange, or transfer, between the psychological and the social order. They also find a split between competing forces or drives (that is, the pleasure principle and the death drive) both in the composition of the psyche and in the foundation of the social bond. And, like Freud, they also find that this split prominently includes a tendency toward both love and death, Eros and Thanatos. Also, many of the critics in this collection follow other general trends in psychoanalytic social theory such as an interest in the relationship between detective fiction and writing broadly understood, as well as an interest in the question of origin, whether it is the origin of the self, the social, of writing, or the origin of psychoanalysis itself.

The collection is divided into two parts. The first part contains five essays that make points about Kristeva's fiction, but focus on one, or at most two, novels to make their claims. The essays are arranged in chronological order, with those essays referring to Kristeva's first detective novel first (Keltner and Bové), followed by those that refer to her last detective novel (Reineke, Restuccia, and Ziarek). The second part contains four essays that similarly make claims about the relationship of Kristeva's fiction and theory, but that do not rely on any one novel to do so.

Stacy Keltner's chapter "Whodunit? Reading Kristeva with the Help of Detective Fiction" opens the collection. It is an example of an account of two of Kristeva's novels (*The Old Man and the Wolves* and *Murder in Byzantium*) as a revolt that shuttles back and forth from the psyche to the social. For Keltner, Kristeva's fiction and her psychoanalytical practice are works of language (and political acts of revolt) against the society of the spectacle. Drawing from her recent book on Kristeva, and from Kristeva's own 1997 work on *Intimate Revolt*, Keltner argues that Kristeva's novels are one instance among multiple Kristevan "works of language" (including psychoanalysis) that in their very multiplicity, and heterogeneity, constitute the promise of revolt. Like Bové, Keltner also argues that Kristeva privileges psychoanalysis and fiction as concrete experiences of meaning and social connection. For Keltner, Kristeva's fiction is not a simple reflection of her theory and vice versa. Neither is her fiction a reflection of normative structures. Instead, she argues, like Brooksbank, Kirkby, and Margaroni (2009), that Kristeva's fiction is "Kristeva's unique response to contemporary social and political life." Keltner argues that if psychoanalysis is an abstract theorization, then it must be put back into its social-historical context, and Kristeva's detective fiction does just that by offering "an interminable return to a (material) past that renews the psychic life of meaning within a particular social and historical context."

Carol Bové's chapter "Revolution Has Italian Roots: Kristeva's Fiction and Theory" follows Keltner's, and it focuses mostly on Kristeva's novel *The Old Man and the Wolves*. Bové describes some of the figures in Kristeva's fiction as places where Kristeva, the writer, grounds the subversive mode of signification that Kristeva, the theorist, calls the semiotic. In other words, the references to Italy and Rome in Kristeva's novels function in a way that is similar to her overall narrative. On the one hand, they broaden the appeal of her theory. That is, they make her theoretical concepts more engaging, more popular, more interesting to a wider readership, perhaps more at home when learning about European commonplaces such as Rome and Italy. On the other hand, the references to Italy also ground Kristeva's fiction in a place with historical characters and with a tradition of aesthetic practice clearly set in a historical timeline, giving Kristeva's theory a similar historical and material foundation. Bové's argument extends some points made in her earlier book, which seeks to make the political connotations of Kristeva's work evident to her readers. It also follows the larger trend within the academic commentary on Kristeva that seeks to politicize her theoretical work (Brooksbank; Kirkby; and Margaroni 2009). When read together with Lechte's essay in this same volume, Bové's chapter is also evidence that the accounts within academic criticism of Kristeva's ideology remain divided.

In "Not a Country for Old Men: Scapegoats and Sacrifice in Santa Varvara," Martha Reineke describes Kristeva's first detective novel, *The Old Man and the Wolves*, as an example of a well-established tradition in literature going back to the poetry of Tibullus that dramatizes the scapegoating of sacrificial societies, which inevitably leads to murder. In the first two sections of her essay, she argues that Kristeva also owes much to René Girard for this account of the social contract to the point of fully replicating Girard's scapegoat sequences. In the third and fourth sections, Reineke turns to what could perhaps be characterized as Kristevan tales of love (the poetry of Tibullus and the *Metamorphoses* of Ovid), which contain an elegiac and compassionate memory that values outsider status and suffering and offer an alternative to the sacrificial economy described by Girard. The essay builds on Reineke's own earlier work on the topics of sacrifice, violence, and the feminine in the work of Kristeva and adds to a compelling trend in the academic criticism that focuses on the religious aspect of Kristeva's work (see O'Grady and Greaney).

Frances Restuccia's essay "Sebastian's Skull: Establishing the 'Society of the Icon' " focuses on *Murder in Byzantium* to make clear the difference between Santa Varvara and Byzantium in Kristeva's fiction. While Santa Varvara stands for a society of the spectacle that encourages acting out the universal death drive, Byzantium stands for a society of the icon that invites us to undergo the experience of the death drive with a mind to make possible a new life. Restuccia argues that Kristeva chooses to transform the fatality of the death drive through representation in her novel *Murder in Byzantium*, rather than act out a lethal death drive that continues to affect her. From this perspective, the novel is a mystical exercise, it is an example of what Restuccia calls a "narrative kenosis," a descent into death, or psychosis, so that the writer can be reborn.

"From the Agency of the Letter to the Agency of the Icon: Femininity and Bulgaria in Julia Kristeva's *Murder in Byzantium*" closes the first part of the collection. In this essay, Ewa Ziarek argues that Kristeva's latest novel subverts the rational epistemology of classical detective fiction with an embodied mode of knowledge—a maternal mode of knowledge based on the sense of taste—that has been overcome by a historical shift away from Eastern Europe and toward Western Europe. From this perspective, Ziarek's work further develops an account of Kristeva's novels as a mode of antidetective fiction found in the academic commentary (see Greaney and Davis), even as it adds to the recent wave of criticism interested in the relation of Kristeva's novels with her past (see Margaroni; Nilsson; and Agoston-Nikolova; as well as Nikolchina in this volume). Ziarek divides her essay into two sections. She describes the innovations of Kristeva's novel to the traditional genre of the detective novel and its implications for its epistemological tradition in the first section. In the second, she raises the stakes of Kristeva's project beyond an interrogation and questioning of the epistemological tradition that gives rise to, and sets the boundaries of, the detective novel. Here, Ziarek unearths the intellectual tradition buried by the detective novel and its companion intellectual projects: an alternative intellectual history grounded on a buried account of the senses of sight and taste.

My essay "*Noir* Analysis: How Kristeva's Detective Novels Renew Psychoanalysis" opens the second part of the collection. In this essay, I argue that Kristeva's fiction is a negative and disturbing poetic practice that is necessary for the development of a Kristevan psychoanalytic practice. More precisely, I claim that Kristeva's detective fiction suggests the need to renew psychoanalysis. More specifically still, I argue that aspects of her detective fiction are drawn from a variety of writers who come together in a "noir series" to suggest a new mode of psychoanalysis: a disillusioned or darker form that suspends the mastery of judgment, a self-questioning mode that turns the analyst and the analysand into partners in crime, and an imperfect, open-ended, turbulent form of analysis that is better suited to the urgency of our modern discontents. I conclude that Kristeva's "metaphysical-crime novels" travel to the dark matter of the unconscious, to the "obscure point" of the noir series, in order to generate a renewed mode of lay psychoanalysis. From this perspective, I follow a trend within academic criticism that tries to better discern the nature of the link between Kristeva's theory and her fiction writing, with the difference that I ask how Kristeva's fiction changes her psychoanalytic theory and practice rather than the other way around.[26]

John Lechte's "Fiction, Analysis, Possession, and Violence in Kristeva's Mirror of Writing" describes Kristeva's novels as a symptom of what Kristeva herself (following Guy Debord) calls the society of the spectacle. Like other academic critics such as Levenson, Lechte states that Kristeva's detective novels are different from the modernist fiction that Kristeva studies in her theoretical work. Her detective novels are not troubled by the semiotic mode of signification, he argues, but rather express an academic and symbolic illusion of control that is symptomatic of the society of the spectacle. He argues that the novels are free from the paradoxes that inhabit classical works of detective fiction such as "The Purloined Letter." Indeed, he compares Kristeva's fiction to a purloined letter, "scholarship for all to see, if only one is prepared to accept what one sees."

Miglena Nikolchina's "Byzantium, or Fiction as Inverted Theory" is concerned with Kristeva's fiction writing and its political context, or with writing under what Nikolchina calls "forms of tyranny." She finds that Kristeva's fiction is both an inversion and an example of a discretion that is necessary under those conditions. Nikolchina suggests that what is at stake in the fiction of Kristeva is an inversion of her theory, the representation of what is left unsaid by the theory, particularly the history of Bulgaria and Kristeva's relationship with her past under a communist regime. Nikolchina brings out the connections of Kristeva's last novel with the work of another Bulgarian writer (Vera Mutafchieva) quoted by Kristeva, a writer, Nikolchina reminds us, who turned out to be an informant under the communist regime. Nikolchina's essay suggests that Kristeva's writing in general, and her fiction in particular, is part of a way of thinking that cannot be separated from Kristeva's past and from a context of tyranny, whether it is the tyranny of Bulgaria before the fall of the Berlin Wall, the tyranny of the West, or the tyranny of Western feminism. She suggests that this mode of writing is structured by a double move that she separates into an initial discretion followed by an inversion. If she locates the discretion in Kristeva's "theory," she speaks of Kristeva's "fiction" as a necessary inversion of it. But the inversions also appear to produce a discretion, in their turn, a discretion that interpellates the reader and asks her to search for what Nikolchina describes as "the true crime of Kristeva's theory" in her fiction. Nikolchina follows and builds her argument on the wake of other critics like Margaroni, Nilsson, and Agoston-Nikolova, who have explored the links between Kristeva's fiction and her Bulgarian past.

Maria Margaroni's "The *Vital* Legacy of the Novel and Julia Kristeva's Fictional Revolt" closes the collection. It is part of a trend in the analysis of Kristeva's fiction that focuses on it as a mode of ethical writing rather than as a genre, and it is part of the trend within academic criticism that finds evidence of a new Humanism in Kristeva's work (see Anna Smith; Rus; and Davis). These writers suggest that Kristeva's writing is founded on a betrayal that must be forgiven, a betrayal that is also at the origins of psychoanalysis as well as of the subject. For Margaroni, Kristeva writes in a radically feminine and strange way, expressing the vexed nature of the origins of writing itself. Margaroni sees Kristeva's feminine writing as the place of a new social bond fraught with contradictory forces. Her novels are expressive of this new bond: they represent a community of others and strangers. From this perspective, Margaroni's essay is also akin to the work of some academic critics on the subject of exile and immigration in Kristeva's novels (see Anna Smith; Agoston-Nikolova; and Raoul). But Margaroni also sees an evolution in Kristeva's thinking about the feminine, which allows for her different understanding of feminine writing, which coincides with Kristeva's decision to begin writing novels. In Kristeva's novels, the feminine becomes a site, a space, a bond that is fraught with contradictory forces (with the death drive perhaps), and this is a disturbance that also constitutes the lowest common denominator for the renewal of both the subject and the community. In short, Margaroni goes further than most in arguing that the human problem for Kristeva is not the knowledge of the self, but how to understand others, and the value of this problem is the emphasis on our connection with the other rather than our difference, even if it is a connection that is fraught and stripped of all idealism.

Notes

1. Over the years, Kristeva has given subtly changing accounts of the "semiotic" mode of signification. In *Intimate Revolt* she emphasizes a transverbal rather than a preverbal meaning or articulation. She writes: "I say transverbal, for to say preverbal leads to confusion: the semiotic is not independent of language, but interferes with language and, under its domination, articulates other arrangements of meaning which are not significations, but rhythmic, melodic articulations" (2002a, 258–59).

2. *Powers of Horror* has been interpreted as part of a trilogy of works that together represent Kristeva's turn toward psychoanalysis; these include *Tales of Love* and *Black Sun*.

3. In *Intimate Revolt*, Kristeva defines the abject as a notion she develops from her clinical experience and as a symptom of a psychical economy where the separation between the subject and the object is not clear: "which also refers to the archaic relationship of nonseparation with the maternal container: the mother being the primary abject" (2002a, 260).

4. Kristeva's other books before the publication of *The Samurai* include *On Chinese Women* (1974), *Language: The Unknown* (1981), *Tales of Love* (1983), *In the Beginning was Love: Psychoanalysis and Faith* (1985), *Black Sun* (1987), and *Strangers to Ourselves* (1988).

5. In *Hatred and Forgiveness*, Kristeva gives a psychoanalytic account of forgiveness as analytical listening and interpretation "that neither judges nor calculates, but is content to untangle and reconstruct" the entangled loves and hatreds that constitute the psyche of the patient (2010, 194).

6. In an answer to a question about the scant presence of signs of her Bulgarian past in her last novel, and referring to her fiction, Kristeva asks in turn, "Is it because the voyage includes its share of betrayal?" suggesting that she betrays that past both in and outside her novels (2010, 300).

7. Kristeva's first novel is widely held to be an autobiographical *roman à clef*, and Elaine Showalter points out that "you don't have to be an initiate into Parisian mysteries to guess at the identities of [the] *samouraï* characters," who include Lacan, Derrida, Foucault, and Barthes, among others (1990).

8. *The Samurai* ends with a reference to both Joëlle Cabarus's and Olga de Montlaur's books. Olga's is titled *The Samurai*. With the end also comes news of the death of Cabarus's father that stops her from writing in her journal.

9. The reader will remember that Dupin, the detective in Poe's story, solves the mystery of the Rue Morgue by deducing with an animal intelligence described by the narrator as "diseased" (1970, 145) and reverse (or "a-posteriori"), that an "Ourang-Outang" is responsible for the brutal murder of Madame L'Espanaye and her daughter.

10. I borrow the term *roman noir* from Kristeva, who uses it to name a form of fiction writing that is breathless, anguished, and even totally crazy ("*complètement givré*," 2005c, 619), a form at which women writers of police investigations, Gothic novels, and modern whodunits excel, and which seeks to name a "sensorial enigma" (2002c, 163).

11. Since joining the European Union, France has become a part of a community of nations that agrees that the death penalty should be abolished worldwide (Simon and Blaskovich, 20).

12. In her essay, Margaroni studies Kristeva's notion of Europe and characterizes Kristeva's detective fiction as a form of Benjaminian allegory (2009, 108).

13. *The Samurai* was translated into English in 1992, *Old Man* in 1994, *Possessions* in 1998, and *Murder* in 2006.

14. To be fair, Showalter goes on to write, "*Les Samouraïs* is an interesting and daring fictional debut by an adventurous thinker who is always breaking new ground" (1038).

15. The most quoted feminist and postfeminist critiques of Kristeva's theoretical works are by De Lauretis, Fraser, and Butler.

16. *The Samurai* has also been described as a *roman à clef*, a detective novel, a novel of hipness, and has also been compared to *Femmes* by Philippe Sollers, to *Lost in Translation* by Eva Hoffman, and to novels by Barbara Taylor Bradford, Judith Krantz, and Jacqueline Susann. *The Old Man and the Wolves* has been described as a philosophical novel, as a *nouveau roman*, and has been compared to *Rhinoceros*, by Eugène Ionesco, and to an Isaac Babel story. *Possessions* has also been described as a psychological thriller, an intellectual detective story, a mystery, and philosophical novel. Reviewers have negatively compared it to Agatha Christie's novels. *Murder in Byzantium* has also been described as a mystery novel, a historical mystery, a hybrid novel, a conceptual and historical detective novel, and an erudite and portentous mystery novel. Reviewers have also compared Kristeva to Ian McEwan and her novels to *The Da Vinci Code* by Dan Brown.

17. With this caveat, I mean to suggest that there is some division among academic critics well versed in psychoanalytic theory regarding the beneficial effects of this writerly therapeutic practice. For a compelling and contrary view, see Walsh Other academic critics similarly familiar both with Kristeva's fiction and with psychoanalytic theory who also express reservations about Kristeva's novels include Raoul, Greaney, and Margaroni (2009).

18. See, for example, Kristeva's *Black Sun* as a melancholy account of feminine sexuality "because the female infant cannot abject the maternal body without abjecting herself" (Oliver 2002, 300).

19. Referring to psychoanalytic forgiveness, Kristeva writes, "In these postmodern times of religious clashes, which are times of endless war, it might be useful to remember that psychoanalytical interpretation, by revealing multifaceted hatreds, offers itself as the ultimate lucidity of pardon, which psychical life needs in order to continue living, quite simply, without necessarily absolutely ceasing to hate" (2010, 194).

20. In *Desire in Language*, Kristeva defines the paternal function as a "permanent go-between" from an imaginary discourse of the self and a discourse of transcendental knowledge: "a pulsation of sign and rhythm, of consciousness and instinctual drive" (1980, 139).

21. These fields emerged in large part thanks to the publication of the bestseller *Hunger of Memory* by Richard Rodríguez in 1991, and of *Borderlands/La Frontera* by Gloria Anzaldúa in 1987.

22. The few examples of critical commentary in academic journals on *The Samurai* include: Renard, Kolocotroni, Levenson, and Atack.

23. There are more than a dozen books dedicated to the theoretical work of Kristeva including (in order of publication) those of White, Adriens, Lechte, Oliver, Anna Smith, Reineke, Anne-Marie Smith, McAfee, Sjoholm, Nikolchina, Bové, and Keltner.

24. Similar comments can be found in Atack, Kirkby, West, and Greaney.

25. Chen then goes on to apply concepts that appear both in Kristeva's theory and in her novels (concepts such as love, melancholia, abjection, time, maternity, and the body) to her own study of the differences between postcolonial, French, and Anglo-American modes of feminism.

26. For examples of critics who ask how Kristeva's theory affects her fiction writing, see Chen, Kolocotroni, de Nooy, and Davis 2003.

PART I

1

Whodunit?

Reading Kristeva with the Help of Detective Fiction

S. K. Keltner

Barely mysteries, if you watch enough nighttime detective dramas, you can time the mistaken leads, twists of plot, and final discovery by the minute hand. Its most popular manifestations reinscribe ideological norms (us/them; justice/criminality; truth/perversion; good/evil; purity/impurity); produce and maintain the banality of violence and horror; and confirm the voyeur-spectator's moral sense of self, even while he or she enjoys the spectacle of erotically charged images and acts. The inquiry that makes the protagonist a detective carries us into the heart of a crime that fascinates us at the same time that it offends (and often confirms) our own morality. And yet, their intrigue may reveal more than a modern society beset with ennui. Rape, murder, incest, abuse, abduction, torture—when presented in the form of a detective story—allows us to confront the darkest secrets and anxieties of modern life. Despite its risk of mystification, detective fiction may also promise transformative experiences. This is Julia Kristeva's double thesis: detective fiction is *both* a privileged signifier of the spectacle *and* a privileged cultural site capable of transforming the psychic life of meaning.

In her first detective novel, *The Old Man and the Wolves* (1991), Kristeva describes the allegorical city of Santa Varvara in the language of Guy Debord's "society of the spectacle."[1] She continues to favor the language of the spectacle in her subsequent detective novels—*Possessions* (1996) and *Murder in Byzantium* (2004)—as well as in the critical works of the same period. Kristeva presents the thesis of the spectacle in an image: a sprawling modern metropolis that glitters and dazzles in spite of, or on condition of, its underworld—gritty, sordid, mean streets, which call to mind the setting of a hard-boiled detective novel or film. In *New Maladies of the Soul* (1993), she describes the virtual city thus: "I am picturing a sprawling metropolis with glass and steel buildings that reach the sky, reflect it, reflect each other, and reflect you—a city filled with people steeped in their own image who rush about with overdone makeup on and who are cloaked in gold, pearls, and fine leather, while in the next street over, heaps of filth abound and drugs accompany the sleep or the fury of the social outcasts" (1995, 27; 1993, 49). She asks, "What might one do in such a city? Nothing but buy and sell goods and images, which amounts to the same thing, since they both are dull, shallow symbols" (ibid.). In the detective novels, Santa Varvara represents this city that could be any existing city, any future city, and all spaces in between: "Santa Varvara expands in all directions. . . . Everywhere? But where exactly? You want to locate Santa Varvara on a map? But it's impossible, you know. How can one locate the global village? Santa Varvara is in Paris, New York, Moscow, Sofia, London, Plovdiv, and in Santa Varvara too, of course—it's everywhere, I tell you, everywhere . . ." (2006b, 64; 2004a, 115).

The city of Santa Varvara concretely stages Kristeva's thesis of the spectacle, which she calls in *The Sense and Non-Sense of Revolt* (1996) the "implicit horizon" and "present context" (2000c, 4; 1996j, 10) of her concern to examine the fate of meaning in contemporary societies. The spectacle signifies the dominance of the mass media in everyday life, the "education" of children by television, the domination of political campaigns by news cycles and media coverage, and the silencing of global injustice by the government-media-corporate oligopoly. The spectacle is not a determinate phenomenon identifiable *within* society or reality, but rather the transformation of reality itself into spectacle, which reduces sensuous, social, and historical experience to the dominance of and mediation by visual representation. The spectacle thus describes modern experience and the entire realm of social activity, including the institutions, social and political practices, and ideological beliefs that support and ensure the economy of the spectacle. It is our (global) *situation*. The economy of the spectacle raises commodity to a new level of abstraction free of any use-value. That is to say, the object's value lies solely in its function as an image.

For Kristeva, the society of the spectacle embodies two new important characteristics affecting the life of meaning. The first concerns the status of power; the second concerns the status of the individual. Concerning power, Kristeva says that the new world order effects a new "schema" and "new regulation of power and transgression" that favors the functioning of "business, speculation, and Mafia activity" (2000c, 5; 1996j, 11). Not only are traditional and modern conceptions of power rendered meaningless, but so too are outdated terms like "fascism" and "totalitarianism." Contrary to the identifiable sources of power in past social and political formations, the society of the spectacle renders power invisible. In place of systems of real production, there is stock market speculation and the falsification of wealth; in place of laws there are measures; in place of culpability, public menace; in place of fault, damages; in place of responsibility, liability; in place of trials, delaying techniques; in place of justice, media theatricalization (ibid.). The new regulation of power does not shrink from calling itself "progress" and "democracy" and "liberal society." But, the "so-called liberal society" that we have attained is ultimately a "power vacuum." The primacy of the new world market economy over bodies, relations, and solidarity point to the replacement of the subject with a new patrimonial individual—literally, I am simply the property (*propre*, self) inherited from my ancestors, the past, my genes. Ethical and political questions concerning my being are thereby reduced to questions concerning whether my patrimony should be "remunerated or free" (2000c, 5; 1996j, 13): "whether 'I' can enrich myself or, as an altruist, forgo payment in the name of humanity or whether 'I,' as a victim, am dispossessed of it" (2000c, 6; 1996j, 13). For Kristeva, the only cultural and personal possibilities that remain are regressive fundamentalism or consumer culture. The spectacular reduction of subjectivity in the context of a new regulation of invisible power effects a psyche and a culture bereft of meaning. Kristeva asks *who* would revolt and against *what*?

Kristeva's deployment of Santa Varvara as the "image of contemporary life" emphasizes social history as one of the major organizational elements of psychic life (1995, 28; 1993, 50). Under the dominance of the spectacle, self-relation, relations to others, and relations to the social-historical world are governed by the accumulation and exchange of images. In *The Old Man and the Wolves*, the most suspicious character, Vespasian, who has "yellow eyes" (1994, 5; 1991, 16), is described by his wife, Alba, as "made up of a vast number of different images. A traveling exhibition of masks, each artificially constructed for an equally artificial scene" (1994, 72; 1991, 107). The residents of the spectacular city are *virtual, spectacular subjects*. The goal of personal and social life, under the sway of the spectacle, becomes a competition of images for the sake of social power, gained by whatever means—deception, violence, crime. In *The Old Man and the Wolves*, Alba goes missing; she and her husband, Vespasian, both plot to kill one another; the rebellious Old Man is poisoned; and a woman, uncannily similar to Alba, is drowned. In *Possessions*, everyone in Santa Varvara is capable of having murdered Gloria Hanson, and it turns out that the murder is a four-part act with four actors (an overdose by Gloria herself; strangulation by her husband; stabbing by an escapee from the local mental institution; and finally, beheading by Gloria's son's speech therapist). In *Murder in Byzantium*, Sebastian Chrest-Jones, a (secret) Byzantine scholar violently in search of his own roots, murders his mistress and disappears; and Number 8, a serial killer, is purifying the city of the members of the New Pantheon, a corrupt religious mafia. In all of her novels, the crimes themselves, some of which remain "officially" unsolved, are not limited to the particular acts or possible acts of violence. The real mystery in *The Old Man and the Wolves*, for example, is not a single or set of crimes, but a mass metamorphosis of its residents into actual and potential, *virtual* criminals. The "wolves" of *The Old Man and the Wolves* are "the people in the street, on the streetcars, in the shops, in the hospital" (1994, 30; 1991, 48). In Santa Varvara, everyone is a criminal suspect—and yet, it seems, no one is. The Almighty Dollar, big hair, makeup, furs, gold, pearls, and a leather-gloved hand shot J.R. In such a city, who could have a soul?

With the reduction of personal and social life to the presence of the image, the primary "relation" the spectacle effects is *separation* or *alienation* (from the object, activity, and social and historical meaning of production). Debord calls separation "the alpha and omega of the spectacle" (1994, 25), concluding that "the spectator feels at home nowhere" (1994, 30). Kristeva's presentation of the society of the spectacle, in both her creative and critical works, affirms Debord's conclusion. She describes alienation, for example, as "the by-product of the spectacle" (1994, 102; 1991, 144). Nevertheless, Kristeva introduces a psychoanalytic dimension of analysis to that of Debord's own, thereby deepening the account of the spectacle by developing a description and account of the alienation of the modern subject in her own social-psychoanalytic terms. Kristeva's concern for suffering subjectivity leads her to analyze the alienation or separation the spectacle effects as the destruction of meaning—the collapse of psychic space and the disintegration of social and historical relations.

Kristeva confronts the loss of meaning directly in relation to the spectacle's destruction of the modern subject's capacity to create and sustain a psychic life of meaning. Psychic life, she insists, is "blocked, inhibited, and destroyed" by the spectacle: "More than just a commodity or a new variant of the "opium of the people," the current transformation of psychic life may foreshadow a new humanity, one whose psychological conveniences will be able to overcome metaphysical anxiety and the need for meaning. Wouldn't it be great to be satisfied with just a pill and a television screen?" (1995, 8; 1993, 17–18). Kristeva's dark irony demonstrates the danger in which she interprets psychic life to be in. The spectacle affects subjectivity by emptying it out, normalizing it, turning subjects into homogeneous automatons. For Kristeva, the "*alter ego* of the society of the spectacle" (1995, 29; 1993, 52) is "an amputated subjectivity" (1995, 7; 1993, 16) who lacks the capacity to represent and to question. The dominance of the image in contemporary, global societies thus effects the "spectacular reduction" (1995, 7; 1993, 15) of psychic life, giving rise to what she calls "new maladies of the soul." The new maladies of the soul—"phantasmatic inhibition," "false personalities," "borderline states," and "psychosomatic conditions," for example—are not reducible to traditional classification systems. Importantly, what they all share is "the inability to represent" (1995, 9; 1993, 18): the contemporary subject would be "an actor or consumer of the society of the spectacle who has run out of imagination" (1995, 10; 1993, 20); the "end result of the spectacle," she says, is "the halting of representation and questioning." For Kristeva, the spectacle effects, at the level of the individual, the loss of the psychic life of meaning, which implies a reduction of both personal and social relations to the economy of the image.

Kristeva's description of Santa Varvara and its inhabitants emphasizes the banality of modern society, which leads to nihilistic despair and its subsequent violence—both of which constitute the dark underbelly of the glittering, dazzling city of the image. Speaking of the figure of Alba as one figure of the modern subject in *The Old Man and the Wolves*, Kristeva says, "[w]e are basically dealing with the image of a *depression* that integrates aggression but under the ruinous guise of an erasure of meaning" (1996d, 166). For Kristeva, the loss of meaning affects subjectivity in the form of despair and/or violence. The fictional characters of the detective novels embody the failures of social functioning and the condition of the modern subject, rather than individual "anomalies." Alba represents a nihilistic, depressive position in relation to the spectacle. Kristeva says, "[a] true depression of meaning itself takes place, and the insignificance into which the melancholy person sinks is not merely an individual, 'pathological' occurrence. Because of its amplitude, it assumes the seriousness of a societal event, a civilizational crisis" (1996d, 167). In the language of the semiotic/symbolic distinction, the spectacle signifies a social and historical crisis in which the symbolic is divorced from the semiotic, resulting in the emptiness of cultural representation and, thereby, semiotic impulses without symbolic form. The spectacle signals the fate of the modern subject in a world constituted by the loss of signifying capacities. Incapable of questioning, imagining, and sublimating affective life, the modern subject imbibes the standardized images of media culture, which regulates and normalizes the life of meaning (or its lack thereof). As a result, "I" am no longer a subject, but rather a virtual repetition of the spectacle, permanently excluded from the questioning of power and the creation of ethical life, except as a complicit consumer, powerless and without guilt, or as the exploited "damages" of inter- and transnational "dealings."

Detective fiction is presented as a privileged signifier of the spectacle. In *The Old Man and the Wolves*, Septicius Clarus ("aka Scholasticus, aka the Professor, aka the Old Man," 1994, 5; 1991, 15) describes the spectacular city of Santa Varvara as a violent "whodunit that ends in a massacre" (1994, 102; 1991, 145). In *Murder in Byzantium*, Stephanie Delacour, the lead protagonist and Kristeva's alter ego in the fictional works, describes it as a "crime novel run wild" (2006b, 64; 2004a, 115). And yet, detective fiction also opens the possibility of reflection and imagination—an *inner life*—in a spectacular society that thrives on their repression. Detective fiction, Kristeva insists, embodies an opportunity to confront what the spectacle represses, transforming its "spectators" into seekers of truth, like budding Oedipuses. Kristeva's detective novels not only present the virtual city and the virtual subjects shaped by the society of the spectacle. They also reevaluate the significance of detective fiction in terms of its capacity to invoke transformative experiences of that which it is also in danger of perpetuating, that is, the spectacular reduction of psychic life. The detective story, even in its risk of mystification, is privileged as an experience and enactment of a revolutionary dynamic. For example, in a chapter of *Intimate Revolt* entitled "Fantasy and Cinema," which is devoted primarily to the cinematic image, Kristeva privileges the form of interrogation enacted by detective drama. She claims, for example, that Eisenstein's films "evoke the detective novel or the horror film" and that Hitchcock might be "the quintessential filmmaker" (2002a, 77; 1997, 112). Nevertheless, the difference separating the spectacular detective structure of prime-time crime drama and that of an Eisenstein or a Hitchcock lies in their effects. If the effect of the spectacle is the inability to represent, the effect of Poe, Eisenstein, Hitchcock, and Godard, for example, must be sought in their creation of "a certain cinema, an other cinema" that "seizes us" in a particular kind of image: "the specular," which is to be distinguished from "the spectacle" (2002a, 69; 1997, 110).

The "specular" is neither the visible image nor foreign to it. Kristeva theorizes "the specular" according to Freud's logic of *Phantasie*. Fantasy, Kristeva says, reveals the logic, as well as the risks, of the imaginary. Kristeva examines fantasy through a return to Freud's notion of *Phantasie*, which refers to the concrete crafting of representations. She defines it as an "imaginary scenario in which the subject depicts in a more or less distorted way the fulfillment of a desire" (2002a, 64; 1997, 101). For Freud, fantasy refers to "particular imaginary formations" and not to an abstract "field of imagination" (ibid.) or a general "faculty of imagining" (2002a, 63; 1997, 101). Importantly, whereas one might interpret Freudian fantasy as a reduction of imaginary formations to biological or bodily instincts, Kristeva emphasizes the irreducibility and complex relation between representation and desire. Fantasy reveals that representation must be understood in relation to the influx of bodily desire and, conversely, that the signifier is always already embodied. Between "flesh and the word . . . fantasy is precisely what emerges at the crossroads" (2002a, 65; 1997, 103). The crossroads of fantasy reveal two important specificities of the Freudian notion of fantasy: first, psychical reality is irreducible to material reality; second, fantasies are themselves complex formations that, Kristeva says, "prompts us to think of psychical life as a life of multiple and heterogeneous strata, as a polyvalent, layered psychical apparatus," which suggests an "interdependence and translatability among all levels of psychical life" (2002a, 65–66; 1997, 104). Thus, for Kristeva, neither biological, instinctual impulses nor social, symbolic codes alone are the ultimate source of fantasy. Fantasy, rather, emerges at the crossroads. It would seem that the society of the spectacle, since it is a society of images, would constitute a nurturing space for fantasy. Kristeva, however, says the exact opposite. For Kristeva, the society of the spectacle is actually hostilely and paradoxically opposed to the creation of fantasy, and the new maladies of the soul affected by the spectacle are characterized by the destruction of the faculty of imagination (2002a, 67; 1997, 107). The specular, in distinction from the spectacle, is a dynamic put in play by the inscription of material affectivity. The specular image of cinema functions as a troubling of the society of the spectacle. That is, it returns us to the image's originary threshold of meaning and being. In her own creative work, Kristeva privileges detective fiction as a modern form of this troubling.

All detective and crime fiction embody at least three essential elements: the mystery, which may or may not contain a crime, a protagonist-detective, and an investigation. These three elements are organized according to two co-constitutive stories: (1) the story that has already happened, that is, the mystery/crime that remains an enigma, and (2) the narrative that constitutes the plot, that is, the interrogation that uncovers the hidden story. Though all detective fiction contains these two levels in its formula, detective fiction may be further divided according to the presence or absence of what Charles J. Rzepka in *Detective Fiction* (2005) calls a "puzzle element," which presents the mystery "as an ongoing problem for the reader to solve, and its power to engage the reader's own reasoning abilities" (2005, 10) and, he later adds, the reader's imaginative capacities. According to Rzepka, these stories are ones that constitute a special relationship to the reader and her or his experience of the text. Contrary to much detective fiction, which reveals a solution of which the reader has already become suspicious prior to its being made public, the introduction of a puzzle element is one that delays the resolution of the mystery and enables multiple, imaginative constructions of the hidden story, on the part of the reader as well as the detective. The narrative constructions of the veiled story hidden at the heart of the detective story are enabled by engaging the reader's imaginative capacities. Detective and reader are joined in a search to solve a riddle through the recovery of a story. However, the effect is not simply the experience of resolution, but the prolongation of the moment in which the imaginative constructions are reduced to a single one (the story's end that gives sense to the beginning and middle of the plot). That is, the experience of reading engages our desire to create meanings.

Kristeva's work introduces a fifth element of detective fiction: the "proper [*propre*] inquiry." The "proper inquiry" of detective fiction embodies what Rzepka calls "the puzzle element," but it further engages the subject's identity uncertainties. The quest for meaning can simultaneously challenge and transform the spectacular ego. In this, it differs from the spectacle of detective fiction insofar as the subject comes to recognize impurity, criminality, evil not as distinct from herself or himself—that is, as the Other—but as part and parcel of one's own untenable identity. The "proper inquiry" that constitutes the demystifying power of the detective story, whether experienced on the screen of the cinematic image or that of our own dreams, is represented in the very mystery and organization of Kristeva's first detective novel, *The Old Man and the Wolves*. The "proper inquiry" that is the detective story in *The Old Man and the Wolves* begins only in part 2, after "The Invasion" of Santa Varvara. The detective story begins when the narrator as narrator enters the novel. Part 2 opens thus: "That's how the tale of the Old Man and the wolves might begin, as seen from a distance by a hidden, anonymous observer, the author in disguise. But if the master of ceremonies should reveal himself and include himself in the story, whether dreamlike so far or literary, plausible or grotesque, is ipso facto transformed into a quest after mysteries, a police inquiry" (1994, 63; 1991, 97). The "inquiry proper" begins only once the role of the author is put into question and made into that of a policeman or an archeologist. Kristeva's use of the phrase "proper inquiry," draws on the sense of the French word "*propre*" which means "the self." The proper inquiry is an inquiry into the self. The "sordid passions," "strange phantoms," and criminal events of the tale come to be seen as implicating the narrator's own quest, which lives from, Kristeva says, "anxiety, fear, sleeplessness, stupidity, bestiality, brutality, crime . . . And who knows what else?" (1994, 65; 1991, 99). The "proper inquiry" of detective fiction, for Kristeva, effects a return to one's own unconscious, where what is projected as other comes to be seen as the same and may thereby be worked through. This process exemplifies Kristeva's psychoanalytic concept of revolt as a return to one's past through one's unconscious.

In her second detective novel, *Possessions*, the "proper inquiry" of the detective novel described in *The Old Man and the Wolves* is redescribed as examining one's *possessions*. Santa Varvara, as the spectacular city of crime, is the place to which Delacour continually returns—having lived there for a brief time as a child and having returned many more times as a journalist. When she arrives in Santa Varvara to investigate the murder of Gloria, she admits to feeling as if she'd never really left. She confesses to "a physical yet shameful affinity with some kind of wickedness": "It's as though I were inhabited by another person, vague but impossible to get rid of, whom I'd rather ignore but who in fact possesses me" (1998c, 15; 1996h, 27). Possession is always possession by sensation—possessed by love, by hatred, by suffering, by sensible excess. Stephanie examines her possessions in order to prepare herself "for the task of working as a detective" (1998c, 106; 1996h, 142). As an epigraph to one of her chapters in *Murder in Byzantium*, Kristeva quotes Patricia Highsmith's confession in *Plotting and Writing Suspense Fiction*: "Perhaps I have a strong criminal tendency buried deep within me, otherwise I wouldn't be so interested in criminals and I wouldn't write so often about them. . . . A suspense novel is quite different from a detective novel. . . . Its author will take a much greater interest in the criminal mind, because the criminal often takes up the whole thing from start to finish and the writer has to get down what happens in his head. Unless one is attracted to him, one does not succeed" (quoted by Kristeva 2006b, 89; 2004a, 149). By examining her own possessions—for example, from her "satisfying hatred" before Gloria's beheaded body to her own erotic *jouissance*—Stephanie avoids both "a good conscience" and "crime." The examination that enables Stephanie to confront and interpret her own emotional trials opens a third option: thought, sublimation, or self-determining meaning.

In *Murder in Byzantium*, the "proper inquiry" of *The Old Man and the Wolves* and the examination of one's possessions in *Possessions* takes place as Delacour's own private Byzantium. For Kristeva, Byzantium's iconography offers an alternative economy of the image. The icon is an inscription, a graph, a sensible trace, not a spectacle. Byzantium is presented as "the opposite of Santa Varvara" (2006b, 67; 2004a, 117), an "intimate strangeness" (2006b, 69; 2004a, 121), "the unnameable" (2006b, 69; 2004a, 118), Stephanie's own little "madeleine cake" (2006b, 71; 2004a, 123), the source of her "detachment" (2006b, 73; 2004a, 125). Byzantium is nowhere, no place. It is related, instead, as "a detective story" (2006b, 84; 2004a, 143). As a detective story, Byzantium is "only imaginary" (2006b, 82; 2004a, 140) and "a question of time" (2006b, 88; 2004a, 147), an "odd future anterior" (2006b, 83, 88; 2004a, 141, 147): "No, don't look for me on the map, my Byzantium is a matter of time, the very question that time asks itself when it doesn't want to choose between two places, two dogmas, two crises, two identities, two continents, two religions, two sexes, two plots. Byzantium leaves the question of time open and time as well. Neither hesitation nor uncertainty, nothing but the wisdom of what happens, of time passing, a passing passenger, future anterior" (2006b, 88; 2004a, 147). Kristeva's search for Byzantium is thus not a return to rescue the historical truth of Byzantium. There are, Delacour says, "only imaginary Byzantiums" (2006b, 82; 2004a, 140).

Because Byzantium is always "only imaginary" it easily functions as an *eidos* for multiple interpretations. In *Murder in Byzantium*, two characters follow the hermeneutical trace of Byzantium: Sebastian Crest-Jones and Wuxian, the Chinese immigrant and twin-brother of Fa Chang, the pregnant lover and murder victim of Sebastian. Sebastian Crest-Jones is described as consumed by interiority; Wuxian as "the man without interiority" (2006b, 239; 2004a, 359). Sebastian seeks to recover the memory of his ancestors in an attempt to solidify his identity; Wuxian seeks to purify the city of a corrupt religious mafia that claims authority over historical destiny. Sebastian's search is no antidote to Wuxian's own. While it opens onto the past, it seeks a historical truth recovered only through the murder of his future in the body of Fa Chang. Time is thus a principal figure of the novel. More correctly, the *Zeitlos* (the outside-time) is the principle figure, and it is first presented as the (non)time of crime, of murder. The criminal, the detective, and the reader all exist in a suspended time. In *La Haine et le pardon* (2005),[2] Kristeva says, "Crime fascinates us because it reveals a psychic functioning authorized by the suspension of time, and, in the instant of the criminal gesture, is itself excluded from human time" (2005b, 626). An outside, "abysmal" time of murderous impulses ravages both Sebastian and Wuxian. Stephanie's Byzantium is neither the historical past nor a sedimented conception of the future, but "an odd future anterior."

The journalist-detective must exist in the interval of sensible timelessness and the time of the narrative. The murderous gestures staged by the crime novel are the projections of the violence of the narrator and the reader themselves. But, as a counterpoint to the outside, "abysmal" time of the murderous impulses that ravage both Sebastian and Wuxian, there also exists "a splendid variant of outside-time" that one discovers in the figure of Jerry, who embodies, Kristeva says, "the best of the *Zeitlos*" (2005b, 628–29). By adopting Jerry, the autistic son of her murdered friend Gloria (cf. *Possessions*), Stephanie encounters a relation that suspends the genealogical time of history. The relationship between Stephanie and Jerry invites the reader to reflect on the imaginary and symbolic function of maternality beyond the celebration of biological, historical, and geographical origins (2005b, 636). Delacour credits her attachment to Jerry as a form of connection that engages her "feminine sensibility" extraneous to the spectacle. By staging the connection as a chance encounter, rather than as a biological fate, Delacour's relationship to Jerry offers an image of motherhood as a privileged model of an attachment, rather than as the natural, biological source of feminine sensibility. The "feminine sensibility" of Kristeva's hero is parallel to Kristeva's conception of feminine being as a boundary being at the threshold of meaning and being. It is not the effect of maternity, but maternity can be (though is not always) one expression of it. The affective/symbolic connection freed of biological roots and historical destiny distinguishes Delacour's connection to Jerry beyond the linear time of history.

Delacour's "feminine sensibility" must be understood in relation to Delacour's nomadism and foreignness, expressed in Delacour's second motto: "I travel myself." Delacour is a foreigner in Santa Varvara both physically and psychically. She owns no language, no soil, no past, no future. In this, she shares the same fate as some of the inhabitants of Santa Varvara, including Sebastian. Sebastian's search for his genealogical roots concludes with a new disclosure of Byzantium that allows him the satisfaction of "[pasting] the pieces of himself back together in another world" (2006b, 182; 2004a, 277). He can then retire as a killer and withdraw for a Coke at a Pizza Hut with Santa Varvaran dollars to tantalize a prostitute (2006b, 181–82; 2004a, 276–77). Stephanie's restlessness does not lead her to search for biological, historical, or geographical roots—*another world*—to settle her own identity uncertainties. Her nomadism opens onto a *sensible strangeness*: "I don't hunker down inside myself because that deep center gets found out. I pass instead into the in-between, neither depth nor surface, and take up residence in that emptiness I call strangeness" (2006b, 63; 2004a, 112). That strangeness is the place of her relationship to Jerry, her delaying tactics as a journalist, the source of her writing and her investigations. Delacour's nomadism, like Sebastian's and Wuxian's, is conditioned by her social-historical situation, but she turns toward the interior to find her strangeness to herself as *another time* outside time, a sensible time where borders become permeable and give way to new choices, new connections, new beginnings that displace the borders of identity certainty—a psychoanalytic experience.

A psychoanalytic dimension is introduced into Kristeva's detective fiction through the comparison of the lead protagonist, journalist-detective Stephanie Delacour, with other, spectacular characters caught in an empty and violent cycle of barbarism and banality. Speaking of Stephanie Delacour in an interview with Bernard Sichère concerning *The Old Man and the Wolves*, Kristeva says, "the character of the journalist-detective introduces a certain psychoanalytic tonality in the book. Without this interior space . . . no working out of truth is possible. No investigation, no knowledge. Some based their aesthetics, for example, on Goethe, others on Rousseau, or Rimbaud. I consider myself a contemporary Freud" (1996d, 166). In the same interview, she says, "Police investigations, mystery thrillers make the unveiling of cruelty plausible, almost bearable. That is why I intend to pursue the mystery genre—a game. A way of continuing analysis" (1996d, 171). In each of her detective novels, Stephanie is able to confront, resist, and describe the society of the spectacle precisely due to her reflective and interpretive capacities. For Kristeva, the detective novel opens the path to a psychic rebirth, which is why she classifies her own detective fiction as a form of revolt.

If Kristeva relates the interrogative revolt of detective fiction, which carves out a psyche within the violence of the spectacle, to that of psychoanalysis, it is not the version of psychoanalysis we've come to expect. Indeed, the parallel might suggest a psychological reduction to an ideological normativity of subject constitution. In her detective novels, the protagonist, Stephanie Delacour, is not a psychoanalyst, but a journalist-detective, and the budding psychoanalysts, who portend to have all the answers, fail to discover any truth insofar as they reduce all other characters and actions to normative structures. In *The Old Man and the Wolves*, Vespasian—a spectacular, virtual, imagistic character—diagnoses the Professor, Septicius Clarus, as nothing but Freud's "Wolf Man." In *Murder in Byzantium*, psychoanalysis is presented as empty dinner-party banter. If Kristeva presents psychoanalysis in such a reductive light, it is because she seeks to distinguish her understanding of psychoanalysis from its popular reception. Kristeva's own psychoanalytic practice, she claims in *New Maladies of the Soul*, attests to the singularity of each individual. Indeed, she claims that the psychoanalyst who fails to discover a new malady of the soul (beyond the classification systems of traditional psychoanalysis) in each patient does not appreciate the singular uniqueness of each of her or his patients (1995, 9; 1993, 19). In her critical works, Kristeva accords considerable importance to rereading Freud as a revolutionary in matters of the soul. The proper inquiry she presents in her detective fiction may be understood as an enactment of the temporal structure of meaning production she discovers in Freud. The detective story is a riddle in which there is a meaning sensed, but hidden, a storyteller with a purpose, but with an elusive object.

It is not simply Delacour's journalistic and detective activity that distinguishes her. Detective fiction and investigative journalism are not in themselves immune to the spectacle, but (more often than not) serve a mystifying function. For example, Delacour's editor at the *Evenement de Paris* appears within the novels only as a form of pressure to "get the story." He "lectures" her on the "no exit" of the spectacle (2006b, 77; 2004a, 132) and continually complains of her delays. Delacour confirms his sentiment by admitting that whatever is exposed through journalistic-investigative activity will not upset anyone. Instead, it will simply fuel a new movie, a new television show, a new novel, a new autobiography. In the spectacle, the image absorbs everything. However, Delacour believes that her "little investigations" propose an exit, "one that passe[s] through the interior" and is achieved by unearthing what lies "underneath the image" and what "the image strives to put to sleep": the drive (2006b, 77; 2004a, 133). Psychoanalysis is privileged by Kristeva in its function as an experience of language in which drives and affects are integrated into psychic life. By returning to the analysand's own past (both historical and affective), psychoanalysis effects psychic renewal beyond the good conscience that separates me from abject crime, as well as beyond criminal enjoyment without remorse. The work of language experienced in psychoanalysis, as well as in writing and literature, traverses the most violent impulses, giving them representation and thereby integrating them into the whole personality. When thought and meaning are but a sham, the result is violence (toward oneself and/or others; emotional and/or physical). Kristeva's thought is that by giving meaning to drives and affects, we can be liberated from acting on them. Delacour claims that she can avoid crime, by writing about it. Her motto is: "I investigate, therefore I am" (ibid.). Kristeva claims that the privileged terrain for exploring the rehabilitation of psychic life is the novel, which offers a "minimal variant of revolt": "It is not much, but we may have reached a point of no return, from which we will have to re-turn to the little things, tiny revolts, in order to preserve the life of the mind and of the species" (2002a, 5; 1997, 10). For better or worse, Kristeva's contribution is the excavation of such "little investigations" or "tiny revolts" experienced in psychoanalysis and works of art.

Kristeva's privileging of psychoanalysis and fiction as concrete *experiences* of meaning and social connection, rather than as mirror images of one another or of normative structures, raises anew the question of the significance of Kristeva's unique response to contemporary social and political life. As a theory, psychoanalysis remains "abstract," that is, *incomplete*, insofar as it theorizes formative structures and processes of psychic life. In order to understand its concrete significance, it must be put back into its social-historical context—both as a clinical experience and as a theoretical construction. Detective fiction, like psychoanalytic experience, offers an interminable *return* to a (material) past that renews the psychic life of meaning within a particular social and historical context. Kristeva seeks to identify and resuscitate a culture and experience of revolt in terms of concrete experiences that are at once social and historical, and thereby shared, on the one hand, and yet material, unique, and irreducible, on the other. Nevertheless, while Kristeva addresses social and historical realities, one may legitimately question the relevance of her psychoanalytic and aesthetic position to larger social and political formations. Indeed, rather than engaging social and political philosophy proper, Kristeva multiplies her examples of revolt by not only writing novels, but also by recounting the trials of her patients, writing autobiographical confessions, and examining the lives and works of artists, philosophers, theologians, psychoanalysts, and saints through book-length and essay-length biographies and critical essays. Anyone looking for a positive social and political philosophy concerned with identifying the nature of just social and political institutions and frameworks for the future will be grossly disappointed by Kristeva's refusal to offer one. One may then ask how Kristeva's novels should be understood and how her decision to multiply individual examples of revolt should be measured. If we all just work on ourselves a bit or read a novel, we'll all be okay? Such questions may have the unfortunate effect of leading one to abandon Kristeva at this juncture: to criticize her models for lacking any real engagement with the future of just social and political institutions and frameworks; or to extend her models of revolt to the social and political level. However, before concluding that Kristeva's thought lacks any real relevance to social and political thought proper or that Kristeva simply failed to extend the significance of her work to the level of social and political realities, it may be useful to examine her refusal to theorize politics in this way and to reevaluate the social and political implications of her persistent concern to identify concrete instances of revolt.

Kristeva's interest in the renewal of revolt is tied to her concern to examine the ways in which the future is closed off by traditional social symbolic systems, not only in their failures to provide meaning, but also in their privileging of progress, production, and development according to sedimented conceptions of the future. In *Intimate Revolt*, Kristeva goes so far as to say that "[w]hat makes sense today is not the future" (2002a, 5; 1997, 11). In lieu of the "future" as that which we seek to determine and achieve, Kristeva proposes "revolt" as "the questioning and displacement of the past" (ibid.). The future that Kristeva seeks to challenge represents the burial of the past, space, materiality, alternative temporalities, and new modes of connection embodied in the concept of revolt. At the start of *The Future of Revolt* (1998), she says, "The need for connection might establish another politics, some day. Today, psychical life knows that it will only be saved if it gives itself the time and space of revolt" (2002a, 223; 1998b, 11). Kristeva thus ties her thesis of revolt to a necessary *suspension* of a sedimented conception of the future. In *The Future of Revolt*, Kristeva offers an alternative sense of the future embodied in her concept of revolt. Kristeva's renewal of the concept of revolt indicates a material temporal process by which the future is opened to plural and diverse possibilities of meaning and connection. Playing on Camus' rebel, who says, "I revolt, therefore we are," Kristeva says, "I revolt, therefore we are *to come* [*à venir*]" (2002a, 224; 1998b, 12). "To come" is the literal meaning of the French term for the future—*l'avenir*. The shift from "I" to "we" in this formulation points to the forging of connections accomplished by revolt. Revolt is not simply a rebellion against some power effecting a separated position, but a process by which new modes of connection are made possible. Thus, while Kristeva insists on the suspension of a certain conception of the future, she ties the concrete possibilities of the future to the emergence of new experiences of meaning and modes of connection. Rather than speculatively defining the nature of just social and political arrangements from transcendental arguments and a privileged epistemic perspective, she seeks concrete instances of revolt emerging from the lived experience of actual social and political realities. "The future," she says, "if it exists, depends on it" (2002a, 5; 1997, 11).

Notes

1. Major elements of this essay also appear in my *Kristeva: Thresholds* (London: Polity Press, 2011).
2. All translations of *La haine et le pardon* are my own.

2

Revolution Has Italian Roots

Kristeva's Fiction and Theory

Carol Mastrangelo Bové

This essay examines the presence of Italy in Julia Kristeva's fiction and theory: "Giotto's Joy" (1972), "Motherhood According to Bellini" (1975), "Stabat Mater" (1977), *The Samurai* (1990), and especially *The Old Man and the Wolves* (1991). Italy, including ancient Rome, becomes a fundamental component of her thought and connecting link between her fiction and theory especially in her second novel and in one of the most literary and celebrated of her essays, "Stabat Mater." An examination of Italy in Kristeva sheds light on the development of the influential, prolific writer, identifies her second novel as a critical moment in her psychoanalytic writing, and helps to evaluate her strength as a novelist. I will examine what seems to be a central problem posed by her work, that her analysis of the semiotic tends to reinforce gender stereotypes. Kristeva uses Italy and Rome both to raise the issue of an identification with a feminine figure in a theory of the semiotic and to ground this theory in the history and material conditions of European culture.

Some critics including Jacqueline Rose and Judith Butler have stated that Kristeva's elaboration of the semiotic feminine—a category fundamental to her writing and linked to Italy and Rome, as my essay will demonstrate—is rife with stereotype. In *Sexuality in the Field of Vision*, Rose has written eloquently on Kristeva's work prior to her turn to fiction and calls attention to the problematic category of the semiotic and its potential for stereotyping women and relegating them to abjection and masochism. With this reservation, Rose nevertheless praises Kristeva's work because it recognizes the persistence of such stereotypes in fantasy and the challenges posed by unconscious drives underlying psychic and social structures (1986, 164).

Kristeva's and Rose's psychoanalytic approaches take care to include components sometimes found lacking in such writing (and in its tendency to universalize) and demanded by recent work in literature, criticism, and theory: historical analysis and an understanding of women as active participants shaping their lives in different ways. Rose, for example, though not uncritical of Kristeva's theory of the semiotic, writes to some extent in her wake, as does this essay, and has cogently examined the psychic formations underlying the Israeli/Palestinian conflict. Such psychoanalytic writing recognizes that contemporary dilemmas including violent conflicts among and within nations and within severely troubled individuals continue to require a psychic realignment and an ethical reflection capable of modifying the events that threaten our well-being. Martha Reineke's essay in this collection cogently analyzes the peace-oriented philosophy underlying Kristeva's thought including *The Old Man and the Wolves* and indicates its debt to René Girard's seminal work.

What is at stake in Kristeva's writing and in her efforts to create an ethics that addresses conflict is the need for the individual to awaken the semiotic capabilities within. That is, briefly stated, to recreate the early symbiosis with the mother that, in order for the child to learn to speak, must also include an identification with the father, the masculine authority figure upon whom the social contract is based. In this process, the child comes to understand the mother (and father) as hybrid entities (see Bové, 14, for a fuller explanation). The language that one speaks incorporates both sexes to the extent that linguistic signs include both (1) the semiotic: signifiers, words themselves, the sounds and ambiguities linked in psychoanalytic theory to the maternal body and (2) the symbolic: signifieds, the dictionary meanings or referents connected to masculine authority. Kristeva's effort to dramatize the dangerous challenge that the individual confronts in trying to recreate symbiosis makes *The Old Man and the Wolves* a particularly strong novel.

In *The Samurai* and *The Old Man and the Wolves*, Kristeva uses Italy, as she had earlier in her theoretical writing, to construct a sensuous language capable of renewing the link to the mother. The element of her theory that enables her to write her most riveting and compelling fiction, the threat of a breakdown resulting from the failure to achieve an identification with the mother, is not central to *The Samurai* and is relegated primarily to Carole and Martin, two minor characters in this first novel (Bové, 100–01). This threat is also absent in the three instances of her nonfiction examined here. It does emerge in her second novel, *The Old Man and the Wolves*, and compels a rethinking of European and American psychic formations and their impact on individual and sociopolitical structures.

Kristeva finds an unorthodox expression of desire for the mother in Giotto and Bellini (Bové, 37). In "Giotto's Joy" (1972) she demonstrates the ways in which the painter's innovations in line and color constitute a practice that is both artistic in departing from tendencies to realist painting, and ideological in aligning itself with the growing Florentine upper middle class. She writes with feeling about instinctual drives, including the relationship to the mother, enabling Giotto, in the clearest example from the essay, to contest orthodox representation of Christian narrative in his fresco's scroll: he represents it rolling back to reveal a more secular human hell. She also focuses on the use of color in one of his paintings to show how it undercuts a perspective that would restrict the viewer to a single point of view. Giotto's painting allows the spectator to enjoy multiple perspectives and does not conform to contemporary movements toward realist representation.

Kristeva's analysis links Giotto's efforts to loosen contemporary rules concerning his art to sociopolitical and ideological developments challenging medieval hierarchies and Christian thought. She calls attention to the fact that mythical characters appearing with Mary, Christ, and Saint Francis resemble contemporary peasants, for example. During this period of significant change, nominalism and Averroism challenge Christian dogma. For Kristeva, Giotto's painting is part of the larger context including the expansion of the thirteenth-century Florentine upper middle class, which provides intellectual and economic support for Giotto and other innovative painters in the decades to follow.

Giotto engages the senses, emotions, and the mind in his use of line and color both in themselves, in their Catholic subjects (the Madonna, hell, etc.), and in their subversion of the artistic, sociopolitical, and ideological constraints of his time. The model for his art is verbal narrative, which, among all of the arts, may be the most significant for Kristeva, given that words are necessary for the thought and psychic structures, including the dynamics between symbolic and semiotic, that underlie all artistic creation: "storytelling . . . relies on . . . the kinetic pleasure everyone feels in following a sequence of events. . . . it's another version of contemplation, an algebraic form of orison, logic transformed into prayer. Then the novel opens out into philosophy, and the interfusion of one with the other abolishes the frontiers once drawn up between the different genres for the benefit of lazy schoolboys" (1991, 99; my translation). Words are also the stuff of stories that she places at the center of these theoretical remarks embedded in *The Old Man and the Wolves* in part because she may believe that narratives are an ideal form for raising theoretical and political issues. They constitute a dynamic pleasure for virtually everyone and for this reason engage the reader's critical thinking. Furthermore, as Kristeva learned from Bakhtin, narrative is dialogic, structured in relation to another to whom it is addressed and thus by its very nature designed to engage multiple voices, including the symbolic and the semiotic.

In "Motherhood According to Bellini" (1975), Kristeva also examines Bellini's work on the model of familial stories unfolding out of psychic formations. She focuses on his portraits of women as child- and male-oriented figures from Byzantine through Renaissance humanist icons. His Madonnas' color and light set within nonrealistic perspectives release desire in and through the portrait of the mother as apparent support of patriarchal cultures. A subversive presence in European painting, Bellini's mothers exist in contradistinction to mainstream depictions of women best exemplified by Da Vinci as man's sexual object and parent to new members of the social order. In this context, Bellini's canvases link Renaissance painting to that of Poussin, Cézanne, Matisse, and Rothko. Kristeva examines Bellini's 1515 Venus in a way many observers would not otherwise understand, in fact, examining her as a cipher in motion and demonstrating how the artist breaks apart realist perspective using the play of colored light created by the mirror that the nude woman holds at an angle. Bellini thus creates an impossible third dimension as the eye moves from her face to the mirror she holds in front of her, to the mirror on the back wall.

In her article on "Renaissance Painting and Psychoanalysis," Mary Bittner Wiseman states that for Kristeva, Bellini reveals two shifting perspectives on the woman in his 1515 Venus. The viewer sees her and the partial image of the back of her head in the mirror on the wall, an image different from the one Venus sees in the mirror she holds and that reveals the entire back of her head and hand reflected in the wall mirror (Wiseman, 112).

According to Wiseman, Kristeva's elaboration of the maternal constitutes an important contribution to psychoanalytic theory on women given that Freud and many psychoanalytic writers focus very little on them and pay far greater attention to the paternal. Wiseman takes Freud's impasse in his case study of Dora as the point of departure for her study of Kristeva's approach to the Madonna in Renaissance painting. In Kristeva's essay on Bellini, the Madonna fascinates, as Raphael's Madonna had fascinated Dora, by enabling a replaying of the connection to the mother understood not as the support of the social contract but as a figure with multiple possibilities for expression subverting paternal authority. Unlike Da Vinci who would more likely paint a child-oriented, conventional female, Bellini uses luminous color, for example, to depict her otherworldly pleasure. Kristeva also places his painting in its biographical context, paralleling the dynamism of his work and personal life: it is during this time that Bellini marries and becomes a father.

Wiseman's essay makes clear the ways in which Kristeva's writing on Bellini is historically grounded in France of the 1970s, in Vienna at the turn of the twentieth century, and especially in his biography and in Italy during the Renaissance. Kristeva uses fifteenth-century Florence to give her study of Bellini an intellectual and social context and to examine his portrayal of the Madonna with more precision, for instance, in comparing his portraits to those of da Vinci.

In "The Body Politics of Julia Kristeva," Judith Butler faults "Motherhood According to Bellini" along with other essays included in *Desire in Language* for seeing maternity as a teleological phenomenon making it virtually impossible for women to be agents in the shaping of their lives. For Butler, "Kristeva reifies maternity and then promotes this reification as the disruptive potential of the semiotic. As a result, the paternal law, understood as the ground of univocal signification, is displaced by an equally univocal signifier, the principle of the maternal body which remains self-identical in its teleology regardless of its multiplicitous manifestations" (Butler 1993, 175). In my reading of the Bellini essay, Butler's critique seems unjustifiable: Kristeva sees the mother not as an object and essentialist category but as a shifting subject with the potential for a variety of modes of being: virgin, otherworldly goddess, mother, writer, among others.

Marilyn Edelstein's careful reading of "Stabat Mater" (1977) corroborates that Kristeva's writing is in fact historical in her documentation of the psychic and social needs served by the Virgin Mary in her various forms over time. Edelstein also points out that one can "almost divide Kristeva's critics into those who excoriate her for privileging the semiotic and those who do for privileging the symbolic" (à la Butler) (37). The fact that the maternal subject is not reified but multiple, functioning in significant ways in both the semiotic and symbolic realms, may explain this division.

In "Stabat Mater," for instance, Kristeva sees childbirth as an engagement in the social contract and thus as a step beyond masochism. The essay, arguably her best known and most poetic, uses fundamental elements of her theory to analyze motherhood, including the categories of the semiotic, the symbolic, and nature, as I have explained (Bové, 7, 14, 91). According to this theory, women live in danger of psychosis, a psychic formation that is masochistic to the degree that women allow themselves to become engulfed by the semiotic and its links to the body during the period of language acquisition. It is an identification with a father that is crucial in this period in order for the child to develop the ability to recreate symbiosis within language.

Kristeva demonstrates the implications of the early Italian category of "woman" for the malaise of contemporary cultures and especially for women's dissatisfaction with motherhood. The dissatisfaction derives from society's denial of women's humanity, her double character. She is "rational mind" in the sense of participant in the social order as mother, wife, and daughter, a triad crystallized in Dante's *Divine Comedy.* She is also "body," including the particular pleasure afforded by the senses, emotions, and psyche—a pleasure deriving from the character the social order often refuses her once she has signed its contract.

Here Kristeva gives careful attention to the history of the Virgin Mary as a matriarchal, goddess-like figure linked closely to the body *and* language, associations derived in great part from the Catholic cult of Mary with notions of the virginal and matriarchal goddess imported from the Eastern Orthodox Church. In this context, the Virgin is often sexless and integrally connected to life in the sense of the spiritual redemption that Christ won back for human beings. In Kristeva's account of the influence of western European Catholicism on the Eastern Orthodox Church, virgins originally linked to the body become sexless enablers of spiritual redemption.

In the essay overall, Kristeva raises the question of a woman's hybrid character, made up of psychic formations deriving in part from 1) primary narcissism, that is, the moment when she is still symbiotically connected to her own mother's body and on the threshold of language acquisition, and from 2) the social contract allowing her to become engaged once she acquires language and, if she becomes a mother, gives birth to new members of society. In a kind of prose poem printed alongside the essay and in parts of the essay itself, Kristeva stages a temporary break with the contract and its more conventional discourses of love that characterize the essay as a whole. The concluding lines mesh with the more emotional and literary qualities of the poem:

> Women bearing the desire for childbearing, for stability. . . . Women available to enable our species, endowed with speech and knowing itself to be mortal, to endure death. Mothers. Because a heretical ethics, distinct from morality, a herethics, is arguably and primarily what makes it possible to endure death by making connections, by thinking. Herethics is *a-mort, amour. Eia mater, fons amoris*. . . . Let's listen to *Stabat Mater* once again, and the music, all of it . . . engulfing the goddesses and hiding the necessity for them. (1983, 327; my translation)

In an essay in which she creates an identification with a maternal figure via the poetic description of a visceral experience, her concluding words evoke that figure one last time in language that is both poetry and prose. "Stabat Mater" affirms a heterogeneous life in the body and in speech linked to Italy via Catholicism's category of the Virgin and exemplified in Pergolesi's baroque celebration of love for the mother in his music as the title borrowed from the composer indicates (*There Stood the Mother*). While the essay would be stronger with some analysis of the music, "Stabat Mater" is compelling both as theory and as literature. Kristeva incorporates fundamental elements of her psychoanalytic thought, the categories of the "maternal" and "paternal," for example, in the hybrid style of a cultural theorist and poet, appropriate in an examination of woman's double character. She conveys the sense of an identification with the mother in the threatening and enigmatic quality of these lines ("the music engulfing the goddesses, hiding the necessity for them") and in the sensuality of the music that together recreate the symbiotic relationship. Kristeva also suggests the role of language in women's hybrid character to the extent that the writers and composers convey notions of the feminine in the form of signs, both verbal and musical, that is, Catholicism's category of the Virgin and Pergolesi's music. Edelstein too emphasizes the double character of the mother in the last lines, connected as she is to both death and love (Edelstein, 36).

Italy next appears in Kristeva's writing in the portrayal of a minor character, Carole, in *The Samurai* (1990). Like her other three novels, this one embodies her theory in a fiction that often resembles a philosophical tale though more autobiographical and with less satire and humor than Voltaire's. The two protagonists—Olga, the student from Eastern Europe who is establishing herself as a brilliant writer in Paris, and Joëlle, the psychoanalyst and the narrator, who is among the most respected in her profession—manage to achieve the identification with the mother that is integral to their successful work. That is, they lead lives that seem to incorporate the fundamentals of Kristeva's ethical system based on the tension between semiotic and symbolic languages. Part of Joëlle's narration is in diary form. On one level, she is communicating only with herself and, as Miglena Nikolchina points out in her essay in this volume, offers an "intimate" style contrasting with Joëlle's more social style in imagining/narrating Olga. Yet, Joëlle's words in her journal permit us to see her character as parallel to Olga's, and especially, to Kristeva's: Joëlle reveals social, intimate, and conflicted components of the novelist herself.

In *The Samurai*, Kristeva uses Italy, including reference to two of the same artists, Giotto and Bellini, as she had in the essays, to construct a sensuous language capable of renewing the link to an androgynous imaginary mother. Olga's friend, Carole, a graduate student, suffers severe depression as she struggles with writing; an even more depressed boyfriend, Martin; and a cold, sadistic mother who has hurt her for years. Fortunately, she spent her summers with her Italian grandmother, Rosalba, in Fiesole, near Florence, as a young girl and revisited the city with her friend Olga the preceding year. Rosalba, fittingly named to call up Fiesole's flowers and the fragile dawning of emotional well-being in Carole, loves her granddaughter and introduces her to pleasurable moments together. They share the beauty of the roses, their color and smell, and of the Virgin to whom they offer the blooms, lighting a candle before her image. This reference directly links Kristeva's theory and fiction, connecting Carole's pleasure to the Roman Catholic Church's cult of Mary examined in "Stabat Mater." In an especially well-crafted passage reminiscent of Colette's *La Maison de Claudine*, Rosalba searches for Carole, calling her name while the granddaughter listens, lost in a sensuous romp through the warm, fragrant grass and lilacs, as Colette, playing in the garden in summer, had heard her loving mother calling out to the children (1994a, 5).

Writing to her friend Olga, Carole recreates these rare and joyful Italian scenes. Facts and language are lost in movement in grass and flowers approaching sexual arousal. Carole asks, "Or was it the lavender? I don't remember" (1994a, 202). She dives into the lilacs whose curvy round clusters (*touffe* ["bunch"] is also a word for pubic hair), thick and sweet-smelling, induce her to relax and almost sleep. Carole mentions her feet as if they were a rabbit's paws meeting and cuddling up in the warm grass and blooms.

Once again Kristeva uses Italian sources to express the semiotic feminine, for instance, Giotto's frescoes in Carole's telling of her strong emotional response to the graceful peasant-like images of Mary and Christ and the unsettling perspectives created in his palaces. Are the frescoes those of Giotto or of his school? She cannot be sure of the facts and can express her pleasure in neither French nor Italian (1994a, 202).

Italian roots, especially those of her grandmother, lead Carole to experience pleasure in the flowers and in the cult of the Virgin. Rosalba and Olga, Carole's friend, come close to helping her to lift herself out of depression. The episode narrating the friends' exchanges shows Carole's attempting to articulate the project that is her life on the model of Olga's. Kristeva depicts this attempt in Carole's creative linking of the landscape and Giotto's peasants to their counterparts in China where Olga is traveling and writing. Kristeva adds legitimacy and hope for her recovery to Carole's experience of Italian art despite her frequent instability by implicitly connecting this experience to one of the most reliable characters in the novel, Olga's husband Hervé. While traveling in Venice near the end of the book, he enjoys the beauty of Bellini's Madonnas no less than Carole appreciates Giotto and in terms similar to those that appear in "Motherhood According to Bellini."

One year later, Kristeva presses Italy—more precisely, its ancestor, Rome—into service in writing her stronger, haunting novel, *The Old Man and the Wolves* (1991). As the title suggests, the old man, Septicius, lives in an Eastern European country invaded by wolves who arrive from the north and who also emerge from the country's own citizens. The wolves resonate on many levels attesting to Kristeva's growing strength as a creator of complex, compelling narratives. The animals represent the transformation of Rome into a corrupt and barbarous place, the tyranny of the Soviet army in Eastern Europe, of the Nazis, and of Western capitalism after the fall of the Berlin Wall, a general moral decay, and the death drive. Given his antimilitarist character, the old man's name is ironically that of a Roman prefect of the imperial bodyguard. Septicius is also a Latin professor and the only one to see the wolves as a threat, until a Parisian reporter, his former student, Stephanie Delacour, arrives in the country to cover human rights violations. In a darker tone than Ionesco's *Rhinoceros*, the novel like the play reveals a proliferation of animals as the citizens lose their humanity. Among the wolves is the cruel Doctor Vespasian, bearing the name of a Roman emperor, and unfortunately the husband of one of Septicius's favorite pupils, Alba.

Once the principal protagonist, Stephanie, arrives, the novel takes on the shape of a detective story as she tries to determine whether the dead body of a young woman recovered on the beach is that of Alba. In the concluding chapters, Stephanie becomes convinced that Septicius has been murdered. These chapters also read as a memoir on two levels: Kristeva herself mourns her father who had recently died, while Stephanie reflects on the death of Septicius and of her own father years earlier. She returns to her Latin Quarter apartment regretting that she has allowed herself to take on the qualities of a wolf, but claiming to continue to resist, like Berenger at the end of Ionesco's play.

In "The *Trial* of the Third: Kristeva's Oedipus and the Crisis of Identification," Maria Margaroni writes convincingly on the strengths of *The Old Man and the Wolves* both as fiction and as an integral part of Kristeva's theory. While Margaroni does not examine the presence of Italy in the novel, she does show that the novelist/theorist's incorporation of the symbolic and semiotic in the narrative are valuable contributions to literature and theory. For Margaroni, Kristeva's writing is not distorted by stereotype and/or reification as, for instance, for Butler (175). Like Wiseman's, Margaroni's essay demonstrates the strengths of Kristeva's writing as an influential psychoanalytic approach to art. Refuting Butler, Margaroni cogently analyzes *The Old Man and the Wolves* in a global discussion of Kristeva's contributions to cultural theory especially to the Oedipal complex understood as three movements, one of which is the recreation of roots in "the archaic and the timeless force of the drive" (60), another way of describing the semiotic feminine.

Kristeva appears to be aware of the difficulties of distinguishing between "masculine" and "feminine" and displays an understanding of how the paternal functions that is arguably as nuanced as Freud's, for instance, in his essay "Femininity." Furthermore, the paternal presence in *The Old Man and the Wolves* is an androgynous figure not unlike Freud's father of individual prehistory (Bové, 123). In other words, Kristeva appears to subsume the figure of the father within that of the mother in a hybrid parental figure underlying the narrative.

Stephanie and the old man, whom the narrator and author present for the most part in positive terms as hybrid, maternal characters, see Rome before the collapse of the empire as a place and time resembling Santa Varvara. Abusive sex, aggression, murder, materialism, and apathy increasingly characterize both societies. The principal allusions to Rome appear in Septicius's study of the poets Ovid and Tibullus. Septicius reads Ovid's *Metamorphoses* as the representation of the frightening transformation of the civilization that was once alive. He sees Hecuba's metamorphosis into a bitch gouging Polymestor's eyes in particular as glaring evidence of decay. For Septicius and the narrators (first an omniscient third person, then the first person, Stephanie) who describe the old man, Tibullus's elegies sadly recreate an ephemeral sensuality and love. With references to America embedding the story in part in material, historical conditions—Santa Varvara is Santa Barbara in the original French—and to Western consumerism, the examination of Rome offers the possibility of understanding the degeneration of contemporary society including France and the United States. Threatened by the lust, violence, greed, mean-spiritedness, and banality of the Eastern European country whose citizens often pass their time bickering and watching bad television, Septicius turns to Roman poetry for help. Here, unlike the protagonists of *The Samurai*, the main characters', Septicius's and Stephanie's, spirit and ethical stance are under siege, as the metaphor of the barbaric invasion of wolves and the characters' confessions, make clear.

The narrator describes Septicius's obsessive quotations of and references to Ovid's and Tibullus's texts as a fascination with the musical qualities of their verse, that is to say, the material, emotional, and sensual characteristics of the signifier. The old man listens to a beautiful melody that is dangerous because it expresses humiliation and abjection, in the case of Ovid's *Metamorphoses*, or death, in the case of Tibullus's elegies. Beginning with Ovid (who also provides the novel's epigraph) and Tibullus, Kristeva grounds Septicius's sensitivity to music in Rome and Italy. As the novel reveals later, he is a member of the liturgical choir and admires Gregorian chant, arguably the most important music of the Roman Catholic Church in Italy that the communist authorities sometimes allow in order to convince foreigners that freedom of expression exists in Santa Varvara. He is also a lover of Billie Holiday's singing, not explicitly associated with Italy but described in Italian (the narrator makes frequent mention of her "vibrato," or wavering of pitch to express emotion—Italian being the language of musical terminology), and sharing its sunshine ("On the Sunny Side of the Street"), and exoticism ("a whole different world"). Replaying symbiosis with the mother in narrating Septicius's experience of Holiday's singing, as in describing his enjoyment of Roman poetry and of Gregorian chant, Kristeva writes: "the voice of Billie Holiday overwhelmed the Old Man's ear and all his organs. It sounded now husky, now shrill; it was full of sighs and strong rhythms. Physical perfection" (1991, 122; my translation). Such music serves to remove him from the inhumanity, violence, and mediocrity of the wolves.

The narrator implies that the Roman authors incorporate their country in the verses as a no-man's-land in danger of destruction. Ovid and Tibullus, like the old man and Stephanie's father, live in such a no-man's land to the extent that they live through their music, languages, and nomadic personalities without displaying the tribalism growing in both countries. Septicius understands this and the fact that the invading wolves have made his country equally vulnerable to disgrace, abjection, and death. He feels himself attacked by the wolves from within as well, in danger of losing his comprehension of and critical attitude toward the evil that is around him. In the end, Septicius's fascination with Rome and also with Billie Holiday enables him to resist the wolves. Significantly, he dies after having nightmares of the animal, including Ovid's Lycaon, but, at the very end, welcoming the African American singer's husky vibrato into his ears.

The principal threat of psychic breakdown in the novel pursues not Septicius, though his life otherwise bears substantive similarities to hers, but Stephanie as she struggles to understand the invasion of Santa Varvara and the possible destruction of a psychic formation and an ethical system that allow her to live a creative and pleasurable life. One of the best examples of the danger she faces occurs when she sleeps with the monstrous Vespasian in order to learn more about Alba's disappearance and possible death. Here, she comes to hate herself in the throes of abjection ("I found myself hating us both") and later, on the penultimate page of the novel, declares that she herself has become a wolf.

The novel ends with her claim that she will be able to continue to resist the wolves. Given her regret that she has become like them, the end of the novel may be asking how she might learn from the professor and his Roman authors in order to shape her psyche and ethics to best confront the dangerous threats posed by inner drives and social structures seemingly beyond her control.

In conclusion, the embedding of Italian cultural history in her writing—including painting, music, and poetry—enables Kristeva to raise the issue of how one might identify with the mother without destroying oneself as a speaking subject, that is, while retaining a tenuous link to the social contract. She uses Italy to emphasize the foreign and its potential for recreating a connection with the feminine that ultimately embraces and overcomes abjection. References to Italian culture seem to be part of the global effort in her work to highlight distance, abjection, and the foreign—characteristics of "the feminine"—in order to become a combative nomad.

Like Bulgaria in Nikolchina's essay on Kristeva's writing in this collection, Italy is a complex category enabling her to talk about the identification with the mother that underlies psychoanalytic thought. Ovid, for example, is not primarily to be celebrated as part of Rome's poetic tradition but rather to be reexamined for the music of his verse and the ways in which his *Metamorphoses* both punish and immortalize dynamic individuals. He is a vital part of the context for reading the old man and Stephanie and their inner struggles with good and evil. Kristeva tells the story of their effort to live with dignity and joy against the backdrop of Italy and Rome, helping the reader to grapple better with the psychological dilemmas of contemporary life.

3

Not a Country for Old Men

Scapegoats and Sacrifice in Santa Varvara

Martha Reineke

She gave them human shape;
her stock was marked by hatred of the gods,
by cruelty and eagerness for slaughter;
you would have recognized their bloody nature.

—Ovid, *Metamorphoses*, lines 18–21

In a conversation with Bernard Sichère about *The Old Man and the Wolves* (Kristeva 1994), Julia Kristeva explains that fiction is more effective than theory in addressing the malaise of individuals today. For Kristeva, *The Old Man and the Wolves* is "anchored in a pain to which allegory aims to give significance without fixing it, having it vibrate, in an oneiric way, according to each reader's personal framework of ordeals and choices" (Kristeva 1996c, 165). Aligning the relationship forged between an author and her reader with that which develops between a psychoanalyst and her analysand, Kristeva defines both sets of relationships as narrative practices that can free individuals from malaise.

In this essay, I explore these practices as I focus on the role played in the novel by frequent references to Ovid's *Metamorphoses* and Tibullus's poetry. Functioning as touchstones in the novel, Ovid and Tibullus's works illuminate incidents of lethal violence that dominate the novel's narrative. So too do they suggest avenues by which conflict could give way to life-giving compassion. I begin by linking the tale of Lycaon's feast in Ovid's *Metamorphoses* with the novel's narrative. Employing René Girard's theory of violence as a critical heuristic,[1] I show how wolves in both stories portend a contagion of conflict that devolves into incidents of scapegoating or sacrifice. Just as Ovid has "resolved to tell of creatures being metamorphosed into new forms," so also does the Old Man draw on Ovid in order to show that the wolfish strangeness the citizens of Santa Varvara seek to exclude is actually constitutive of their being (Ovid 2005, 15; Kristeva 1994, epigraph). Eschewing narrative authority, Ovid offers only clarity of perception; nevertheless, his insights expose the wolves as tokens of fracture in the human psyche.

Holding a mirror up to wolves in order to illuminate the conflict that besets humans, Ovid also guides the Old Man away from deadly violence. When Ovid likens Lycaon's transformation to a work of art, suggesting that Lycaon has become "the very picture" of a wolf (*eadem feritatis imago est*),[2] he offers the Old Man a leitmotif for revelatory acts of perception from which the Old Man will draw life-saving insights. As the Old Man "breathes new life into Latin tomes," creating a kind of music—"corporeal, clear, precise"—he accesses healing alternatives to the wolves' assaults on the citizens of Santa Varvara (Kristeva 1994, 149, 151).

Introduced to a new way of seeing by Ovid, the Old Man finds in Tibullus resources on which he can draw to mend the fractured human psyche. In the second half of this essay, I suggest how the wolves could regain their humanity were they to appeal to these resources. As the Old Man recites Tibullus's words, they reverberate through "an interior space sculpted by mourning" (Kristeva 1996c, 166). An outsider who bears what Kristeva describes as the "full weight of his psychology, his affects, his fears," Tibullus suffers and confronts death (Kristeva 1996c, 170). However, Tibullus also evokes healing powers of nonsacrificial memory. Those who hear Tibullus, dream with him, are able to access transforming alternatives to sacrificial scapegoating that open them to connection with others.

Wolves, Scapegoats, and Mimetic Theory

The novel begins with an invasion of wolves in Santa Varvara. These "gray-coated, sharp-nosed carnivores, slinking singly or in packs through houses and gardens," wear people's faces and utter human speech (Kristeva 1994, 7). Yet, apparently only the Old Man can see or hear them and smell their musky odor. Only he observes the marks their claws have made on the land and on the throats of "animals, birds, even women" (Kristeva 1994, 4). The Old Man is Septicius Clarus, a classics scholar.[3] Like his Roman namesake, the praetorian prefect who accompanied Hadrian to Britain to build a wall against the barbarians (Birley

2005, 121–23), the Old Man takes on a protective mission in Santa Varvara. He keeps watch from his window, and his "unwavering vigilance . . . prevents the wolves from approaching his house" (Kristeva 1994, 12).

The wolves' invasion of Santa Varvara, which has inspired the Old Man's watchfulness, lends itself to an analysis grounded in Girard's theory of mimetic rivalry and scapegoating, for the victims of the wolves' violence are scapegoats. According to Girard, individuals who are targets of mob violence are innocent of crimes of which they are accused; nevertheless, they are perceived to be guilty and are slain. Indeed, because Girard understands that scapegoating lies behind acts of human sacrifice, Girard equates them.[4] In *The Scapegoat*, Girard identifies several characteristics or "stereotypes" of this deadly victimization. Drawing his definition of a stereotype from an early method of printing in which multiple copies of a document are produced from duplicate impressions of an original typographical element, Girard lays out unvarying features of scapegoating that reoccur across time in diverse cultures and locales. An initial indicator that scapegoating may develop in a community is *a breach in the social order* (Girard 1989, 14). A community is caught up in some kind of crisis not of its own making: a plague, an epidemic, a cosmic or political disturbance. Santa Varvara is experiencing such a breakdown of order due to the ongoing murderous rampages of wolves, whose violence is reminiscent of the plagues that beset Europe in earlier centuries (Girard 1989, 14). A second stereotype emerges as individuals subsequently seek out the origins of disorder and look for its cause (e.g., Jews were blamed for the plague). In the absence of social stability, *conflict among community members develops and spreads.* Individual is set against individual, neighbor against neighbor, as each sees the other as a potentially lethal threat. In time, such a contagion spreads in Santa Varvara. Truly, people are dying and those who are not already dead have begun to look different—even wolf-like.

Girard's theory is especially helpful for understanding how violence in Santa Varvara is both microcosmic *and* macrocosmic, engulfing individuals and the wider society. Girard observes that every human is drawn toward what another human desires because of a more basic desire to be like the other; for each human imagines that another can confer on it a plenitude of being that it lacks (Girard 1979, 146–47). However, because the other also lacks being, both individuals mirror each other in their desires, and both are caught up in an increasingly fraught competition for being. Inclined toward mimetic rivalry, they become even more vulnerable to its excesses in the presence of social disorder. As disruptions in society exacerbate a sense of lack, relationships become more contentious (Girard 1979, 160–61). In Santa Varvara, Vespasian and Alba embody just such a threatening mimesis. Once desirous of each other's being, the couple is beset by a violent enmity that escalates simultaneously with the spreading wolf menace.

The novel's narrative attests to a mimesis that transitions gradually into rivalrous and deadly violence. When they first meet, Vespasian and Alba discover in each other a way to redress lack and experience a wholeness of being. Although he is a successful army surgeon, Vespasian is consumed by self-loathing and enraged that he is insufficiently appreciated by others (Kristeva 1994, 38–39). When Alba meets Vespasian and is enthralled by him, he feels valued. In turn, Alba, an immigrant, desires an enhanced social standing she believes will come to her as the wife of a high-ranking military officer. But the elevated social status Alba seeks proves elusive. She loses ground even as Vespasian, mirroring Alba's own sense of inadequacy, lashes out at Alba with increasing frequency. Once each other's cherished model, Vespasian and Alba now regard each other with violent antipathy. That each perceives the other as a threatening, nonhuman monster links Vespasian and Alba with the social unrest unfolding around them. Vespasian is attacked by a wolf that injects its venom into him. His eyes change, "They're yellow now, like the eyes of an animal" (Kristeva 1994, 8, 5). A witness to her husband's metamorphosis, Alba too "is necessarily contaminated." One day, instead of words, "the barking of a dog" comes from Alba's mouth (Kristeva 1994, 51). Embodying on a small scale the violence spreading through Santa Varvara, Alba and Vespasian's interactions promise to become deadly.

The denouement of the couple's relationship has an expressly contemporary cast, for Vespasian and Alba exude an overwhelming sense of emptiness. The narrator of the novel observes that a lover typically "selects an idol or at least a fetish to adore. But Vespasian had no inner shrine at which to worship: he had fenced it round with frontiers, and inhabited an area with reversible borders and merely temporary thresholds" (Kristeva 1994, 50). Alba speaks candidly of her husband: "He was no one, not really a person at all. We think those who hurt us are devils. But no—all we see is a mask with no one behind it" (Kristeva 1994, 100). Alba and Vespasian's mimetic desire is emptied of all affect except the most deadly.

The army surgeon and his wife are like their neighbors in this way. Bombarded by media images, the Albas and Vespasians of Santa Varvara convey no feelings for others or display any depth of expression. In an earlier era, the residents of Santa Varvara would have been satisfied to seek in each other a fullness of being even when it led to monstrous rivalry; now, eye-to-eye relationships are supplanted. Screen images—television, computer, and mobile phone—are the preferred site for the negotiation of mimetic desire. Observes the novel's narrator: "the choice is between active monsters and monstrous insignificance (*monstre actif ou monstrueux d'insignifiance*)" (Kristeva 1994, 51; Kristeva 1992a, 82). Thus, even as Vespasian and Alba are swept into a vortex of violence, Kristeva would have her readers think expansively about violence. The wolves, Kristeva states, "symbolize everyone's barbarity, everyone's criminality" (Kristeva 1996c, 165).

At this point, we may anticipate that a third stereotype that Girard claims is featured in every scapegoating scenario will emerge in Santa Varvara. Girard writes that community unrest builds until it eventually polarizes around one, apparently random victim who is believed by the others to be the cause of the problem. *The one around whom all the others circle is the scapegoat* (Girard 1989, 20). Although the mob latches onto its victim seemingly by chance, Girard identifies *stereotypic victim marks.* Individuals who are attacked typically are outsiders by reason of gender, nationality, or religion; they are likely to stand at either the highest end of a society (as do Oedipus and Marie Antoinette) or at its lowest end (as do lynching victims in the American South). Victims may walk with a limp or have another physical disability; often they are suspected by their persecutors of having a predilection for incest, orgies, or other rule-defying behavior (Girard 1989, 20–22). From the perspective of a neutral outsider, the victim of scapegoating is wholly innocent of all charges; from the perspective of the community that aligns as a mob against the victim, the victim is responsible not only for all that threatens the society but also for the peace that will follow his or her death (Girard 1979, 85–88).

The mob banishes or, more typically, kills its victim. After the sacrifice, a community previously divided and under siege engages in a celebratory feast. In this final moment, another stereotype emerges: *the scapegoat is salvific.* Just as the scapegoat has been the source of absolute threat, so also in death is he or she the locus of restorative power that returns the community to peace. Ever after, the community will see itself as captive of a sacred power that lies beyond them. Thus, for Girard, the sacrificial death of the scapegoat is a founding rite, creative of human society (Girard 1979, 306–07). Over time, when humans are again caught in a cycle of violence, *religion* emerges in the form of *rituals of sacrifice* that recreate in domesticated form the original violence against an innocent victim; *culture* emerges as *myths preserve the logic of scapegoating,* justify the actions of the mob, and confirm the guilt of the victim (Girard 1979, 235, 257–58; Girard 1987, 105ff.).

Thus, Girard would not be surprised that Ovid's tale of Lycaon, hearkening back to Greek myth,[5] offers Septicius a mirror in which to view the vortex of violence into which Vespasian and Alba are swept. Indeed so closely does the present mirror the past that the professor becomes disoriented: "Was he in the first century . . . dreaming of the metamorphosis that took place in human beings as they entered upon a new era, a new age just as steeped in brutishness as the old? Or was he in the present, in Santa Varvara . . . ?" (Kristeva 1994, 120). Past and present stories join, as if enclosed in a poetic quatrain. Lycaon's tale begins with a sacrificial *feast* and ends with a *man* becoming a wolf; Vespasian's story begins with a *man*—Vespasian—becoming a wolf, "a real Lycaon" (Kristeva 1994, 60), and subsequently ends with a violent "feast." That each narrative features an outsider—a Molossian and the immigrant Alba—brings to view the sacrificial mechanism that they share.

Ovid attests to this mechanism and its pervasive power when he tells us that humans, born of the remains of giants whose own desires led to their destruction, are beset by problematic desire from the moment of their creation. Envious of the gods' being and unwilling to accept their own lack of being, these humans are violent. Moreover, humans' first efforts at social interaction, memorialized by Lycaon, man-become-wolf, are founded in sacrifice. Significantly, this sacrifice takes the form of scapegoating. Rather than engage in civil discord, this race of humans picks one victim—the Molossian outsider—to dismember, kill, and cook.[6] Scapegoating ending in alimentary sacrifice also is definitive of the contagion of violence that threatens to destroy Santa Varvara.

The Old Man forecasts this sacrifice when he predicts that Alba and Vespasian's conflict-ridden marriage is "bound to end in murder" (Kristeva 1994, 50–52). A few days after the Old Man's warning, a crowd gathers on the street. The authorities have "fished out the body of a woman" from a lake (Kristeva 1994, 92). Clothed in a suit with black dots on a white background that matches one of Alba's suits, its face is blue, bloated, and spattered with mud, the body bears a preternatural resemblance to a gigantic trout. The crowd spies a bite mark on the victim's neck. "The wolves," cries the crowd; "probably stabbed by her lover," someone utters (Kristeva 1994, 85). Back at Vespasian and Alba's apartment, the table is set for a dinner that Alba never serves. One of her specialties—trout marinated in wine and served up with herbs and fresh ginger—has been left "to rot in the oven" (Kristeva 1994, 87). The reader understands that, just as the Molossian outsider's death was celebrated with a feast, Vespasian has "feasted" on a different dish this evening.

Tasked with the responsibility of investigating the mysterious death of the young woman at the lake is Stephanie Delacour, a French journalist and former student of Septicius. Girard's theory sheds light on Stephanie's observations, enabling us to recognize that she is reporting an act of scapegoating and sacrifice. After all, as described by Girard, scapegoating inevitably progresses toward the death of an innocent victim who often is an outsider. In Santa Varvara, suspicion has fallen on marginal foreigners such as Alba. Already, her father and mother have been killed. Although the death at the lake initially does not look like an act of mob violence, as is typically associated with scapegoating, Stephanie discovers the body under such circumstances. As Stephanie walks toward the scene of the crime, she observes something she describes as "odd." Crowds on this street are an uncommon occurrence because there are no stores in the neighborhood to attract groups (Kristeva 1994, 84). Nevertheless, Stephanie has to press through a throng to view the body. As a result, the death Stephanie investigates fully replicates the stereotyped sequence of events that Girard has labeled scapegoating.

The Very Picture of a Wolf

With the death of the woman at the lake, a double for Alba,[7] the professor's protective mission reaches a critical juncture. He is all but alone in his capacity to see that Santa Varvara may yet be consumed by the spreading violence. What lifts Septicius above the mob, enabling him to perceive the threat the wolves pose when others are inured to their violence? How is he able to distinguish the innocent from the guilty and the wolves from their victims when all around him a contagion is obliterating differences? Ovid's *Metamorphoses* supports the professor's faculties of discernment, for even as the *Metamorphoses* recounts Greek and Roman myths, which Girard would claim uncritically attest to scapegoating and justify mob violence, Ovid does not preserve the authority of myth when he tells these tales. Indeed, as Joseph Solodow reminds us, the narrator of the *Metamorphoses* asserts that his stories may not be reliable (Solodow 2002, 64–68). Because the narrator distances himself from the myths of which he writes, Septicius can find in the *Metamorphoses* the maneuvering room he needs to move away from the violence that threatens Santa Varvara. When Ovid likens Lycaon's transformation to a work of art and suggests that Lycaon has become "the very picture" of a wolf, Ovid highlights elements in his writing on which Septicius can draw to expose scapegoating. Metamorphosis transforms that which is personal or individual, and therefore potentially inaccessible to judgment, into *a perception that can be grasped* (Solodow 2002, 213–14).

Ovid is a rich resource for the professor. For Ovid, violence is associated with the *loss of speech*. As Lynn Enterline observes, Ovid is preoccupied with stories that "testify to the power, failure, and disturbing unpredictability of the human voice" (Enterline 2006, 11). Beings who lose their voices or whose voices fail to effect the change they seek are regularly associated by Ovid with the metamorphoses about which he writes. The speechless face is one most alienated from its previous existence (Enterline 2006, 15–16). Lycaon exemplifies Ovid's sensitivity to the importance of embodied speech. Lycaon is the first character to lose his human shape, and that change is signaled by a change in the shape of his lips. His foaming mouth, recalling rabies-infected animals, marks Lycaon's transformation from human to animal (Enterline 2006, 43).

Ovid also is fascinated with the productive possibilities of speech and silence. Song is a focal point, for the narrator claims to be "singing" his stories. Persons typically are more aware of their bodies when singing than when speaking. Recognizing their voices as instruments, they focus not only on words but also on their mouths, diaphragms, and lungs. Singers are sensitive to where they form the words in their mouths: their tongues' proximity to their teeth and the way their lips form around their teeth are critical to the tone and quality of the sounds they emit. Sharing the speech of figures in the *Metamorphoses* with his readers, Ovid expresses a keen awareness not only of the figures' tongues, lips, and breath but also of his own (Enterline 2006, 41). Thus, when Ovid "resolves to tell of creatures being metamorphosed" he asks that the gods "*breathe* on these my undertakings" (Enterline 2006, 206, emphasis Enterline's)." The mind is moved to speak by drawing breath from somewhere else. Anima (mind) is linked also with air or breath: breathing marks the possibilities of life just as death is associated with the exhaling of breath into the wind (Enterline 2006, 50). On the one hand, speech signals death, for one dies when the breath of speech passes for the last time from one's lips; on the other hand, when taken up by others, speech garners one a kind of immortality. Ovid alludes to this aspect of speech when, in the concluding passages of the *Metamorphoses*, he describes how his words and songs will be spoken or sung by others who will revivify them with their lips and breath (Enterline 2006, 54; Ovid 2005, 554).

Yet even as Ovid testifies to the enduring power of speech, *how* songs are revivified remains an open question for him. Often, the lips of persons—silent, protesting, uttering monstrous words—become the occasion in the *Metamorphoses* for a direct critique of fantasies of coherent, meaningful, death-defying speech. Ovid names the image of a person whose lips are silently contorted or from whose lips spew nonsensical words as *os*: "a face deprived of the capacity to speak." The affective power of such faces makes them a recurrent presence in the *Metamorphoses* (Enterline 2006, 16). But even though Ovid displays keen insight, he is unable to break fully with the tales he tells; he does not expose the scapegoat mechanism. So also do the rays of discerning light from Ovid that reach into Santa Varvara not free Septicius from the violence these rays illuminate. Septicius's access to a nonsacrificial alternative to scapegoating must await his encounter with Tibullus.

Nevertheless, Septicius learns from Ovid that the human capacity to attain a critical distance from scapegoating is sustained by our bodies: sensory experiences rather than analytical thought found our capacity to replace sacrifice with nonviolent connection with others. Thus, with Septicius's powers of perception sharpened by his reading of Ovid, he takes the measure of threats to Santa Varvara. Newly sensitive to mouths of its residents, the professor reads faces and looks for the *os* of those whose visages signal that they have fallen victim to the wolves. He spies "furry cheekbones lengthening into muzzles, with lips drawn back to reveal the fangs of wolves"; he observes the face "of someone who might have been a man if his ears hadn't been so hairy and his eyes so phosphorescent"

(Kristeva 1994, 35, 120). So too does the professor become increasingly attentive to the speech of Santa Varvara's inhabitants, for Ovid has taught him that loss of speech is symptomatic of a loss of humanity. A series of exchanges between Alba and Vespasian to which Septicius has been privy is illustrative: "'Work!' (Vespasian.) 'Power.' (Alba.) 'Exactly!' (Vespasian.) 'So what about boredom?' (Alba.) 'What is it?' (Vespasian.)" (Kristeva 1994, 56). Meaningful connections are missing from the words they throw at each other; their inability to converse signals that their humanity has been replaced by wolfishness.

Alerted by Ovid's songs to the deadly tenor of his time, Septicius recognizes the importance of countering life-denying with life-affirming voices. Breathing life into Ovid with his own lungs, the professor seeks to enliven Santa Varvara with the very air of the ancient civilization that was inspirited by the voices of its poets. Asking his students what has become of these men, the Old Man answers his own question: "I think they've undergone a metamorphosis. Into what? Into us. Into you" (Kristeva 1994, 58–59). Others disparage Septicius for clinging to the past; but all he has sought to do "via metamorphoses and elegies set down in a dead language that he rehabilitated was to create a kind of music" (Kristeva 1994, 16). Repeatedly, "the bustling crowd of metamorphoses in his mind divested itself of matter: 'sine materia, exercitium arithmeticae occultum nescientis se numerare animi.' It was a kind of airy music which carried him away" (Kristeva 1994, 22).

With Septicius, Kristeva lays the foundation for a telling criticism of contemporary society. Engaged in a protective mission in Santa Varvara, the professor enhances our awareness of threats not only to Santa Varvara but also to every present-day locale (Kristeva 1994, 51). Moreover, with the Roman poets, Septicius discovers that, just as violence is associated with the loss of speech, alternatives to violence and scapegoating emerge with the recasting of speech as transformative "song." But how can the professor's critical perception, in which he has been tutored by Ovid, become a starting point for action against wolves in Santa Varvara or elsewhere? Septicius locates in Tibullus's poetry an alternative to wolfish violence. However, after Septicius becomes one of the wolves' victims, the nonsacrificial praxis that he has discovered in Tibullus is attested to only indirectly, as it is refracted through memories of others.

Men of Sorrow

Although calm follows incidents of scapegoating, Girard's theory suggests that violence eventually returns; when conflict resumes, new scapegoats are sought (Girard 1987, 103). When the Old Man dies under questionable circumstances after having been hospitalized, Girard's insights are confirmed. The Old Man seems an unlikely scapegoat; in contrast to Alba, a marginal outsider, he is a revered professor from whom others in his city have sought advice. But, according to Girard, scapegoats emerge at both ends of the social spectrum, for social marginality features among those at the pinnacle of a society as well as at its bottom (Girard 1989, 18). Indeed, around the time the mass graves are discovered, people are "starting to be frightened" of the Old Man (Kristeva 1994, 10). As he "withdrew into his own aura of wisdom and honor" in the face of a widening contagion of violence, the citizens of Santa Varvara "intensified his isolation with their hints, their furtive looks" (Kristeva 1994, 11). The Old Man becomes the object of hostile gossip in Santa Varvara's bars. One day someone whispers, "I think talking about this sort of thing—the wolves, I mean—only makes them more real: you have to believe in them, and so you have to do something about them. . . . He's just trying to provoke the wolves, that's all. Our hero must be starting to get bored with his books!" (Kristeva 1994, 24). Stephanie seems aware that a contagion of violence in Santa Varvara has placed the Old Man especially at risk: "the weak, the old, and the handicapped don't usually arouse pity . . . they provoke the distorted rages, the masked hatreds, the monstrous acts of vengeance that are revealed to us in our dreams, when the hypocrisy of the day no longer operates" (Kristeva 1994, 11–12). Although the Old Man's death is the work of only a few wolves, Stephanie asserts that "it had been in everyone's interest to get rid of Septicius Clarus." Vespasian and Alba had wanted him dead because he knew too much about their violent relationship. The nurses at the hospital had wanted him dead because they were badly paid and disliked elderly patients. The wolves had wanted him dead "because they were wolves." Further, the Old Man is described as being Christ-like, which evokes images of an innocent victim, a scapegoat. He was, Stephanie recognizes, a "single visionary" who could perceive the "extreme limits of being" (Kristeva 1994, 126).

At Septicius's funeral, that the professor's powers of perception have transferred to Stephanie becomes evident. She notices that, rather than mourn the Old Man, those attending the funeral are transfixed by a poised and perfectly coiffed woman, a plastic surgeon who is Vespasian's colleague. Stephanie previously has dubbed her "the Face-lifter" (Kristeva 1994, 78). At the funeral, only Stephanie finds the Face-lifter's visage monstrous. Observing her mouth closely, seeking what the professor would have called her *os*, Stephanie notices that the Face-lifter never speaks; instead, she emits the "laugh of a hyper-efficient madwoman" (Kristeva 1994, 129). For Stephanie, the Face-lifter's perpetual smile and laugh are reminiscent of the "red lips as white and shiny and massive as a kitchen sink" of a sculpture at the Santa Varvara fountain.

The Face-lifter and her sculpture-twin also are reminiscent of Medusa in Ovid's *Metamorphoses* (Ovid 2005, 154–56). As described by Andrew Feldherr,

Medusa is noted for her *commutative powers*: "each person who has gazed at the face of the Gorgon becomes a wondrous image, able to freeze and transform new viewers in turn, sentencing them to death as well" (Feldherr 2010, 325). Citing Girard, Feldherr labels these powers a "contagion" and suggests they announce an impending "sacrificial crisis" (Feldherr 2010, 327–29). So also are the Gorgon-like powers of the Face-lifter decidedly transmissible. Just as those who gaze at the Gorgon "absorb the stony nature directly from the image" (Feldherr 2010, 327), so also do those who attend the Old Man's funeral absorb the Face-lifter's monstrousness into their own being. Stephanie knows that this very evening, emulating the Face-lifter as they stand "in front of their halogen-lit mirrors," the residents of Santa Varvara will pull "all sorts of faces to arrive at the right look" (Kristeva 1994, 129).

Up to now, as commentator Anna Smith notes, the wolf has served as an image of violence in Santa Varvara: the "impulse in society to savage the outsider who is different" (Smith 1996, 191). So also has Santa Varvara been depicted as a society flattened by torpor and banality. At the funeral of the Old Man, these features of life in Santa Varvara are joined. An innocent victim has been scapegoated, and no one has acknowledged the crime or cared. As Stephanie recognizes that the residents of Santa Varvara are inured to injustice *and* incapable of mourning, hopelessly infected "by monsters *and* monstrous insignificance" (Kristeva 1994, 51), she makes a decision that signals a turning point in the novel. In the aftermath of the funeral, Stephanie discovers memories of her past coming back to her; "suddenly," she feels like writing about them (Kristeva 1994, 130).

As Stephanie takes on the role of diarist, the "duplication (*dédoublement*) and dissemination of identities," first visible in the doubling of Alba, the professor's student, with the dead Alba of the lake, now extends to the Old Man (Kristeva 1996c, 165; Kristeva 1992a, 76). In a sudden proliferation of old men, Stephanie's memories of Septicius blend with those of her father, a friend of the professor and ambassador to Santa Varvara. So also is Stephanie's voice amplified when her recollections are joined with Kristeva's memories of her own father's life and death.[8] The poetry of Tibullus magnifies the voices of the old men, sustains their daughters' memory-work, and introduces themes that point beyond scapegoating toward human relatedness not founded on sacrifice. The most important of these themes attests to a form of memory that exposes scapegoating and recalls us to our common humanity. In contrast to memories founded in a sacrificial economy that justifies scapegoating, this *nonsacrificial memory* is founded in positive mimesis. Unlike relations based on acquisitive mimesis, which revolve around rivalries, relationships grounded in positive mimesis express love, genuine intimacy, and compassion. Further, entry to positive mimesis is through embodied human experience.

When Septicius forges a connection between Tibullus and the work of nonsacrificial memory, he echoes Freud who, in *Civilization and Its Discontents*, likens the history of Rome to human memory. Acknowledging that much of the earliest topographies of Rome are lost in rubble, Freud suggests that, if Rome were a psychical entity rather than a habitation in space, all layers of history could be held together at once: "the same piece of ground would support the church of Santa Maria sopra Minerva and the ancient temple over which it was built. And the observer would perhaps only have to change the direction of his glance or his position in order to call up the one view or the other" (Freud 2005, 34). So also does Septicius point to an ancient city's landscape to suggest the power of nonsacrificial memory to counter violence that, on the macrocosmic level, is destroying Santa Varvara and, at the microcosmic level, is shattering the psyches of its residents. He tells his students that Tibullus and Ovid today may be found "in the original texts, of course; in the ruins of ancient palaces and churches" but also "in the thoughts of people. There are still traces of their old selves in them, in you . . ." (Kristeva 1994, 59).

Thus, the professor asks that we associate violence in Santa Varvara with the collapse of a psychic space that previously supported human relationships grounded in recognition rather than rivalry. The degeneration of humanity into beastliness is an expression of a *loss of memory for relationship.* In its absence, connection with others is impossible. Caught up in scapegoating, we do not remember that we could live differently. Confronted with a crisis of memory, Kristeva suggests that we can turn toward the past in a "reactive, nostalgic fashion," or we can explore "a grafting (*à greffer*) of what comes from another culture, another mentality," onto our own time (Kristeva 1996c, 169; Kristeva 1992a, 81). With *The Old Man and the Wolves*, Kristeva chooses the second option in order to move toward "an experience of sorrow and hurt that originates elsewhere and is perhaps liable to awaken other effects" (Kristeva 1996c, 169)." Tibullus's poetry is such a "grafting." From the first pages of the novel, his poems establish a vascular connection between past and present, gradually fusing ancient rootstock with contemporary scion. Late in the novel, Tibullus's poems have the strength of a mature graft, enabling those who grieve in the aftermath of sacrificial violence to awaken other effects.

Early in the novel, Septicius connects with Tibullus's poems through sensory-driven encounters. Rather than read Tibullus in his study, Septicius happens upon Tibullus in natural settings. For example, out for an autumn walk, he finds that Tibullus's words "slip in amongst the leaves." Moreover, "the pleasure he got from the bright-hued season was that of taste and touch. All the shades of brown and yellow and red entered into his skin, warmed his throat, filled his eyes, inducing the overwhelming sense of fulfillment that cannot be adequately expressed except in song." The poem's "resonance reconciles

Septicius with lost time" (Kristeva 1994, 13–14). Mirroring Septicius's outdoor locale, the rural setting of the poems further frames the encounter between the poet and his readers in terms of mood rather than place (Michael 1968, 16–17). Where Ovid often uses the landscape to signal impending violence in the text, Tibullus's poetry offers nonsacrificial access to a world that is tactile, sensorial, and somatic. Indeed, Tibullus is fascinated by the power of touch: words such as "hands, feet, and hair" are common to his poems (Putnam 1979, 11). By invoking the past, in memory traces accessed through the body, Tibullus's poetry grants access to a psychic space that is all but absent from the environs of Santa Varvara where a monstrous plastic sculpture graces the public square, abject horror haunts the lake, and surface effects of a media-driven spectacle replace embodied human experience.

Two additional themes in Tibullus's poetry—*outsider status* and *suffering*—are important in the novel. Although these motifs are readily associated with scapegoating—the scapegoat is typically an outsider and is made to suffer by an attacking mob—they take on a different meaning in Tibullus's writings, forming a constellation of alternatives to violence. Associated with Tibullus, these themes recall an earlier time preserved in our capacity for nonsacrificial memory. Tibullus redefines the notion of an outsider when he describes himself as a farmer. He claims not to speak as an authority or to count as patrons an elite audience (Cairns 1980, 28). Standing outside the door to the household of his love, Delia, he also is an outsider to family relationships. Quoting Tibullus, the professor says Tibullus has "no mother here to gather up my incinerated bones in the folds of her mourning veil; I have no sister to bestow in my ashes the perfumes of Assyria and weep with unbound hair beside my grave" (Kristeva 1994, 15).

Tibullus's outsider status leads to *suffering*. However, as he describes his pain, suffering born of love is shown to differ from pain experienced sacrificially. Most notably, Tibullus suffers from the remoteness of the woman he loves, Delia. The poems that summon Delia and speak of the rural life they will enjoy depict also the separation they will experience because of death. Even as he asks Delia to come close in order to make her one with him, Tibullus knows that "soon death will come, its head shrouded in darkness" (Kristeva 1994, 60; Tibullus 2012, 4). The poet does not fear death itself; he laments only that he may encounter death without Delia. Further, Tibullus contrasts his suffering with that caused by war, which he understands to be caused by greed. Greed, Girard would remind us, is rooted in mimetic rivalry. Tibullus contrasts the world of acquisitive desire that regularly becomes violent with the simplicity and contentment of rural life (Michael 1968, 13).

A third theme in Tibullus's poetry is *connection with others*. Septicius celebrates the connection of which Tibullus writes and distinguishes it from Alba and Vespasian's conflict-ridden relationship. Acknowledging that Tibullus's relationship with Delia also founders, the professor nevertheless asserts, "There used to be links between people, and yet they weren't bound." Tibullus's embodiment of freedom achieves balance, drifting neither toward a binding passion nor toward indifference (Kristeva 1994, 58). The classics professor attributes to Tibullus's era the "dawn of connection" when persons forged "a sacred bond both passionate and pious—by which I mean respectful" (Kristeva 1994, 15). But also it was "free, questioning, skeptical, intellectual . . ." (Kristeva 1994, 97). Thus, after losing Delia to another lover and encountering difficulties along his way, Tibullus revisits earlier themes in a new poem, still moving toward connection. Words can't offset the suffering that he has encountered in his life, but the promise of relationships can (Putnam 1979, 99). Squabbles of rural life are acknowledged; however, the poet now makes family—husband and wife, son and daughter—the "touchstone" against which all challenges of life are measured. Writes Tibullus, "Peace lifts to the sun the hoe and the plowshare; darkness covers the soldier's broken weapons with rust. Merry with drink, the farmer drives homeward with his wife and children through the sunny dust" (Tibullus 1968, 62, Book I, Poem 10). In celebrating the ordinary, what Stephanie calls "the happiness of simple folk," Tibullus exemplifies living according to "*quodlibet ens*," which Septicius always translates as "a being that matters, no matter what" (Kristeva 1994, 145–46).

For Septicius, the poems of Tibullus provide direction: love of another *no matter what* has the power to counter the violence that besets Santa Varvara. Tibullus's poems create a kind of music, one that "emerges from a brutish cacophony, refining it into duration, expectation, and promise. The promise of harmony, perfection. Epiphany (*l'avent*)" (Kristeva 1994, 16; Kristeva 1991, 31). Pointing to an alternative to scapegoating, Tibullus counsels that the space between sensation and language to which his poems grant access is vital to connecting with others in spite of suffering. The narrator suggests that Tibullus anticipates Christ (*pressentant Jésus*) (Kristeva 1991, 29), and the Old Man, embracing Tibullus's vision, is described by Kristeva as "a man of sorrows, in a certain way, a Christ-like figure" (Kristeva 1996c, 170).[9]

Tibullus's prefiguring of Christ and the Old Man's Christ-likeness should not lead us to ascribe a sacrificial theology of atonement to *The Old Man and the Wolves*. The Old Man's suffering and death are not salvific for others. Of what Christ-likeness does consist for the old men in her novel is signaled by Kristeva in *Tales of Love*. Echoing Girard, Kristeva establishes a context for understanding the Christology of *The Old Man and the Wolves* when she asserts that sacrifice stems from "the law of the social contract." Just as Girard claims that human society originates in sacrifice, so also does Kristeva assert that sacrifice creates meaning for "a social group that has been offered it and on which that social group is dependent for its being" (Kristeva 1987b, 142–43). Elsewhere, Kristeva draws explicitly on Girard (Kristeva 1986b, 213 n. 21) to explain that the "socio-symbolic contract" that is fundamental to the formation of any society is based on "the expulsion of an excluded element, a scapegoat" (Kristeva 1986b, 202). In *Tales of Love*, Kristeva again follows Girard when she expressly distances Christ from this system of scapegoating. Referencing Girard's *Things Hidden since the Foundation of the World*, Kristeva says that love offered by Christ is "very far removed from the classical concept of sacrifice" (Kristeva 1987b, 142, 395 n. 16).

In drawing on Girard for her own understanding of the dynamics of Christ-like behavior among the old men, Kristeva rightly understands Girard's claim in *Things Hidden since the Foundation of the World* that the crucifixion of Jesus is *not* a sacrifice. To be sure, elements of scapegoating that Girard has labeled stereotypic in their unvarying regularity are visible in Gospel accounts of Jesus's life and death. The Gospels do describe social disorder, an intensifying conflict, mob action that polarizes around one individual, and escalating violence that culminates in the death of Jesus. On the surface, the Gospels replicate the structure of myth, making Jesus's crucifixion a story of sacrificial scapegoating. But, for Girard, the Gospels differ from myth in a most profound way. In myth, the stereotypical elements of scapegoating, stacked one on top of the other, show the victim of mob violence to be *guilty*; in the Gospels, these stereotypes collapse and shatter, revealing Jesus to be *innocent*. In this way, building on an antisacrificial trajectory already evident in the Hebrew Bible, the Gospels fully expose the scapegoat mechanism and offer an alternative to the mythic justification of sacrifice: a revelation of a loving God who sides with victims. Writes Girard, "To say that Jesus dies, not as a sacrifice, but in order that there may be no more sacrifices, is to recognize in him the Word of God: I wish for mercy and not sacrifices. . . . Rather than become the slave of violence, as our own word necessarily does, the Word of God says no to violence" (Girard 1987, 210). Girard states that the Gospels understand that God does not work through violence: the "non-sacrificial economy" that Jesus sets forth is "a Kingdom of love" (Girard 1987, 197).[10] Continuing to follow Girard in the development of her own nonsacrificial Christology, Kristeva asserts that love offered by Christ comes as a gift that "assumes total suffering and loss" but manifests itself non-sacrificially in the form of compassion shared among members of a community, a community that stretches to "include neighbors, foreigners, and sinners" (Kristeva 1987b, 146–47).[11]

In a sacrificial economy such as Santa Varvara, outsiders typically bear the marks of victims and suffer as victims. But in the nonsacrificial economy to which the old men testify, outsider status and suffering are revelatory. As Pamela Sue Anderson notes, exiles (outsiders, aliens, foreigners) have a privileged perspective because they view the center from the margins of speech, community, and consciousness. On the periphery, the old men (Tibullus, Stephanie's father, and Septicius Clarus) can see from a distance what is "eating away at the center of the social-symbolic order" (Anderson 2000, 114–15). Although those on the margins of society are the most vulnerable when scapegoats are sought—the wolves seek them first—when these individuals persist, they stand as witness to an alternative social *and* psychic order. Thus, notwithstanding that the Old Man's death exemplifies scapegoating for the residents of Santa Varvara, the novel offers intimations of a nonsacrificial economy for those who, in embracing the songs of old men, receive from them a gift of compassion.[12]

With their lives and words, Kristeva's old men offer compassion as an alternative to sacrifice (Kristeva 1994, 173). If they can be said to save others, it is through this gift, not through the violence they suffer at the hands of others. Compassion points to the possibilities of *connecting with others* nonviolently. The form of connection proffered by the gifts of the fathers is described by Kristeva as *Einfühling*; the bond becomes one of identification (*Einfühling*), and "because of that very fact its name is love. Not sacrifice" (Kristeva 1987b, 143). So also does Kristeva characterize this bond in terms of empathy and Christian *agape* (Kristeva 1997a, 178–79). But are the citizens of Santa Varvara open to such a gift? Or will Santa Varvara and other like environs remain beset by vicious scapegoating?

The Alchemy of the Word

Near the end of *The Old Man and the Wolves*, Stephanie writes in her diary that, although she never anticipated it, her sojourn in Santa Varvara has opened up possibilities. The memories and stories of the past to which the old men—Ovid, Tibullus, Septicius, her father—have testified are enabling her to emerge from the debilitating environment of Santa Varvara. No longer caught between Santa Varvara's Scylla and Charybdis—rapacious wolves and engulfing whirlpools of ennui—Stephanie discovers, much to her surprise, that these men have handed down to her a way of going forward: "from this void new forms will be born. It's up to you now, Stephie" (Kristeva 1994, 176). Confronted with the devastating loss of the Old Man to the wolves, Stephanie yet stands in receipt of a possible future: compassion, connection, life with others.

Stephanie's insights are as old as Tibullus's poetry and as contemporary as Kristeva's conversations with clients in her psychoanalytic practice. Writes Kristeva:

> . . . I believe we must reinstate a notion of the psyche and the soul that avoid the two major detours the psychoanalytic movement has taken, the first of which seeks to thrust psychic space into biology (which makes it closer to psychiatry) and the second which considers

> psychic space to be a product of language alone and disregards the signs emitted by the body. (1996f, 86)

Kristeva recognizes that human efforts to break open cycles of scapegoating require complex interventions in conflict that do not bifurcate human experience along dualistic lines, juxtaposing an animalistic violence of the human body to a perfected rationalism of the human mind. As a consequence, she emphasizes the healing powers of empathetic identification: *Einfühling*. Further, Kristeva understands that when we seek alternatives to violence, narrative traditions shared by literature and psychoanalysis are critical to our interventions.

Through what process do stories become a source of hope for writers and readers, analysts and analysands? How are memories that are attuned to compassion rather than to sacrifice drawn forth from narratives? Kristeva identifies two features of narratives that help us access nonsacrificial memory: *embodied human experience* and *relationships founded in acceptance rather than rivalry*. When a reader gets caught up in what Kristeva calls "the alchemy of the word," reading is not exclusively an act of comprehension and cognition; rather, according to Kristeva, through reading one recovers "his own memory, his own body," and this can be "revitalizing." Such memory work, Kristeva suggests in an interview, resembles the analytic process (Kristeva 1996a, 221) for therapeutic narratives promote forms of relationship that can unlock healing powers that Girard would associate with positive mimesis and nonsacrificial memory.

Kristeva draws on Arendt to explain how storytelling is a relational activity. Narration relies on two factors: we exist among others (*inter-esse*) and, through them, we are able to form memories and offer testimony (Kristeva 2003, 73). That others are necessary for storytelling to be meaningful is not only a condition of creative exposition but also a condition of human life. Together, the narratable and exposable features of our lives make possible transformation. As philosopher Adriana Cavarero states most eloquently (also commenting on Arendt):

> Only in the improbable case of a life spent in perfect solitude could the autobiography of a human being tell the absurd story of an unexposed identity, without relations and without world. The existent is the exposable and the narratable: neither exposability nor narratability, which together constitute this peculiarly human uniqueness, can be taken away. The one who is exposed generates and is generated by the life story—this and not—another—which results from such an exposition. (Cavarero 2000, 36)

But even as she makes shared narratives fundamental to relational being, Kristeva identifies acute challenges that interrupt storytelling. Suffering decouples what should be joined: when we have been traumatized by physical or psychological violence, we have no memories to turn into stories or we are unable to construct meaningful narratives. Active relationality, in which someone elicits a story from another, plays a crucial role in recovery from trauma. As Colin Davis observes in summarizing Kristeva's commentary on Arendt, when someone hears another say, "tell me a story," that other has mediated a previously insurmountable gap between "what cannot be called back to memory and what can be narrated" (Davis 2003, 141). Psychoanalysis and literature thus share a common function: to bridge the gaps and ruptures in being which have been brought on by traumatizing violence. The relationship between analyst and analysand, writer and reader, turns on an invitation to "tell a story" that can recreate our humanity and effect healing.

Crucially, Kristeva shows how embodied memory is decisive also to efforts to access nonsacrificial engagement with others through narratives. Although novels purportedly are conveyors of signs, writers and readers of novels are led by narrative back into body practices that trauma previously has prevented them from accessing. Thus, Ovid's *Metamorphoses* is not unique in attesting to the transformations of bodies; conversing with Vassiliki Kolocotroni, Kristeva identifies revelatory potential in other literature as well (Kristeva 1996a, 220). For Kristeva, literature taps into memories and memories access not only signs but—as Ovid has demonstrated so compellingly—perceptions. With ideas joined with embodiment, narratives allow for "a permanent come-and-go that remakes the personality as a whole" (Kristeva 1996a, 220).

So also in analysis, when an analyst identifies with an analysand, the connection that the analyst forges draws not only on the analysand's biography and memories but also on "transgenerational memory and imagined sensation" that "mobilize the analyst's entire psychical apparatus." As a consequence, transference and countertransference effect healing through a kind of "transubstantiation" (Kristeva 2002a, 61). According to Kristeva, Maurice Merleau-Ponty provides language for understanding this process, common to the narrative practices of writers and readers, analysts and analysands, when he attests to the reversible and chiasmic relationship among embodied individuals that connects "the perceiver and the perceived, the feeler and the felt." Reminded by Merleau-Ponty that "touch is always tangible, sight is visible, matter is the body, and the same is other," Kristeva understands that, in relating to each other, we "become flesh" (Kristeva 2002a, 61).

Merleau-Ponty asserts that there is no name in traditional philosophical reflection that designates flesh, for it is not matter or psychic material. Flesh is an "element" in the sense of being "a general thing, midway between the spatio-temporal individual and the idea, a sort of incarnate principle" (Merleau-Ponty 1969, 137–38). Flesh brings the presence of Being where there is a fragment of being. Adhering to location, flesh offers facticity; it sustains beings' presence with things. Being is not out there in front of me but surrounds and traverses me: my being is formed in the midst of Being. As a consequence, the fleshly exchange that give me things, gives me the other. The fission of the sentient and the sensible that makes my body capable of communicating with things also founds transitivity between my body and that of another. Speech does not break with the flesh but accomplishes the intentionality of being-in-the-flesh by other means (Merleau-Ponty 1969, 153).

I am formed in the midst of Being. Moreover, as a consequence, I share a connection with others. Writes Merleau-Ponty:

> It is said that the colors, the tactile reliefs given to the other, are for me an absolute mystery, forever inaccessible. This is not completely true; for me to have not an idea, an image, nor a presentation, but as it were the imminent experience of them, it suffices that I look at a landscape, that I speak of it with someone. Then, through the concordant operation of his body and my own, what I see passes into him, this individual green of the meadow under my eyes invades his vision without quitting my own, I recognize in my green his green, as the customs officer recognizes suddenly in a traveler the man whose description he had been given There is here no problem of the alter ego because it is not I who sees, not he who sees, because an anonymous visibility inhabits both of us, a vision in general, in virtue of that primordial property that belongs to the flesh, being here and now, of radiating everywhere and forever, being an individual, of being also a dimension and a universal. (Merleau-Ponty 1969, 142)

In describing how the flesh connects us with others, Merleau-Ponty could be describing Septicius who, on an autumn walk, hears Tibullus whispering among the trees and feels that Tibullus is with him when bright leaves fall on him in a "shower of sweet smelling tongues of flame" (Kristeva 1994, 13). Tibullus's poetry enables Septicius to access an opening to being in the flesh that reconciles him to lost time, a time not carved out by sacrifice. A sacrificial economy, fueled by mimetic rivalries that beset those who lack being, provides only for metamorphoses that deprive us of our humanity. By contrast, a nonsacrificial economy that emerges from positive mimesis—compassion become flesh—opens up possibilities for a transubstantiation in being. The compelling message of *The Old Man and the Wolves* is that the memory work we undertake in our narrative practices can establish pathways for such healing transformation.

Writing in her journal about the old men—Ovid, Tibullus, Septicius, and her father—Stephanie has remembered in hopes that she can create a bridge to a meaningful future. Writing *The Old Man and the Wolves*, Kristeva has remembered in hopes that, in exploring a psychic space etched by mourning, she can experience healing in the aftermath of her father's death. Reading this novel, those who participate in the memories it evokes may yet hope to glimpse alternatives to aspects of their own experience that mirror life in Santa Varvara. In all these ways, Kristeva has offered entry through her novel to key moments of an aesthetic and therapeutic praxis that plumbs the healing powers of narrative.

Notes

1. Kristeva regularly references Girard. Although John Lechte attributes the theme of sacrifice in Kristeva's work to Bataille (Lechte 1990, 74), Girard's theory of sacrifice figures in her work (Kristeva 1984, 249 n. 91; 250 n. 100; Kristeva 1982, 213 n. 4; 215 n. 17; Kristeva 1986b, 213 n. 21; Kristeva 1987b, 395 n.16). Michael Payne confirms my assessment in citing Girard's influence on Kristeva (Payne 1993, 182). So also does Stephen Bann suggest in his foreword to Kristeva's *Proust and the Sense of Time* that Kristeva's theory of subjectivity is informed not only by Lacan but also by "the speculations of René Girard, whose achievement she was one of the first to salute" (Kristeva 1993a, x).

2. The idiom is suggested by Joseph Solodow. (See Solodow 2002, 206.)

3. Kristeva calls the professor the "Old Man" when she is describing his interactions with the residents of Santa Varvara. When he is engaged in communicating the past, breathing new life into the figures of the Roman Empire, she calls him "Septicius Clarus."

4. Girard offers a particularly clear commentary on this point in his recent book *Sacrifice* (Girard 2011).

5. Girard would find of particular interest also that one of the oldest renderings of this myth has Lycaon serve Zeus a dish created from the sacrifice of Lycaon's son. According to Girard, child sacrifice is one of the most ancient expressions of the "victim mechanism." Abraham's near sacrifice of his son Isaac is cited by Girard as an example. (See Girard 2001, xv.)

6. (Ovid 2005, lines 220–335). Ovid writes that Jupiter destroyed with a flood the race of humans that had originated from the bodies of the giants. If so, one could posit that the second creation of humans was less violent. For his part, Girard understands that humans are uncomfortable with acknowledging that human society begins with sacrifice. The truth of origins is glossed over and obfuscated by myth (Girard 1987, 103–04). For his part, Feldherr argues that Ovid's mythic stories also obscure any clear separation between the two "races" of humans. They share the human form in common; further, as the story of the second creation progresses, that rivalry with the gods persists is clear. The "second" race of humans "reduplicates" all the questions raised about the first race. The flood resolves nothing about the nature of humanity (Feldherr 2010, 126–28).

7. Kristeva never states that the young woman at the lake is Alba, the student of Septicius; instead, she is "Alba's double" (Kristeva 1994, 108). Late in the novel, when Alba is observed by Stephanie "hand in hand with Vespasian" (Kristeva 1994, 126), Stephanie continues to honor the memory of Alba of the lake. In Kristeva's interview with Sichère,

she explains that "the duplication and dissemination of identities refer to the obvious fact that we are experiencing contemporary culture in a process of metamorphosis" (Kristeva 1996c, 165; Kristeva 1992a, 76).

8. Kristeva suggests that she is replacing "a hidden, anonymous observer," the author in disguise, with a "master of ceremonies" who will "reveal himself and include himself in the story" (Kristeva 1994, 63). In Kristeva's interview with Sichère, she comments that she wrote the novel in the aftermath of her father's death, which occurred "in a Sofia hospital through the incompetence and brutality of the medical and political system" (Kristeva 1996c, 163). Especially when scenes are not explicitly placed in Santa Varvara and refer to incidents from Kristeva's own life (as in a visit Kristeva made to the cathedral in Sofia with the president of France), that Stephanie and Kristeva's father are one is clear.

9. The "Man of Sorrows" is a prevalent theme in Orthodox icons of Christ. Writing about icons (Kristeva 2000b, 153), Kristeva says that an icon is not an image. Images "inscribe" meaning; icons "manifest" meaning: "the icon is a graphein, a sensible trace, not a spectacle." The origin of the term "man of sorrows" is from Isaiah (52:13–53:12). This figure, assumed by Christians to be an anticipatory reference to Christ, is also the focus of an antisacrificial message within the Hebrew Bible. The man of sorrows is an outsider to the community; he becomes despised by them and appears to have a disfigured face from whom others hide; he bears the pains of that community, is crushed by that community even though he has not been the source of that community's suffering and has done no violence; and he becomes the source of healing for the community. But the text of Isaiah is not myth: myths justify mob action; but, in the text of Isaiah, the persecutors recognize that the suffering servant is innocent of the charges for which he has been held culpable (53:9). In myth, Gods do not challenge scapegoating; in Isaiah, Yahweh sides with the victim. Although human violence is not wholly supplanted by Yahweh, Yahweh does not have his servant repay violence in kind. In this way, the power of violent mimesis is broken in the Hebrew Bible as it is not in myth. See Raymund Schwager (Schwager 2000, 126–33).

10. Girard discusses at length that the historical religion of Christianity has frequently ignored the message of the Gospels and regularly has been a primary instigator of cultural scapegoating (see for example, Girard 1987, 224–62). Christianity also has developed theologies of atonement in total forgetfulness of the Gospels' message. These theologies reinstate a God who wants human sacrifice. In order to satisfy this God, even his son must die. But God is not the problem that theologies must resolve; rather, mimetic contagion among humans that mutates into scapegoating is the problem. With Jesus, theologians are given a new task by God: to disseminate the Gospel message that has exposed the truth of sacrifice and revealed a God who defends victims and offers love (Girard 2001, 150). That, in its history, Christianity has not absorbed or acted on the nonsacrificial message of Christ is a focus of critical exploration for many students of Girard (see, for example, Swartley 2000).

11. Kristeva is sympathetic toward much of the Christian story. However, even as she recognizes its antisacrificial message, enabling her to draw close to Girard, she is not a Christian apologist. She discusses that the message of Christian love comes at a price: the disavowal of the human body. Christian love becomes implicated by its theologians

in a worship of a Father who welcomes us "as pure spirit, as name, and not as body" (Kristeva 1987b, 144). *Powers of Horror* is Kristeva's extended commentary on problems that have accrued to Christianity over the centuries because of its choice against corporeality. In seeking to join Hebraic flesh (a body bounded by the law) with the pneumatic body (that flesh subdued), Christianity has created the "lining and the cloth of one and the same economy" (Kristeva 1982, 124–25). But that economy, fundamentally sacrificial, moves Christianity away from its antisacrificial origins, creating a history with onerous consequences for those within Christian history who most obviously represent the body. For further discussion of this sacrificial history, see my *Sacrificed Lives* (Reineke 1997, 93–102). For nonsacrificial alternatives that Kristeva observes Christianity has retained see Reineke (1997, 189–90).

12. Kristeva does not associate these old men with the Oedipal father or with Lacan's Law of the Father. But with a weakening of the paternal function and a flattening of affect not only in psychoanalysis but in the larger world, analysis needs to rely on other forms of paternal agency that help subjects reconnect to affect and meaning. This task calls for imaginary fathers—the old men of her novel. See Kelly Oliver for a discussion of how access to psychic space is linked with the imaginary father. In discussing Kristeva's concept of "intimate revolt," Oliver explains how, for Kristeva, access to our bodies and to meaning depends on the possibility of "metaphorical transference" to which a "loving third," the imaginary father, makes a critical contribution (Oliver 2005, 82–84).

4

Sebastian's Skull

Establishing the "Society of the Icon"

Frances L. Restuccia

"Flesh reveals in death its smelly truth that the living try to perfume away and cover up."

—Julia Kristeva, *Murder in Byzantium*

Julia Kristeva's Byzantium is all about time, rather than a place on a map. The female protagonist of her novel *Murder in Byzantium* (2004), Stephanie Delacour, comments: "A foreigner and a woman, I know that I come from Byzantium, a place that has never existed with any credible reality except in my soul" (Kristeva 2006b, 64); her "Byzantium is within [Anna Comnena's] fifteen books—an imaginary chronicle" (Kristeva 2006b, 87). The novel also offers the following description of the concept:

> Byzantium is the color of time; don't look for it on a map. Modern misanthropes who nurse their depressed feelings with tourism believe they meet up with it in Greece or Turkey—some go as far as the Balkans, but. . . . Today Byzantium is nowhere; it is noplace, except perhaps on the tingling skin of the Bosporus . . . or perhaps the sulfur exhaled by the Black Sea around Nessebar when the sun goes down and the women depart. . . . Only passing epiphanies such as these . . . give an idea of what this odd future anterior of Byzantium was, is, and will always be. A wine of intrigue and tenderness, savors

> and pains, an intuition of mixtures and meetings. But not a place, no, not any place. (Kristeva 2006b, 83)

On the one hand, *Murder in Byzantium* focuses on Santa Varvara, or the society of the spectacle, which for the most part precludes the time outside of time or timelessness—as the Spectacle is characterized by speed as well as by the type of image Kristeva describes as having lost its "inscription in the flesh," and as operating "just at the surface of the retina," "without substance" (Kristeva 2012, 56). On the other hand, the novel engages "Byzantium" or timelessness. But timelessness manifests itself in two antithetical ways in this book: propelled directly by the death drive, it erupts in crime and, in particular, murder; timelessness also takes the form of blossoming or flowering.

To Kristeva, because we are (at least in part) unconscious beings, we need to experience what she refers to as "the event," which happens at the temporal/atemporal intersection of the word/language, and the flesh/biology. The problem is that globalization has abolished such events, leaving the death drive—which gets expressed beautifully through the event—to explode somewhere. Hence "humanity has become more homicidal than ever." "Made delirious by the acceleration of the spectacle" (Kristeva 2010, 279), we kill. Speed; empty images that dictate fantasies to us (for profit) rather than enable us to cultivate our own (for the enrichment of our psychic lives); and all-consuming consumption, it might be said, convert the death drive to crime. It turns out, then, that a monstrous form of timelessness erupts in Santa Varvara, the very place where timelessness is disavowed. The question of what lurks beneath the spectacular image sets the narrator of *Murder in Byzantium* off on a rant:

> It's the drive, my friends, that the image strives to put to sleep. . . . "Stop, drives are no longer in!" one of my lovers used to snort, . . . before popping another ecstasy tablet that turned him off of sex entirely. . . . "Watch what you're going to say, your drive to think is making me ill!" complained another who had a very low resistance to castration anxiety. But he's not the only one, the whole spectacle society has a very low resistance in this area: one is advised not to think, it curbs the appetite of every consumer, and it hurts. Let's play Who Wants to Be a Millionaire? instead. Let's win at . . . the stock market. . . . Under the screens, the crime. (Kristeva 2006b, 77–78)

The detective novel is "the fruit of [the] explosion of the death drive" (Kristeva 2010, 279) and a counterweight to the virtual society of the spectacle. In *Intimate Revolt: The Powers and Limits of Psychoanalysis*, Kristeva defends detective fiction, mildly, as "a popular genre that keeps the possibility of questioning alive" and that "basically tells the reader, 'You can know'" (Kristeva 2002a, 4). But, after noting that when people stop reading, they still are inclined to turn to detective novels, she also describes this genre as possessing the potential to alter subjectivity. The detective novel is a "low form" of what Kristeva calls "revolt," that is, the subject's "return/turning back/displacement/change" (Kristeva 2002a, 4–5).[1] And with *Murder in Byzantium*, it seems that Kristeva has stepped up the idea of the potential power of the psychoanalytic detective novel, illustrating that such novels, by virtue of their polyphonic structure, can produce "events" resistant to virtuality, insofar as they allow the reader to dissolve, to transubstantiate, and then to undergo resurrection, through sublimation of the death drive. Rather than succumbing to the violence of death, the detective novel is a literary genre especially suited to modulate the death drive as a way of "grappling with our passions and our mortality," as Kristeva urges us to do through certain forms of representation (Kristeva 2012, 10).

The detective novel would appear to acquire such power by including murder as a matter of course, a way intrinsic to the genre of inviting the reader to pass through a certain "arc of Nothingness." Here we have a genre that one reads deliberately to confront murder and even decapitations, a genre that reflects them, and in turn offers the opportunity to meditate and reflect on them in order to preclude their enactment: "It's in writing the crime that one avoids it" (Kristeva 2006b, 78). (In *Murder in Byzantium*, a continuation of Kristeva's earlier fiction, Jerry is an orphan since his mother, Gloria, was decapitated. Gloria, a translator, loses her head in Kristeva's previous novel, *Possessions*, which begins with this crime committed by multiple murderers, also in Santa Varvara, an "imaginary town . . . emblematic of the global village" [Kristeva 2002a, 4]. Bridging the two novels, a reference to Gloria appears on the first page of *Murder in Byzantium*. Stephanie reminds us that, thanks to "previous assignments," she knows Santa Varvara "by heart": "sunny air saturated with hydrocarbons and jasmine, skeletons in the closets of political parties and petroleum companies, *women decapitated*, such as [her] dead friend Gloria Harrison, who devoted herself to translating literature in a country where no one reads any more because of television" [Kristeva 2006b, 1–2, my emphasis].) In detective fiction, murderers are destroyed by reflection of as well as on them, as their real power is transformed into literary representation. They resemble Medusa figures whose deadly trajectories are turned around against them through literary expression, just as "Medusa's gaze kills, but it is the *reflection*—the figure of splitting in two, of representation—that finally kills Medusa" (Kristeva 2012, 30).

Like Guy Debord, in *The Society of the Spectacle*, and Giorgio Agamben, especially in *Means without End*, *Profanations*, and *Nudities*, Kristeva condemns our so-called society of the spectacle, in which "power is vacant and values corrupt." "[M]an has become a simple conglomerate of organs, no longer a subject but a patrimonial person, someone belonging to the patrimony, financially, genetically, and physiologically, a person barely free enough to use a remote control to choose his channel," a person bombarded by entertainment, performance, and show culture (Kristeva 2002a, 4). In *Murder in Byzantium* (and here we get a glimpse of the porous border between Kristeva's theory and fiction), she asserts that "The non-stop exhibition of intimacy, televising of values, and execution of our passions" form a society where "The flutterings of the heart have been taken over by the flutterings of spectacle," and where "a desire for death" is cultivated by the raising of children on video games (Kristeva 2006b, 64–65). Drugged on Prozac and Zoloft, consumers merely bandage their psychic wounds; speech has no meaning; self-reflection is nonexistent, and the written word ignored. We can deduce from this list of the inadequacies and abuses of the spectacle some reasons why Kristeva writes novels: the "recounting of affects," she comments, is "an unbeatable antidepressant" (Kristeva 2010, 277).

But this narrativizing process is by no means superficial, a mere recounting of a story of pain and woe. Kristeva promotes what she calls the "novel of the subject" that descends into "the folds not of the Ego but of the subject" (Kristeva 2010, 273). In fact, experiencing such a novel, the reader's ego is meant to be destabilized; the novel of the subject is "a piercing through" (Kristeva 2010, 274), a return, an intimate revolt. The reader is put into sync with his or her sadomasochism; in the novel of the subject, "[r]eading meets the death drive" and "destroys the mask of surface identity"; a "menacing brutality" is engaged (Kristeva 2010, 286). Here too, as with skull rituals and images of beheadings, as Kristeva elaborates in *The Severed Head: Capital Visions*, we have the "condition for the representation of what allows us to stand up to the void," that is, the "ability to represent the life of the mind, psychological experience as the capacity for multiple representations" (Kristeva 2012, 4–5). In other words, the novel of the subject establishes a double *relation* to the death drive: the drive is freed into the text that operates in its service, at the same time that the signs of this text effect and celebrate distance from the drive.

However, it is because we are now, in our contemporary spectacular world, pressured by an unrepresented death drive, a drive festering under the screens, that characters in *Murder in Byzantium* find themselves identifying with serial killers. In the novel, that is, Kristeva first exposes the "wrong" or destructive kind of timelessness. Police Commissioner Rilsky, whose job it is to find the killer of eight members of a cult called the New Pantheon, senses "this serial killer in his skin, his muscles, his head" (Kristeva 2006b, 32) and later proclaims to himself, "the serial killer [is] really [me]!" "[H]e made an 8 with his finger" (Kristeva 2006b, 54), indicating his connection to, or perhaps even envy of, the serial killer's experience with infinity or timelessness (the killer's trademark being this infinity sign). Through this identification, the novel implies that now we are *all* capable of killing, of behaving also like Professor Sebastian Chrest-Jones who snuffs out his lover, Fa Chang, merely because her pregnancy might endanger his research. "He was becoming more and more excited by Fa and this desire frightened him. Sebastian had the feeling that he would never be able to get rid of her, that she would never let go, never leave them alone, neither him nor his field of dreams, including his research, his precious investigations that led him to Byzantium and his novel: *The Story of Anna* . . . his obscure quest" (Kristeva 2006b, 13). "Is each of us a potential killer?" the novel asks. Are we not all drawn to the "hole" that murder carves "in time" (Kristeva 2006b, 30)? When Sebastian squeezes Fa's throat, he loses "all sense of time." Yet he feels "no particular emotion. Just indifference toward this crumpled little body," to the point that he can insouciantly "thrust his thumbs into the eye sockets of the foreigner" (Kristeva 2006b, 14).

Here Kristeva unveils the murderer's unconscious craving for timelessness; but at the same time, we observe *murder's* lack of depth. Even murder, this most radical of evils, in the society of the spectacle turns out to be meaningless and unsatisfying, a trivial gesture with no psychic impact. One day, Number Eight, the novel's serial killer, Xiao Chang, a Chinese immigrant intent upon purifying the contemporary world but lacking interiority himself, decides to kill "because he was feeling an irresistible urge to vomit" (Kristeva 2006b, 147). By strangling the pregnant Fa Chang, Sebastian nonchalantly commits, in fact, matricide. (Performing such an act mechanically, without feeling or meaning, would appear to be blasphemy against Kristevan theory, which regards "matricide" as "our vital necessity, the sine-qua-non condition of our individuation, provided it takes place under optimal circumstances" [Kristeva 1989, 28].) Likewise, Number Eight kills mechanically, in a line—one New Pantheon figure after another. Even more strikingly, from a psychoanalytic point of view, this particular serial killer's goal of purification attempts to place death itself "outside." He believes that "[h]e will expel it . . . by evacuating the twisted individuals of every species" (Kristeva 2006b, 212). Militating against Kristevan psychoanalysis, this serial killer aspires to depart from the self by following an ancient Chinese notion of " 'long life,' 'to die without perishing,' " by achieving "a state without time and space in which there is *no place for death*" (Kristeva 2006b, 211, my emphasis). Here we have a murderer on a linear trajectory, killing to expunge death. The point is twofold: because the society of the spectacle shuts out timelessness, murder becomes psychically attractive and erupts; but murder too is caught in the spectacle's web. Like all contemporary crime, murder turns out to be a mere "acting out" rather than the psychically nourishing kind of engagement with timelessness that grants a *relation* to lack, the unsaid, the Heideggerian Nothing in Being. Murder thus fails to facilitate our standing up to the void through a making use, or putting into play, of the drive.

That is, Kristeva favors an imaginary capturing of fear that appeases it, and creatively "restores it to the symbolic order," which (in her view) follows Christian art in its deployment of the image. Kristeva curiously regards cinema as the "apogee" of "Catholic astuteness that makes man in spite of his disquiet 'walk in an image[.]' Christian art, in the half-light of churches, knows, multiplies, and exploits this fascination: calm reigns before images of hell. . . . The image as compensation for anxiety and cultural project: this was already in Augustine" (Kristeva 2002a, 79). Evil, or the nonsymbolized death drive, might, then, be articulated and appeased by the imaginary, or it might end up being the ultimate consequence of the society of the spectacle. For Kristeva, the central ethical question is whether the work of art first "take[s] us for a ride but [second] makes us keep our distance" (Kristeva 2002a, 79) (her preference) or mystifies and banalizes evil. Debord's "society of the spectacle," Kristeva makes clear, is the antithesis of the "imaginary of demystification": "By exhausting representation, being bored in representation, suffocating from its falseness in the ballet of those who govern us (and who trade planes for human rights, for example), by letting himself be invaded by representation, though he knows its strings, modern man comes up against the logic of fantasy" (Kristeva 2002a, 79). "Modern man," in other words, ruins his opportunity to fantasize, and thus to locate his desire, as he allows the spectacle's fantasy to govern him.[2]

We have to turn elsewhere for such playful empowerment, for the chance to indulge in liberating fantasies of our own, to swing from Santa Varvara to Byzantium. Byzantium, a timeless place, where "intimacy blossoms in the unsaid," to quote Stephanie in the novel, must be restored. Again to borrow Stephanie's words: "Intimacy speaks indirectly, transmuted into figures and parables, numbers, symbols, and allusions, and all that is Byzantium." Her Byzantium in a sense "names the unnameable" (Kristeva 2006b, 69). One can reach it, as Stephanie does, through (for example) erotic acts: what Stephanie calls her "strangeness." "The joy of coming," Stephanie theorizes, "is the intimate strangeness that we seek amid the ordinary order of our lives—a strangeness that constitutes us . . . that can transform into a marvelous openness" (Kristeva 2006b, 69). Such nonsentimental love that annihilates the self and plunges a nonself into timelessness (Stephanie sees her "love story" with Rilsky as actually having no story, given that it takes place "out of time" [Kristeva 2006b, 62]), "more a kind of music than a bond," is "the symmetrical opposite of crime's silence" (Kristeva 2006b, 52). Kristeva singles out "the sensory body" as the "true antidote to crime and murder" (Kristeva 2010, 303); the articulated and shared sensory body is for Kristeva a primary safeguard against acting out. Likewise, the Orthodox faith "lets you touch the mystery of the incarnation not with a finger but with your entire body: the Word is made Flesh [especially] in an Orthodox Church" (Kristeva 2010, 302).[3]

Like the Byzantium sphere of the intimate unsaid, the sensory body, and the Incarnation-based icon, Jerry's world is also "incompatible with Santa Varvara" (Kristeva 2006b, 61); conversion from his milieu to the society of the spectacle is virtually impossible. Stephanie's adopted, disabled child, "a fragile flower" (Kristeva 2006b, 2), possesses tenderness and a "wounded voice" (Kristeva 2006b, 62) with the power to eclipse the realities of Santa Varvara, while the savageness of Santa Varvara manifests itself in the way it shrinks and almost causes to disappear "the fragile existence of this adolescent computer nerd" (Kristeva 2006b, 61). In *Hatred and Forgiveness*, Kristeva talks about her involvement in "the vast domain of disability" as a way of being on the "frontiers of living" as well as a means of exploring our shaky identity and staying connected to "our [own] unbearable vulnerability" (Kristeva 2010, 288). Jerry's realm of disability, then, is another Byzantine space, one marked by Eastern Orthodoxy's compatibility with Good Friday rather than the *Gloria*.

Kristeva opts for Eastern Orthodoxy over Catholicism since the "depression that is ravaging our societies, in the West as in the East, seems to find more consolation in Orthodox ritual" than in the Catholic Church (Kristeva 2010, 302). Celebrating the concept of *kenosis*, exalted by the Eastern Orthodox Church, that is, "the annihilation of the divine realized by Christ's descent into hell" (Kristeva 2010, 301), Kristeva identifies the voyage to, and through, death that she urges us to take as an Eastern Orthodox journey to the end of the night. "[T]he Orthodox tradition opens the space for a mystical union, a passionate fusion *in silence* with what defies the intellect," as Maria Margaroni explains in "Julia Kristeva's Chiasmatic Journeys" (Margaroni 2009, 116). Such a Pauline journey (*kenosis* is Saint Paul's term), by taking into account the void, is able to give birth. A radical "hollowing out," *kenosis* carves out a space of iconic representation that devotes itself to inscribing that void, giving rise to it "in the visible" (Kristeva 2012, 55), from where it generates new life.

Experiencing such a *vita nuova* by falling in love, Stephanie opens a Byzantine space in Santa Varvara where she lives among "geraniums and their soil," plays with "little purple flowers," and "seep[s]" into a "lively amber scent that overpowers the heavy fragrance of the neighboring rosebushes." She holds onto "tenacious flowers" "like an energetic or drunken bee or fly, the ephemeral lover of perfumed pollens of innumerable colors" (Kristeva 2006b, 63). Through Stephanie's intoxication with flowers, Kristeva literalizes her metaphor of "flowering," which is the promise offered by the novel "for those with no system, no home, for travelers . . ." (Kristeva 2010, 289). Rilsky even conceives of his passion for Stephanie as having been "always locked inside his dreams—only waiting to blossom" (Kristeva 2006b, 53). He regards his love for Stephanie, and his identification with the serial killer, as "the light and the dark faces of the same abyss" (Kristeva 2006b, 54): one can be driven to murder, or let one's passion blossom.

The metaphysical detective novel itself, we might even claim, is a mystical flower or (better) a flowering mystic. Here we find the timelessness and the unsaid of Byzantium, a "propitious place" where, rather than a clash between religions or assassins, ultimately we have their "recasting into a *bouquet* of psychical landscapes" (Kristeva 2010, 297, my emphasis). Kristeva entertains Durkheim's notion that society is God in order to posit that therefore the novel is "its mystic" (Kristeva 2010, 296). We can begin to comprehend what this startling idea of the novel-as-mystic might signify by noting Kristeva's conception of the mystic. A mystic does not deny death. In fact, she or he identifies with death, and such an identification, Kristeva contends, separates the mystic from the mother, for to relive death is to detach from the lost mother.

In *The Severed Head*, Kristeva tells a story about her childhood that vividly captures this idea. In fact, it is her own Mama who draws a snowman whose head is melting as if, ironically, to send the message to the young Kristeva that an artistic encounter with lack/death—the snowman's cut-off head—offers insurance against collapsing into the maternal Thing. This story is, to my mind, complemented by a childhood recollection that Stephanie shares in *Murder in Byzantium* about her father who enables her to experience an annulment of herself without risk by "being exiled within the invisible of the image." "Shored up in this way, the pleasure of my strangeness knows no limits; I can *melt* with no fear whatsoever . . ." (Kristeva 2006b, 73, my emphasis). In these stories, Kristeva articulates a release from the mother that the father's support enables one to bear. Like the snowman, Stephanie can melt, identify with death, and thereby detach from the mother. Insofar as she is at her father's side, she can locate—or be revealed to—herself through her pleasure in her limitless strangeness. Stephanie/Kristeva illustrates her pleasure beyond the pleasure principle, her being "without personal borders," by way of a photograph taken of the winning goal at a game she attended with her father, in which she appears as a "speck" (a similar photo was taken of Kristeva at a soccer match in Sophia [Kristeva 2010, 275]):

> The miniscule little point there, right there, was me—my head like a pinprick, a micron-sized iron filing held by the magnet of the stadium and the indifferent newsprint. I have never enjoyed any photograph of myself taken by lovers, friends, or professional photographers . . . as much as this one, nor have I felt so certain about the absolutely faithful representation of who I really am as I did when I saw that grainy gray photo. Beyond or short of the real me, . . . it's the annulment of myself that I celebrated in exquisite peace looking at this speck that finally revealed me to myself. (Kristeva 2006b, 72)

Mystics engage in negative thought; yet their experience is one of constant resurrection, a journey into the night of desire followed by the capacity to think, and to connect to others. Cultivating this idea, *Murder in Byzantium* establishes that "One needs to have been as dead as a stone and then to have been remade as a self outside oneself to reconnect with the splendor of the outside world" (Kristeva 2006b, 158). Hence the novel of the subject takes one on a "voyage through negative thought," a voyage through and to death, what we might call a narrative *kenosis*: the reader descends into hell. And one variation on this idea is that the polyphony of the novel can escort the reader into "the psychosis that is the brute reality of globalized humans," as it is revealed by our "generalized criminality" (Kristeva 2010, 296). Only through a descent into Western culture's psychotic inferno can a resurrection from it be imagined and achieved; this paradox provides a model for desiring subjectivity, which in turn is the only way that a "society of the icon" can come into being.

Murder in Byzantium offers the reader an experience of *kenosis* as he or she follows Sebastian on his travels to former Byzantine territories to find his lost ancestor, Ebrard de Pagan, a Latin barbarian passionately beloved and thereby reformed by Anna Comnena, the great Byzantine intellectual-princess and first woman historian. It seems plausible, as Maria Margaroni interprets the novel, that while visiting Boyana, "Sebastian is seduced by 'another way of seeing,' which leads his eyes to the interior and beyond" (Margaroni 2009, 116). He seems, to Margaroni, to comprehend the image as being at the crossroads of the corporeal and the incorporeal. It seems plausible that, after his despicable robotic matricide of Fa Chang in the society of the spectacle, a reformed Sebastian seeks "an alternative beginning," that "his quest for another world-outside-this-world" is "for a reconciliation between East and West," reflected in his vision of "a Crusade of love rather than conquest, a fatal crossing of paths between Anne Comnène, the 'belated Greek of Orthodox Empire,' " and Ebrard de Pagan, and even that Sebastian conceives of a Europe that might someday realize her sisterhood with a repressed Eastern Europe, the former Byzantium (Margaroni 2009, 116). Although he starts out as a murderer in the society of the spectacle, as someone who, "for as long as he can remember sunlight, . . . [had] adored strangling butterflies, Tracy Joneses [Tracy Jones is Sebastian's mother, whose death apparently did not faze him], and Fa Changs" (Kristeva 2006b, 163), Sebastian can perhaps be read as embarking belatedly on an experience of intimate revolt insofar as he returns to his place of origin seeking a lost ancestor, a lost father, and lost self.[4] Just as Anna Comnena apparently wrote her *Alexiad* as a justification of the reign of her father, as well as to search for (and return to) him, there's "a secret motive" behind Sebastian's attraction to Byzantium, as he himself realizes. He hopes "to recharge [himself] by investigating origins," and to return "to an absent father, to the primordial enigma, which one must solve in order to retrieve [oneself] and, if possible, give [oneself] at best a certain shape and weight, to some dream of acquiring in this way an identity" (Kristeva 2006b, 20). Indeed, *Murder in Byzantium* states explicitly that, "[l]ifted out of the ordinary passage of time by the extravagance of his solitude as a bastard and murderer, an intellectual crazy about the past and beautiful things that will never belong to this world, . . . Sebastian is always in search of *nothing in the flesh of the world*" (Kristeva 2006b, 181, my emphasis), leading us to believe that Sebastian was finally on his way to an encounter with an abyss that could have enabled him to face it, and possibly even to have folded it creatively into his life. However, for murdering Xiao Chang's twin sister, Sebastian ends up being murdered himself by the Santa Varvara serial killer in Puy-en-Velay's cathedral, called in the novel the "cathedral of hell" ("Vel- in Velay supposedly has the same root as hell" [Kristeva 2006b, 198]), his intimate revolt cut terribly short.

But it is a propitious journey for us. Sebastian draws us into this hellish church, where we simultaneously follow the serial killer wallowing in his psychosis that, despite his (absurd and misguided) attempt to purify the society of the spectacle, is clearly a product of it. Herein lies a potentially productive space for the reader since, to Kristeva, we can engage one version of the Nothingness in Being through "a familiarity with psychosis" (a foreclosure of the law that serial killing certainly indicates). For psychosis brings us "up against a psychical reality that endangers consciousness"; it exposes us to "the pulse of being. Erasure of subject/object borders, assault of the drive: language becomes tonality (*Stimmung*), memory of being, music of the body and of matter. Heidegger seeks to capture this near psychosis in being, by respectfully visiting the work of Hölderlin" (Kristeva 2002a, 9).

In her work in general, Kristeva looks at philosophy and psychoanalytic theory for traces of "this border region of the speaking being that is psychosis" (Kristeva 2002a, 10). I am suggesting that her treatment of the serial killer in *Murder in Byzantium* is a fictional engagement with this pathological condition, from the first two pages of the novel to Xiao Chang's demise in the "cathedral of hell." Isn't it striking that the opening two pages of *Murder in Byzantium*, titled "Mystery at the Whale Lighthouse"—which describe in detail the ritualistic behavior of the serial killer near the ocean after his seventh murder, and then his return to his apartment to watch TV news of his crime that leads him to smile—are placed outside the formal beginning of the book? This structure itself implies that the serial killer's status exceeds the social order. Traversing the book, he travels from this external space to the infernal French cathedral, where he is shot. The psychotic spaces in which Xiao Chang, alias Wuxian, is situated, along with the murderous behavior he acts out, are limitless sites of "bad timelessness": *wuxian* = "no limit" (Kristeva 2006b, 214). *Murder in Byzantium* engages such psychosis and unfolds its meaning at the level of sensations and drives.

The aim of psychoanalysis as well as of the psychoanalytic detective novel, then, is to escort the subject on a voyage to hell, one that illuminates vulnerability, in order to bring into being "a perpetual rebirth of the subject." "New capacities of thinking," "new bodies," "new lives," and new links have the chance to flower only once the untenable *lack of being* is embodied (Kristeva 2010, 41–42) and subsequently inscribed in our concept of the human itself—so that it can have an impact on our political practice. Contemporary Western civilization (the Spectacle) resists acknowledging trauma. In *Murder in Byzantium*, Kristeva diagnoses this obtuse social condition that she metaphorizes as a "beautiful mask over a monstrous face":

> [the] plaster cast, the bandage, and the mask are called Civilization. There are families that, like the Rilskys, often want to know nothing of evil. No traumatic events, nothing ever happens at the Rilskys, nothing happens now, a nothing that is not everything, one that whispers the unsaid that [is] communicated through headaches, fevers more or less acute, and ulcers. [Rilsky's] conductor father died of it, of nothing. (Kristeva 2006b, 31–32)

There is, then, Nothing and also perhaps the much more terrifying nothing (absolute vapidity) that fails to recognize the Nothing. To Kristeva, a true civilization can emerge only through such an acknowledgment.

Being such a civilization, "Byzantium" (like an icon) embodies the unsaid and the hidden, allowing the visible and the invisible to coincide. It preserves the *lack of being* disallowed by the iconoclastic society of the spectacle, whose insistence on static images nevertheless produces holes that are only dead ends. Murder is the return of that repressed, the malicious consequence of the abolition of Nothing. By representing that murder—the "murder" of *lack of being*—and by literarily killing off its murderer, *Murder in Byzantium*, the novel as mystic, pulls death and the death drive into the symbolic arena, allegorically restoring our *lack of being* by destroying, in effect, the society of the spectacle. (Guy Debord launches his book *The Society of the Spectacle* by stating his very deliberate intention to do "harm to spectacular society" [Debord 1994, 10]; but by exposing psychoanalytically the Spectacle and its discontents, Kristeva offers a more penetrating and effective approach to that same aim.) Sublimating the death drive *in this way*—by crushing the evil of the nonrepresentation of the death drive through its representation—*Murder in Byzantium* creates new openings. "Meaningful murder" can take place (only) in Byzantium, which provides a fertile context for it, one in which the timelessness of murder (and matricide) can have a psychic impact. Sebastian's journey back in time that gets looped together with the present to give a sense of past-present fusion (in the novel the eleventh and twenty-first centuries in a way timelessly converge) allows the final killings to be situated in a Byzantine venue where they can carve out a site of the Nothing—into which the society of the spectacle is then allegorically deposited.

By reconstructing Byzantium through the story of Anna Comnena and arranging a fictional journey to that rich world, Kristeva's novel imagines the possibility of a Byzantine dissolution of the society of the spectacle, thus creating a timeless void, from which all the virtues of Byzantium can spring: the sensory body, intimacy, a marvelous openness, flowering, links to the unsaid as well as to others. Even Police Commissioner Rilsky, albeit with some resistance, is "surprised by the new body that was waking up inside him[,] and the commissioner let it happen" (Kristeva 2006b, 104). When Stephanie returns to Paris at the end, she reenters the timelessness of gardens:

> The Luxembourg Gardens smell a lot like linden even though it's not the season, but that honey scent of linden always surrounds my garden in my sensory memory, in my present impregnated with the past, in my walks with Jerry, doves in the pink walnut trees, bees that confuse their hives with my windows on the rue d'Assas. The fragrance of flowers in bloom, of freshness, of renewal, so light and that yet penetrate glass, iron, stone, my skin, my bones, nourishing me and undoing me. (Kristeva 2006b, 237)

How removed from the Spectacle is this? Is *Murder in Byzantium* not a Kristevan fantasy in which the society of the spectacle, instead of consuming, is itself consumed? Here we have an "event": the flesh made word, that is, dead bodies driven by the death drive transformed into detective fiction, a menacing brutality engaged through a literary reconstruction that enables the Byzantine Empire once again to flourish. Kristeva revives Yeats's famous sailing to Byzantium, as she joins him in celebrating "the young in one another's arms," the heart that "knows not what it is," and in reveling in "sensual music" and gold mosaics to gather us, as well, into "the artifice of eternity."

The novel, I am suggesting, arrives at these Byzantine delights through a murder of its own, a killing, a cut—of the society of the spectacle itself—that renders the novel iconic rather than mimetic and certainly not spectacular. The psychoanalytic power of *Murder in Byzantium* emanates not from a representation that the reader visualizes, but from an experience of *kenosis* that he or she has of the novel as a staging of death and the death drive. Like an icon, this psychoanalytic detective novel is not viewed but experienced, by a reader who is enticed to solve the mystery of the crime, to locate what is hidden, the invisible beyond the visible signs in the text. The reader gradually comes to realize that Wuxian is the killer of the Santa Varvara cult and that he turns against Sebastian (for Sebastian's killing of Wuxian's twin sister). But being allegorical, *Murder in Byzantium* goes further, asking us to consider what its murderers' crimes emblematize. The reader follows Sebastian and Wuxian into the "cathedral of hell," to their deaths—Wuxian puts a "slug in the *skull* of the professor" before he is fired on and killed himself (Kristeva 2006b, 218, my emphasis)—iconically to confront *their crimes*, killings that fail to produce a lack, and consequently fall short of enabling us to situate ourselves in relation to it. But Sebastian's punctured skull is a different story. It becomes another of Kristeva's severed heads: a different "status of the image reveals itself here, which . . . we have now lost in the world of 'the spectacle'" (Kristeva 2012, 4). Kristeva is interested in skulls as works of art and skull worship as a way of "pass[ing] through the 'arc of Nothingness' . . . to move beyond it[.] To forget oneself for a time, project oneself into the animality of the beyond, reconnect with Being" (Kristeva 2012, 22). "The world of feeling," she adds, is one of "cohabitation with mortality: it requires . . . meditation on the terror of the skull and the appropriation of it through the intervention of a reflection or an image" (Kristeva 2012, 24).

Sebastian's pierced skull turns out to be the site of the novel's gaze, like the cuttlebone at the base of Hans Holbein's Renaissance painting *The Ambassadors*, a "skull" that Lacan presents, in *The Four Fundamental Concepts of Psycho-Analysis*, as the constitutive lack—or gaze—of both the painting and the painting's viewer. Here, too, it is through the image of a skull that desubjectification is imaged. As Lacan writes in his Eleventh Seminar: "Holbein makes visible for us here something that is simply the subject as annihilated—annihilated in the form that is, strictly speaking, the imaged embodiment of the *minus-phi* . . . of castration, which for us, centres the whole organization of the desires through the framework of the fundamental drives" (Lacan 1981, 88–89). Kristeva and Lacan come together in featuring the skull as well as in grasping its meaning as the necessity of representing the drive in order to access desire. To Lacan, "the magical floating object . . . reflects our own nothingness, in the figure of the death's head. It is a use, therefore, of the geometral dimension of vision in order to capture the subject, an obvious relation with desire which, nevertheless, remains enigmatic" (Lacan 1981, 92). Desire depends on the opening up of a void. Desire = lack.

As Lacan reminds us, "all human desire is based on castration" (Lacan 1981, 118). But what is even more striking, for our purposes here regarding *Murder in Byzantium*, is that Lacan locates the gaze in icons in particular: "Icons—the Christ in triumph in the vault at Daphnis or the admirable Byzantine mosaics—undoubtedly have the effect of holding us under their gaze." Lacan concludes his discussion of icons and the gaze with a point central to Kristeva's glorification of the icon: "a certain pact may be signed beyond every image. . . . the image remains a go-between with the divinity" (Lacan 1981, 113). Especially icons, Lacan suggests, operate at the level of the gaze, one's constitutive lack, giving the viewer a chance to experience the fascination produced by the separation that causes the break with his/her missing piece and offering an empty base on which to stand. It is insofar as our subjectivity is determined through this fracture that we are *not* "essentially indeterminate" (Lacan 1981, 118). Our not essentially indeterminate subjectivity is propped up by the gaze, and inasmuch as the icon embodies the gaze, the icon anticipates psychoanalysis.

What then, again, is the fundamental crime? The killers in *Murder in Byzantium* murder the gaze. The novel, in turn, kills *them* off, in "hell's cathedral," precisely to engage the death drive so that it can be faced through reflection. A space of Nothing is thus created, puncturing the society of the spectacle, by virtue of the killing of that spectacle, through the demise of its allegorical representatives. By extinguishing the society of the spectacle, *Murder in Byzantium* serves as an icon, which always manifests the cut. The "living being" murdered in banal ways on a daily basis is once again able to breathe as its destroyers are destroyed. The novel exposes an abyss that allows us to seek and produce new reflections on and of it—reflections that give us language to make use of that void, to draw it forth into our creative acts as well as into our most mundane experiences, to inject Eros with Thanatos. Without such a stance, we will only remain anxiously plagued by an invisible presence crying out for our engagements—mundane, creative, and erotic—for a transformation of the society of the spectacle into a society of the icon. Kristeva drops a hopeful hint about this possibility early in her novel: "Byzantium is what remains most precious, refined, and painful about Europe, that which others envy about it and which she has difficulty realizing herself and extending—unless, that is . . . who knows?" (Kristeva 2006b, 64).

Notes

1. To Kristeva, the novel genre, in general, is conducive to such revolt insofar as it is fertile ground for exploring "sensory intimacy" as well as for "meditation" (Kristeva 2002a, 5).

2. In her chapter "Fantasy and Cinema" in *Intimate Revolt*, Kristeva describes fantasy as the "intimate creation of representations" (Kristeva 2002a, 63) that "distortedly admits the subject's desire" (Kristeva 2002a, 65). Boredom in representation works against one's ability to formulate fantasy verbally or pictorially. It allows society's representation to block the creation of imagery of one's own and in turn the bringing to light of one's own desire.

3. It is noteworthy that the chief argument supporting icon veneration during the debates over icons in the eighth century in Byzantium was that "the Incarnation of the Son of God permitted a depiction of Christ as He had been seen on earth": "The holy Church of God which confesses rightly that there is one hypostasis of Christ in

two natures, has been instructed by God to represent Him in icons, in order for her to remember His redemptive dispensation. (Sixth session of the Council of 787)" (Herrin 2007, 111). Iconophiles held sophisticated positions founded on the Incarnation; St. John of Damascus and others thought that Christians could gain a "higher awareness of the divine through the veneration of icons" (Herrin 2007, 114). Kristeva understands the economy of the icon as falling under "neither *mimesis* nor *figure*," emphasizing its (Christ-like) status as "a visible *transition* between the visible and invisible" (Kristeva 2012, 51). No wonder, more than any other type of icon, the mandylions, "maintained in the popular imagination by the symbolism of the cloth and blood, manifest this transitional economy" (Kristeva 2012, 51).

4. Kristeva's concept of intimate revolt entails a turning back to one's past to question and displace it. By recollecting, interrogating, and thinking, one goes in quest of oneself. Intimate revolt involves an activation of "untenable conflict," takes place at the "limits of the representable/thinkable/tenable" (Kristeva 2002a, 7), and thus opens psychic life to infinite re-creation. The subject in revolt experiences the erasure of subject/object borders, *anamnesis*, an interrogation of nothingness, and an assault of the drive for the sake of an eventual psychic restructuring with the goal of rebirth and a renewed link with the other.

5

From the Agency of the Letter to the Agency of the Icon

Femininity and Bulgaria in Julia Kristeva's *Murder in Byzantium*

Ewa Plonowska Ziarek

For the longest time I have refused to engage with Kristeva's detective fiction. I was suspicious of her literary turn; I did not want to be disappointed by a writer whose theoretical sophistication and style I have admired because it was hard for me to imagine that her literary achievements would match her theoretical acumen. What has prompted me to approach this neglected territory in my own readings of Kristeva as well as in Kristeva scholarship[1] at large is not only the invitation to participate in this collection but also my curiosity about the title of the book I chose for interpretation: *Murder in Byzantium*. It was Byzantium, its proximity to and distance from Eastern Europe, that unspoken cultural "background" of Kristeva, that intrigued me. Perhaps I wanted to play a detective game of my own and explore the relationship between Byzantium and Bulgaria, between Western and Eastern Europe in Kristeva's work.

Enfolded within Kristeva's fictional Byzantium, Bulgaria is an object of fascination because Kristeva, this so-called French feminist, remains rather discreet on the subject of her country of origin,[2] a discretion that I understand all too well. More often than not, the specificity of Bulgaria is suppressed in Kristeva's texts or appears under a generalized notion of foreigners and strangers. For example, when asked in the interview "Why France, Why the Nation?" whether she still feels like a foreigner after thirty years of living in France, Kristeva responds: "Of course. It's a paradoxical situation, because abroad I am taken as one of the representatives of contemporary French culture, whereas in France

I am and always will be a stranger . . . it's a question of language, mentality and perhaps a certain personal marginality that writers have always claimed for themselves" (2002c, 45–46). Yet, when this sentiment is echoed in *Murder in Byzantium* by the main character's Eastern European Jewish mother, it becomes a painful accusation of French xenophobia: "You know, my daughter, no one in the world has the contempt for foreigners that we have, we the French. A cold contempt, without the least scruple or bad conscience" (2006b, 186).

Kristeva scholarship in English reproduces this erasure of Eastern Europe. When looking for a "Bulgaria" entry in the indexes of books published about Kristeva, I usually find "Judith Butler" where Bulgaria might have been listed. This ironic coincidence points nonetheless to the questions I want to explore in this essay: What is the relationship between the erased cultural differences and sexual difference? What are the possibilities of resignifying these differences within the genre of detective fiction, as driven by fixed conventions? How can the law of the genre itself, with its preference for rational epistemology and masculinity, be put on trial in order to retrace what this law has erased: the symbolic matricide, the murder of Eastern Europe and Byzantium by the West?

The Law of Genre on Trial

Although, after years of neglect, Kristeva's detective novels have been recently discussed in terms of conceptual issues of revolt, globalization, and the reunification of Europe (see, e.g., Keltner 2011; Margaroni 2009; and Rus 2010a), her revision of the gendered conventions of detective fiction is still ignored. Yet, *Murder in Byzantium*, like most feminist detective fiction, poses the dilemma of gender and literary experimentation within a genre driven by fixed conventions. One of these conventions is the epistemological character of investigation, defined by rationality divorced from the body; the second one is the return of normalization after the solving of the crime. Not surprisingly, feminist critics have questioned whether being a detective is a "suitable" job for a woman (for feminist revisions of detective fiction, see Irons 1995 and Berlund 2000). Given the often formulaic and conservative structure of detective fiction with its emphasis on the rational solving of the disorder that the crime represents, can, as Peter Messet asks, the law of this genre be put on trial? Can the role of the detective, the representative of the law, rational epistemology, and gender hierarchy, undergo a feminist transformation? (Messet 2000).

Some of the most interesting, now classic, interpretations of detective fiction, like Tzvetan Todorov's *The Poetics of Prose*, appeared in the 1970s in response to the rise of postmodern literature. These theories are contemporaneous with Kristeva's *Revolution in Poetic Language* (1984), a text which launches a critique of structuralist linguistics and proposes the redefinition of experimental language in terms of the semiotic, affective economy of the libidinal body. According to Todorov, a fellow refugee from Bulgaria, the task of detective investigation is to explain the past in rational terms. Indeed, as Kristeva puts it, detective fiction is an "optimistic genre" (2006b, 249)—" 'You can know the source of evil' promises the world of detective fiction" (2006b, 227). However, in contrast to historical narrative, the detective story is organized in correspondence with the discursive order of public opinion rather than with the referential order of reality. Represented in Kristeva's novel by a female journalist, Stephanie, this reference to public opinion shows, as Todorov suggests, that the narrative of investigation "must be consistent with another (anonymous, impersonal) discourse, not with its referent" and ultimately with "the discursive law" of the genre itself (1978, 82, 84). In its emphasis on the signifier rather than the referent, detective fiction displays, therefore, the law of the symbolic order as such, or as Lacan would say, "the agency of the letter" (1977)—a point also emphasized in his psychoanalytic interpretation of Poe's *Purloined Letter* (1988). Expanding Todorov's analysis, I would claim that there are at least four levels of law in murder mystery: the juridical law violated by the crime; the discursive law of public opinion (the initial assumptions about guilt) corrected by detective investigation; the rational law of the detection; and, finally, the law of the genre, the symbolic law of discourse itself.

As this brief overview suggests, the structuralist analysis of detective fiction purifies it from the semiotics of affect, bodily drives, and from what Kristeva calls heterogeneous historical practices. Such absence of affect and historicity is, according to William Spanos (1972), the main limitation of detective fiction. By establishing rational relationships between random events, detective fiction transforms the groundlessness of history, which generates anxiety and dread, into teleological, discursive coherence. In the context of Kristeva's psychoanalytic theory, such an anxiety corresponds to the semiotics of abjection—to the objectless state of the drive that subtends but is irreducible to the symbolic world of subjects, signs, and objects. We could say, therefore, that the rational solving of the crime restores the symbolic order by purifying it from the ambiguous, borderline state of abjection (see Kristeva 1982, 111).

Yet, what if the conventions of detective fiction cannot be so easily purified from the semiotics of affect? To question such epistemic purification of the symbolic order, critics like Peter Messet refer to Kristeva's theory of abjection though, ironically, not to her own literary revisions of the genre. Messet argues that the revulsion and fascination provoked by the dead body suspends the symbolic even after the solving of the crime. Indeed, in *Powers of Horror* Kristeva relates not only crime and the corpse to abjection, but, more importantly for our purposes, to the Greek prototype of the detective, Oedipus himself (1982,

84–87). If in classical detective fiction murder disturbs the social order, and the rational solving of the crime restores normalization, Kristeva fundamentally questions and ironizes this paradigm by exploring the knot between the juridical/the symbolic law, affect, and the contradictions of history. In *Murder in Byzantium*, it is not primarily detectives but the abject criminals who function as the purifiers of the symbolic order from the depravity of the world. This ironic co-implication between criminal acts and the symbolic purification of the law blurs the boundaries between the murderer and the detective and exposes the violence of the detection itself insofar as its inductive reasoning seeks to eliminate the enigma of being and the possibility of a new beginning.

The detective narratives in *Murder in Byzantium* are organized around three types of crime. The first murder is committed by Xiao Chang, who calls himself the purifier and has just committed his eighth murder by killing Reverend Sun, the head of the corrupt "New Pantheon" sect. By killing the corrupt fathers of Santa Varvara, Xiao Chang is acting out the incestuous fantasy of an intrauterine reunion with his twin sister, Fa Chang. The second crime, which follows in quick succession, is committed in a moment of rage by an academic historian, Sebastian Chrest-Jones, a specialist in the history of migration and an amateur historian of the Crusades and Byzantium. Sebastian murders his pregnant Chinese girlfriend, the twin sister of Xiao Chang, at the very moment when she jubilantly announces her pregnancy. This crime, which eliminates the possibility of a new beginning, is presented as an uncanny double of the highest academic honor, the honorary degree of honoris causa, which the historian receives at the University of Santa Varvara. Having learned about the murder of his sister, Xiao Chang in turn becomes a detective, tracking and eventually killing her murderer. Finally there are two murders in ancient Byzantium: Constituting the enigmatic paternal origin of the Chrest ancestry, the first murder concerns the legendary ancestor of the Chrests, Ebrard de Pagan, a member of the first Crusade who abandoned his quest in Philippopolis, Byzantium (the present-day Bulgarian city Plovdiv), and married instead a mysterious Thracian woman. Sebastian's quest for the mystery of his paternal origins, the classic "search for the lost father," is thus the reversed mirror image of Xiao's attempts to eliminate the corrupt fathers of the social order, whereas his matricidal rage is the opposite of Chang's longing for the incestuous union with his twin sister. The second murder occurs in the fantasmatic Byzantium: When Sebastian is killed by Xiao Chang, he manages to die in an imaginary Byzantium of his own making.

By displacing the purifying function of the genre from the detective to the criminal, Kristeva's novel also shifts violence from the crimes of individuals to the criminality of the social order.[3] What is criminal in the novel is the pervasive society of the spectacle, capital, and globalization, or what Kristeva calls the world of Santa Varvara. Like a Situationist artist, Xiao Chang, the son of Chinese immigrants, relentlessly exposes and "purifies" this criminality by murdering the most corrupt representatives of the new social order, enshrined as the New Pantheon. Misdiagnosed in childhood as psychotic and abused by his special education teacher, Xiao Chang is a brilliant mathematician, an anti-global activist, and a protector of wild life. An accomplished calligrapher and a poet of infinity, he is both an abject being and the purifier of criminal abjection infecting the social order of normalization. By imprinting the dead bodies with an ambiguous mark that could be the mathematical number 8 or the symbol of infinity, paradoxically, the purifier infects the mathematical purity of the symbolic order itself with abject traces of the corpse and the crime.

In a further ironic twist of the generic conventions, the police commissioner, Rilsky, identifies with the serial killer and considers the purifier to be justified by the criminality of the victims and the corruption of the law: "It is laws that make criminals" (2006b, 212). The son of Eastern-European immigrants, the commissioner knows that the purification of the investigation has an intimate relation not only to the law but also to the jouissance of the crime: The law "exist[s] with these two sides, the pure and the impure, because the law is necessarily schizo, it was Northrop's job to know this" (2006b, 32). By acknowledging the impurity of the law and the criminality of the new world order, Rilsky not only refuses to associate investigation with rationality alone, but, on the contrary, treats detective fiction as a story of life: What matters in both are detours and delays, discoveries of new possibilities and not the closure of the solution. By contrast, his illegitimate cousin, the murderer/historian Sebastian Chrest-Jones, initially believes in the rational explanation of history: "everything becomes rational for the mind of the historian" (2006b, 25). Yet, the historian's belief in rationality is accompanied by depression, the obsessive search for the paternal origin, and the violence of matricidal drive. Consumed by hatred for his own unwed mother, Sebastian murders in a state of rage/panic his pregnant Chinese lover because her pregnancy represents a new beginning: "Fa Chang believed . . . herself to be at the beginning of a new chapter in her life! To become an origin without him, beyond him, despite him" (2006b, 100). By purifying the paternal order from every trace of the maternal body, the rationality of history destroys a new beginning that such traces might enable.

As this brief overview of the novel suggests, Kristeva undermines the binaries of classic detective fiction—criminal/victim, signifier/affect, criminal/detective, crime/law, body/mind, desire/reason—as well as their gender hierarchy. Structuring the symbolic law of the genre, such binaries restore order, normalization, and temporal closure with the solving of the crime. By contrast, the proliferation of uncanny doublings in Kristeva's novel creates uncontainable, indeed, infinite strangeness (see Kristeva 1991a, 169–95), which cannot be eliminated or repressed: The murderers are victims and vice versa; the police commissioner is doubled by the female amateur detective; the law, purification, and murder are intimately intertwined. One of the most striking uncanny doublings manifests itself through the multiplication of sibling relationships, which suggests intimate kinship ties between criminals and detectives: The detective finds out that he is the cousin of the suspect; the twin brother kills in order to avenge his murdered sister; the murderous rivalry between the Byzantine princess, Anna Comnena, and her brother could have ended in fratricide if the assassination plot had succeeded. The Bogomil heresy, explored in the novel, represents this uncanny kinship of good and evil as the ontological principle of creation by the two divine brothers: Michael and Satanael. This intimate proximity between the law and crime requires different methods of detection, a departure from the classical separation between the mind and the body, letter and passion. If, as Hernández Martín suggests, the process of detective investigation is at stake implicitly in every interpretive act (1995, 44), Kristeva fundamentally transforms the stakes of such an act: Her female detective does not want to solve the mystery but to restore enigma and the possibility of a new beginning to historical existence itself.

Perhaps the most important innovation Kristeva introduces to her detective fiction is a departure from the Oedipal structure of investigation. The Oedipal function of the detective and the proto-detective role of Oedipus have been frequently remarked upon by numerous interpreters of the genre of detective fiction, including Kristeva herself.[4] In *Murder in Byzantium*, however, Kristeva diagnoses the matricidal, criminal aspect of the Oedipal investigation, which erases the affective inscription of the maternal body from the symbolic. Sebastian hates single mothers, and progenitors more generally: "Sebastian has adored strangling butterflies, Tracy Joneses, and Fa Changs. You call it murder? No, it's not murder, it's beyond everything" (2006b, 163). This matricidal Sebastian frightens Stephanie because, beyond murder, he seeks to eliminate a new beginning from time itself. The only mother that Sebastian is finally able to find solace in is the Christian iconography of the Virgin Mary: "Mary reassures the warrior, or else she walls his madness inside an impregnable, unsayable . . . innocence" (2006b, 207). At the end of the novel, Sebastian returns to this purified maternal figure, but such return is deadly. In contrast to erotic, desiring and professional women, the Virgin, who rescues believers from sex and desire, is the masculine fantasy supporting war, as was the case with the Crusades. As a kind of fictional postscript to "Stabat Mater,"[5] *Murder in Byzantium* suggests that matricidal Western culture has failed to invent "anything to replace the Virgin Mary" except technology, cloning, or "pediatric psychiatry," of which Xiao Chang is a victim (2006b, 235).

Nonetheless, single mothers multiply in *Murder in Byzantium*: from the unwed mother of Sebastian—or his dead, pregnant lover—to Stephanie, who becomes a single mother by adopting a disabled child, Jerry, whose biological mother, a translator of literature, was decapitated. In this group of characters, Stephanie is the only single mother who is not a victim, but rather the detective and an accomplished woman of letters. And it is she—the aberrant part of the Oedipal triangle—who solves the core of the mystery. Since Stephanie's last name—Delacour—associates her with the law, Kristeva's female detective mediates between the juridical order and art, letter and love, irony and affect, language and the semiotic economy of the drives, and finally between Western and Eastern Europe. Although she can "put anything and everything into words" (2006b, 182), Stephanie is also acutely aware of the limits of the symbolic. By reconstructing the trajectory of Sebastian's journey through his imaginary Byzantium on her own terms, the female detective searches for another language and a feminine intellectual genealogy in order to restore the enigma of being and the possibility of a new beginning.

Another Beginning: Femininity, Eastern Europe, Byzantium

The crucial question Kristeva poses is whether one can "mock" detective fiction "all the while using the minor genre as a platform" for personal and historical memories, which, though inseparable from invention or hallucination, can nonetheless be a source of renewal (2006b, 234). Such an innovative redeployment of detective fiction reinvents both its language and temporality. As Todorov points out, the conventional murder mystery is characterized by the retrospective temporal/epistemological relationship between two stories: The story of the crime and the story of investigation that interprets the first story and, in so doing, also explains how the book is constructed (1978, 135). In Kristeva's novel, however, the closure of the retrospective investigation is transformed into "the vast palaces" of memories (2006b, 234) in order to restore a new beginning to history itself. By rejecting the rational explanation of the past, both the criminal and the female detective embark on an endless re-creation of personal and collective histories, on the search for lost memories or the invention of the past. Yet, the stakes of their traversal of the "palace of memories" are fundamentally different. For the matricidal son, what matters is the recovery of the paternal origin, for the female detective, a possibility of recommencement eliminated by the matricidal killer.[6]

Like Hannah Arendt, Kristeva's female detective turns to St. Augustine's notion of a new beginning: The "man of memory is the man of the beginning: '*So that there would be a beginning, man was created*'" (2006b, 242).[7] By reading Sebastian's historical novel and his travel diaries, Stephanie invents a new character for the murderer: If the first one is a matricidal killer who wants to wipe out the maternal traces of origination, then the second one is an Augustinian subject who succeeds in transforming the violent history of the Crusades into an imaginative story of a love affair in medieval Bulgaria (2006b, 237–42). Unfortunately, Kristeva and her female detective fail to invent a similar second beginning for the serial killer, Xiao Chang. Even though Xiao Chang is a calligrapher of infinity and assumes the name of the Infinite, Wuxian, which means " 'never to be exhausted' " (2006b, 157), in the novel Chang's Taoist promise of infinity is never fully explored or fulfilled; on the contrary, it is destroyed by the killer's persona of the purifier. In fact one has the impression that the rebirth of Sebastian occurs at the expense of Wuxian.

The transformation of the search for paternal origin into a feminine new beginning is limited in Kristeva's novel to the suppressed Bulgarian province of Byzantium, its intellectual history, iconography, and Orthodox Eastern Christianity. One could say that Kristeva's Byzantium doubles as Kristeva's Bulgaria—the historical genealogy of the novel traces Slavic and Hellenic intertwining of cultures in the medieval Bulgarian province of Byzantium: Philippopolis, Boyana, Sozopol, Nessebar. Even the names of the Western detectives, like Popov or Rilsky, or the psychiatrists, like Dr. Moscovitch, are Eastern European, as if to prevent the nostalgic association of Bulgaria only with religion and art. One of the ironies of the novel is that the name of the police commissioner, Rilsky, evokes the most famous Eastern Orthodox monastery in Bulgaria, Rilski monastir, founded in the tenth century by the cave-dwelling hermit St. Ivan of Rila, the patron saint of Bulgaria. Always already a part of the suppressed European imaginary, Bulgaria, with its Hellenic and Slavic past, is a part of multicultural Byzantium: "[T]he Porphyrian genealogy was also a skillful mosaic of wars and weddings between nobles and the invaders, Greeks and Slavs" (2006b, 126). For example, the Bulgarian city of Plovdiv, Philippopolis, now one of many "blind spots" of Western Europe, is described in the novel as "a crossroads for Georgians, Jews, and Armenians, traveling salesmen, cosmopolitan scholars who settled over the three hills of the Thracian city among wine makers and tobacco growers" (2006b, 167). The Bulgarian genealogy has its own bloody history, for example, the cruel blinding of the defeated Bulgarian troops by the Byzantine Emperor Bulgaroctonus (the Bulgar slayer), whose terrifying story is still retold to Bulgarian children (2006b, 126).

The political intervention of such a recovery of the suppressed Byzantium, and the suppressed Bulgaria in Kristeva's own intellectual genealogy, has been stressed by Kristeva's critics like Keltner, Margaroni, and, especially, by Rus (Keltner 2011, 141–48; Margaroni 2009, 115–17; and Rus 2010a, 200–42). Unlike more distant cultures like China, Byzantium and Eastern Europe constitute the disavowed, "the stormy, the desirable, the impossible Europe," which Western Europe does not want to know (2006b, 174). As Kristeva writes:

> The ancients celebrated Apollo, the sun healer, and they called the city Apollonia before the first Christians opted for Sozopol, meaning "the saved city." Saved—Apollo, Anaximander, Aristotle? The sand itself holds the memory of its past along with the fisherman who tread over it, still speaking Greek in this country that has been Slavic for more than twelve centuries now. (2006b, 175–76)

According to Margaroni, Byzantium, Orthodox Christianity, and I would add, Eastern Europe, are Western Europe's intimate but repressed others. Only thanks to this repression, could Western Europe construct itself as Europe proper with its origins in Greece, the legacy of which has been transmitted through Latin Rome and the Western Renaissance, rather than through Byzantium (Margaroni 2009, 115–17).[8] Such an ideological genealogy suppresses Eastern Europe and constructs orientalized Byzantium, associated with decadence, intrigue, and exoticism.

By contesting the hegemony of Western Europe, Kristeva's counterhistory of the impossible cosmopolitan Europe is intertwined with the feminist project of historical recovery and philosophical/imaginative reconstruction of the past. To invent a new beginning, the female detective rewrites the archetypical male murderous narratives—kill the corrupt fathers; find the lost father, destroy the phallic mother; catch the killer—and supplants them with forgotten female intellectual genealogies. In so doing Kristeva makes a double move: On the one hand, she contests the exclusion of Byzantium and femininity from the intellectual history of Europe. The narrative of the detective investigation is interrupted in the middle of the novel by the reconstruction of female intellectual history in the form of a fifteen-volume historical chronicle, the *Alexiad*, written by the medieval Byzantine princess Anna Comnena. Trying to convince the commissioner of the *Alexiad*'s importance for the crime investigation, Stephanie mocks Rilsky, stating that he "cannot imagine a female intellectual before Simone de Beauvoir . . . Am I wrong? Oh, you go back as far as Germaine de Staël too?" (2006b, 115). On the other hand, such a recovery of female intellectual genealogy supplements the symbolic agency of the letter with the enigmatic economy of passion, represented in the novel by Orthodox iconography and the medieval Bulgarian heresy of Bogomil.

The new beginning for the female detective/writer is intertwined with the discovery of the forgotten first female historian in Europe who mocks the "barbarous pretensions" of the Latin West. Comnena's *Alexiad* offers a counterhistory written "from the other side of Europe, from that vestigial Greece of the orthodox and sovereign empire" (2006b, 116). Raised and educated first by the three royal grandmothers, Anna is from birth crowned as the next empress. She receives an excellent education in the Greek classics, history, geography, mythology, and philosophy. Yet, as Stephanie puts it, patriarchy steals her crown when her brother is born. Dispossessed, Comnena becomes a writer only at the age of fifty-five in the aftermath of the death of her father and the failure of the fratricidal plot against her brother. Ostensibly Comnena's writing is an act of mourning for her father, and perhaps a prophetic mourning for the fall of the Byzantine Empire. Yet, since female writing in medieval Byzantium can emerge only after the death of paternal figures, is such writing a lamentation or, perhaps, a female symbolic reworking of patricide? By displacing murderous violence and failed political ambitions into words, Comnena's writing, as Stephanie notes, "would earn her a type of royalty far superior to the perishable political power that the patriarchal costumes had stolen from her" (2006b, 118). Can we imagine Comnena's *Alexiad* as the focus of the fourth volume of Kristeva's trilogy, *The Female Genius*? After *Life*, *Madness*, and *Words*, could there be a volume devoted to female intellect? And perhaps to the impossible origin of an Eastern European feminism?

It is of course ironic that such a female genealogy of the world's first woman historian, intellectual, and, Stephanie adds, the first female troubadour (2006b, 119), is mediated by the novel of a criminal who falls in love with his own narcissistic fantasy of the idealized princess. Sebastian "remakes Anna's history as he pleases to fit his own story" (2006b, 117). What Kristeva shows is that any reconstruction of suppressed female intellectual genealogies is mediated, on the one hand, by the deconstruction of the hegemonic transmission of history and its underlying fantasies, and, on the other hand, by interpretative "love affairs." Like Sebastian, Stephanie falls in love with Anna—"how can you not fall in love with this woman like Sebastian, like me" (2006b, 144)—and recalls the moment in the *Alexiad* when Anna, the historian, compares herself to the beautiful Sappho. To justify these supposedly Sapphic undertones of her investigation, the narrator, in one of the several jokes at Kristeva's own expense, refers to "Kristeva's" claim that "feminine homosexuality is supposedly endogenous" (2006b, 228).

By projecting himself onto Anna's story because "[h]e too is building a reasonable intellectual surface over an abyss of passions, perhaps even of mad delusions" (2006b, 145), the matricidal historian invents a fictional Bulgarian episode of courtly love at the time when "the Bulgarian kingdom is nothing more than a Byzantine province" (2006b, 122). According to his script, Anna, with her brilliant intellect, convinces Sebastian's fantasmatic ancestor, Ebrard, to abandon his Crusade. By turning war into a sacred "jihad," the Crusaders, according to Anna, have forgotten the religious teaching that in the beginning was "love" (2006b, 130). As a counter to female intellect, Sebastian invents a chivalric romance in which Ebrard rescues Anna, floating like a fish in Lake Ohrid, from the pillaging Christian mob. With the woman's erotic body transformed into the mystical fish, the anagram of Christ (2006b, 135), Anna becomes the emblem of both erotic and divine love. After such a passionate encounter Ebrard abandons his military ambitions, settles as a farmer in Bulgaria, and, instead of military violence, chooses a humble anonymity: He becomes "a living being in the anonymous flow of living beings" (2006b, 159). The opposite of the Santa Varvara Lake where he drowns the murdered body of his pregnant lover, the fictional events at Lake Ohrid allow Sebastian the writer at least to imagine the possibility of love as an alternative to his own matricidal violence.

As a counter to this chivalric romance, Stephanie, perhaps in the most imaginative interpretative leap in the novel, looks for the displaced traces of passion in Anna's own text, in particular, in her description of Bogomil's heresy, focused on the execution—burning by fire—of the leader of the sect, Basil the Bogomil, ordered by her own father. Why this long and detailed reference to the Bogomil heresy in the middle of criminal investigation, and in Comnena's history, we might ask.[9] This enfolding of the detective narrative within an Eastern-European religious movement questions the symbolic agency of the letter and the rationality of detective fiction.[10] Anarchical, anticlerical, and anti-institutional, the Bogomil heresy, which flourished in the ninth century and the beginning of the tenth century, rejected the ecclesiastical hierarchy, the state, and church authorities and was one of the few religious movements that was open to women.[11] For a female detective the neo-Manichean Bulgarian heresy provides a secret code to female passions because it still preserves the intimate relation between Good and Evil, which are seen as the two forces of creation, the creation of the spirit/logos and matter/flesh. The kinship between these two forces is represented as the antagonistic relation between two brothers, the two sons of God, Michael, the creator of the spiritual realm, and Satanael, the creator of the material world. Because of this dualism, the Bogomils (*bogomil* means "dear to God,") in Comnena's text are a religious movement defying logos, representing "as yet unrecognized saintliness" (2006b, 144) and perhaps "another reason" (2006b, 143).

According to Stephanie, Anna appropriates the dualist language of the Bogomils, with its strife between the logos and demonic possession, in order to write the dual structure of female melancholy, which hides the daughter's passions and ambitions behind the intellectual tribute to her father. Despite her allegiance to logos, Anna acknowledges the force of the demonic erotic possession of Satanael: "the demons of Satanael persist and fascinate, they make surprise attacks on one's heart and guts and take possession . . . without leaving a memory trace" (2006b, 143). By displacing her own eroticism (and patricidal passion?) onto a long description of the demonic possession of the Bogomil monk, a possession which seems to arise from nature itself (2006b, 144), Anna, the historian of the eleventh century, is "accompanying the heretic in his loss of ordinary reason" and looking "for another reason, that which drives him to defy the historian's father and God himself" (2006b, 143). When Anna interrupts her search for a reason capable of embracing passion and defying paternal logos, she evokes not a paternal authority but the female poetic authority—the authority of Sappho's "modesty" (2006b, 144). Does this double reference to Sappho and the heretical defiance of logos enable the inscription of passion within female intellectual history only on the condition that it is negated, as Freud suggests in his essay on "Negation" (1991, 213–17)?

Through the interplay of heretical dualism and negation, the first female intellectual of the eleventh century encodes her (Sapphic?) passions within the "secret crypt" of her own text (2006b, 145), transmitting the "immense sadness," the story of lamentation beneath the paternal logos, a "pure melancholy spirit calling out, across nine centuries, for the compassion of readers" and of nature itself (2006b, 145). Nine centuries later, this female melancholic spirit resonates with the female detective's mourning the death of her own scientific Eastern-European Jewish mother, the daughter of Russian immigrants: "I have lost my blackbird, the wing that gave me wings" (2006b, 187). Thanks to maternal love, Stephanie supplements her symbolic power of words with imagination and silence "that words are unable to grasp" (2006b, 183). Such silence, however, is not a mark of erasure or repression but paradoxically expands language so that the daughter can "write what one cannot say" (2006b, 184). By creating a welcoming interval between words, maternal love "gives a child well loved or any beloved creature the chance to take wing" (2006b, 186), a gift of a new beginning, and a support for recommencement, which the matricidal Sebastian wants to eliminate from language and being itself. Thanks to such love, Stephanie discovers in the intervals of silence a possibility of dwelling in the foreign language—"my cradle, my country" (2006b, 187)—and finds support for her own journey. Intralinguistic rather than outside language, the maternal interval is a space of potentiality, generosity, and erotic love, which welcomes and listens to another: "[T]o know how to take care of another to the point of letting a stranger who will always remain foreign reach orgasm and yet not become a victim, and certainly without killing him or her" (2006b, 226). Is it ironic that Stephanie's mother, the lost bird, is in the safe keeping of the Chinese serial killer, a mathematician, antiglobal activist, and a birdwatcher?

In the last instance, the mediation between the agency of the letter and the passions/discourse among women—the female detective, her intellectual mother, and the ancient female historian—occurs in Kristeva's novel thanks to the heretical appropriation of Byzantine iconography. In the end, the epistemological agency of the letter and even the dualism of the Bogomils are replaced by the mysterious agency of the icons painted on the walls of Boyana Church, located on the outskirts of Sofia. Built in the tenth century, the church houses one of the most important collections of medieval icons painted in 1259. Kristeva claims that it is at Boyana that the history of European painting was decided with the invention of a new philosophy of the visible in response to the first crisis of iconoclasm: "But," Stephanie asks, "who today knows anything of Boyana and its artists . . . ? Who remembers today that it was in Byzantium at Boyana . . . that the future of painting was decided?" (2006b, 172). The defense of the icon against the iconoclasm of the eighth century articulates a new economy of signification: The relation between the image, model, and meaning is based neither on the imaginary resemblance nor on the arbitrary symbolic but on the affective link between the visible and the invisible, on "the economy of a love of another age, another way of seeing. Love of the Beyond in the eyes turned inward" (2006b, 173). In contrast to the arbitrary relation between the signifier, the referent, and the signified, iconography expresses the intersubjective, passionate relationship between the invisible divinity of the Father and the mystery of the visible incarnation of the Son, with the Son being the living image of the Father. As Marie-José Mondzain demonstrates, the emotional power of the icon—its love and grace—"creates a bond that is neither natural nor artificial," but rather a bond of intersubjective intimacy (2004, 30; see also Mondzain 2004, 776–78) "Forever neglected by the pretentious Occident" (2006b, 172), this new way of seeing and painting provides, therefore, an alternative to the symbolic, discursive verisimilitude of detective fiction as well as to the referentiality of history.

To be sure, in its religious orthodox version, this intimate bond between the image and its model expresses, as Kristeva puts it, "the passion between two men, God the Father and his Son" (2006b, 173). It is this paternal economy of love rather than law that offers Sebastian, the novel's illegitimate son, the possibility of symbolic and semiotic identifications, an inhabitable past, and genealogy. Abandoned by his father, the matricidal son recognizes his own personal hell in the iconic image of "Christ in hell who does not yet believe in his resurrection" (2006b, 173), whereas *The Miracle at Sea*, the Eastern-European version of Ulysses' journey in "the middle of Bulgaria" (2006b, 173–74) signifies his rebirth and offers him the possibility of dwelling in "a world that though *in* this world is yet not *of* this world" (2006b, 182). Yet, in its heterodox fictional version, the passionate relationship between the model, the image, and the beyond, the intertwining of the invisible and the visible, can be transformed into a signification of the enigma of mundane intersubjective relations. The iconic language of intimacy and the enigma of being, of familiarity and foreignness, is reappropriated by the female detective to designate passionate exchanges among women and among cultures. Does Stephanie's/Kristeva's reinterpretation of iconography in the twenty-first century create a new, expanded reason that Anna Comnena was searching for in the eleventh century? Such a reinterpretation is particularly striking in the case of the medieval icon of Dessilava, the wife of the benefactor of the Boyana Church. Like Comnena's *Alexiad*, the icon incorporates heterogeneous Greek, Slavic, and Latin cultural elements into a harmonious composition. In so doing, its language of gestures replaces divine transcendence with profane interhuman strangeness and with the enigma of maternal genealogy: "[I]f one overlooked the diadem and the tunic encrusted with precious stones . . . the moon-faced Dessilava that Sebastian was looking at was the spitting image of his grandmother. There was the same . . . Greek nose, the same round high Slavic cheekbones," and the "Latin" gesture of her hand (2006b, 170). Based on the "living" yet unknown relation between the image and the model (2006b, 172), the female language of the intimate enigma of being facilitates the recognition of strangeness as the condition of being with others. And instead of a new origin, it transports the viewer, like *The Miracle at Sea* in "the middle of Bulgaria" (2006b, 176) into an impossible journey, into a profane beginning.

This capacity to see the intimate enigma of being in the profane world supplants the epistemic search with the judgment and sensation of taste. As the female detective discovers at the end of her interpretative journey and before the recommencement of another, taste is the proto-language of maternal love: "before the code of ideas, that envelope of aromas—in a word, Love. Reread the Song of Songs!" (2006b, 240). Stephanie detects a similar discovery of taste in Anna's chronicle: "Byzantium was definitely a matter of taste, and this was in fact the key to its downfall—Anna knew this all along" (2006b, 179). Pitted against military powers, "taste is an inexorable weakness" (2006b, 179–80). To be sure, this language of "taste" is erased in the matricidal heroic narratives of the West: The men loved by their mothers become criminal heroes—Perseus, Orestes, or Oedipus—who end up killing "the maternal model and then kill themselves" (2006b, 240–41). And yet it is precisely in this "military" weakness of taste that we can still find one of the remaining sources of renewal and community. The Kantian/Arendtian judgment of taste,[12] enlarged to encompass profane sensations, for example, the profane taste of dried sardines in Bulgarian fishermen's huts, creates a new community of shared strangeness. By mediating between ideas and sensations infusing the intervals of language, taste provides a fragile alternative to murderous "male monotheist fanaticism" (2006b, 180). Like the intimate enigma of the icon, this mundane memory of the taste of dried sardines (rather than the Proustian madeleine), restores sensible time "regained outside of time" (2006b, 180). We might call this time, as Kristeva does in "Women's Time," a spatiotemporal unfolding of future perfect, an opening of a new beginning through the traversal of historical, personal, and archaic memories (1986d, 188–213).

By restoring the enigma of being and regaining time "outside of time," the novel transforms the temporal/epistemic closure of detective fiction into a new beginning, which is a narrative sign of infinity: "I'm a journeywoman," proclaims the female detective/journalist in the final page of the novel to a female psychoanalyst (2006b, 249). "There are mothers—not many, it's true—who may help you in this recommencement exercise" (2006b, 240), responds the analyst. In place of a final resolution, the novel leaves us with questions as if Kristeva were to suggest that a good question in fact constitutes a "proper" sense of an ending: " 'Everything's starting over?' . . . 'But for how long?' 'Good question' " (2006b, 249).

Notes

1. The notable exceptions are Keltner 2011; Margaroni 2009; Rus 2010a; Davis 2002; and Bové 2006.

2. The crucial exception is her essay "Bulgaria, My Suffering" (2000a).

3. Peter Messet points to the recent reinterpretation of the genre of detective fiction as the exposure of new cultural conflicts (2000, 125). Spanos also stresses the political implication of detective fiction—it corresponds to technological manipulation and the political will to power (1972, 151).

4. The complicity of the detective and the psychoanalyst has been discussed for example by Patrick Ffrench, "Open Letter to Detectives and Psychoanalysts: Analysis and Reading," in *The Art of Detective Fiction*, ed. Warren Chernaik, Martin Swales, and Robert Vilain (New York: St. Martin's Press, 2000), 234. See also Kristeva 1982, 17.

5. For Kristeva's analysis of the cultural function of the Virgin Mary and its contrast to women's desires for motherhood, see her "Stabat Mater" (1986c).

6. Even though, as Hernández Martín observes, in the more experimental detective novels, for instance those of Borges and Eco, the path from the mystery to solution is not necessarily linear but, through numerous detours and delays, can lead through a labyrinth or through a library as the textual version of a labyrinth, allowing us to eventually emerge from the maze with the solving of the mystery. See Hernández Martín 1995.

7. For Arendt's discussion of Augustine's new beginning, see Arendt (1958) 1998, 177.

8. As Margaroni shows, Kristeva evokes Byzantium and its different understanding of freedom, mysticism, and, especially, iconography, as an alternative to the Society of the Spectacle (2009, 115–17).

9. The *Alexiad* is in fact one of the important historical sources about the Bogomils.

10. According to Holquist (1971), the problem-solving rationality of detective fiction is the antithesis to the mythical structures of modernism—for instance, the Odyssey or the Oedipal drama, deployed by writers such as Joyce . . . or Freud. As Spanos suggests, the experimental narratives of postmodernism, the genealogy of which leads to Kafka's *The Trial*, are self-consciously anti-detective novels insofar as they provoke and frustrate the desire for a solution: "It is, therefore, no accident that the paradigmatic archetype of the postmodern literary imagination is the anti-detective story" (1972, 154).

11. The Bogomil heresy "arose in Bulgaria toward the middle of the 10th century from a fusion of dualistic, neo-Manichaean doctrines . . . and a local Slavonic movement aimed at reforming, in the name of an evangelical Christianity, the recently established Bulgarian Orthodox Church" ("Bogomil," 2011).

12. For Arendt's discussion of Kant's judgment of taste as the basis of political philosophy, see Arendt 1989.

PART II

6

Noir Analysis[1]

How Kristeva's Detective Novels Renew Psychoanalysis

Benigno Trigo

> "I must make progress artificially so that I can focus all the light on an obscure point." Such is Freud's confession to Lou Andréas-Salomé, and it summarizes for me the analytical experience. But also my way of writing a novel.[2]
>
> —Julia Kristeva, *Hatred and Forgiveness*

In an interview soon after the publication of Julia Kristeva's latest detective novel, *Murder in Byzantium* (2004), Pierre-Louis Fort points out that the media repeatedly asks the psychoanalyst-turned-fiction-writer: why a novel? (2005c, 623). In so doing (Fort suggests) the media secretly aims to put Kristeva back in her place, to return her to her academic self, to her self as a critic, and to the more familiar ground of her affiliations with Roland Barthes, *Tel Quel*, and psychoanalysis. In the interview, Fort appears to want to reverse this trend by asking the implicit question: why *not* a novel?

In what follows, I will begin with Fort's question "why *not* a novel?" but only as a means to ask the fiction writer two related questions: "*why* psychoanalysis and *what kind of* psychoanalysis?" More precisely, I will argue that Kristeva's detective fiction suggests the need to renew psychoanalysis at a time when one often hears of its demise on all fronts.[3] I will also argue that Kristeva questions or interrogates psychoanalysis in and through a "*noir* analysis" based on a "negative aesthetics," in other words, a Kristevan form of psychoanalysis of personal and cultural crises carried out in an artistic process that represents a loss of meaning.[4] I will suggest that what distinguishes Kristevan psychoanalysis from Freud's is, on the one hand, her inspiration in her own melancholy poetic writing, and on the other, her work in *noir* detective fiction. And I will argue that Kristeva renews psychoanalysis by aestheticizing its theory and its practice through her early readings of poetry, and then through her later practice as a fiction writer. More specifically, Kristeva renews psychoanalysis by aesthetically traveling through the dark matter of the unconscious to the "obscure point" of a signifying negativity. "*Noir* analysis" then can be summarized as a Kristevan mode of psychoanalysis inflected by, and founded on, the aesthetic practice in general, and by the negativity of the aesthetic practice (or the *work* of art) in particular.[5]

Orpheus Descendant and Triumphant

The question of Kristeva's entrance into the world of fiction writing is an old one. It can be traced back at least to two interviews conducted in 1985, five years before the publication of her first novel, *The Samurai* (1990). It is a question that emerges in the context of Kristeva's account of the modern novel as an intertextual and polyphonic genre, and from her own practice of multiple styles of writing including psychoanalytic theory and literary criticism. It is also a question framed by Kristeva's views on the poetic character of the modern novel, as well as on the difference between narrative fiction and poetic writing.

In the two 1985 interviews, Kristeva describes poetic writing as more regressive and vulnerable than novelistic writing because the former is a more direct confrontation with the loss of meaning, with the object of loss that troubles the self. She describes poetic writing as a journey that she compares to an Orphic experience: a descent into hell, and a "confrontation of the subject with the object of loss . . . that maternal form which may be conjured up as a dead mother, an absent mother" (1996b, 193). She further compares the poetic experience to the "maternal . . . solicitations of sexual pleasure and gratification and, at the same time, risk and loss of the self" (1996b, 193). Therefore, Kristeva's account of poetic writing can be understood perhaps as a direct confrontation, and a close struggle with, what amounts to an archaic mother tongue, identified with what she famously named a semiotic mode of signification, a paradoxical mode that prepares the subject for language even as it puts signification in crisis.

After elaborating on poetic writing, Kristeva goes on to describe modern narrative fiction as a mode of writing that also "incorporates the poetic experience in an intertextual manner" (1996b, 194). That is, modern fiction writing is such by virtue of its intertextuality and polyphonic nature, of its inflection with the rhythms and figures of poetic writing. She also describes the practice of this narrative as "a working out" of the self "in relation to its experience of crisis"

(1996b, 194). She describes it as a descent but also as a reemergence from the journey to the unconscious: an Orpheus triumphant, she calls it. She describes modern narrative's confrontation with the unconscious as more protected than poetry's, as keeping a certain distance, a "means of guiding us most deeply into our crises and farther away from them at the same time," she says (1996b, 194). This distance from the object of loss, from the archaic tongue of a dead mother if you will, or from the crisis and malaise troubling the self, turns modern narrative construction into "a tremendous opportunity for the sublimation of our crises and malaises" for Kristeva (1996b, 194). And in turn, sublimation turns contemporary fiction writing into "a kind of continuous lay analysis," a powerful and profound form of "guiding" and "leading" the self to and through its crises and malaises that Kristeva compares to dreams and to sacred discourse (1996b, 194–95).[6]

Kristeva's Lay Analysis

Kristeva's early description of narrative fiction, both as an opportunity for sublimation and as a continuous form of "lay analysis," underscores the extent to which fiction writing and psychoanalysis are intertwined in her thought, but her description also suggests important differences with Freudian psychoanalysis. The term "lay analysis," for example, is the title of one of Freud's later works, where he argues against subsuming psychoanalytic training under medical school training (*The Question of Lay Analysis*, 1926). For Freud, psychoanalysis must remain "lay analysis," or nonprofessional in the sense of nonmedical, in order to preserve its independence of focus and training. In his pamphlet, Freud suggests that the term "lay analysis" was shorthand for a scientific form of analysis applied in a nonmedical field (1989, 684). "Sublimation," on the other hand, is a better known psychoanalytic concept that appears throughout Freud's work, but one that the psychoanalyst left undertheorized or in a "primitive state," according to Laplanche and Pontalis (1973, 433). It essentially refers to a variable capacity of the sexual instincts to be diverted, defused, attracted, deflected to nonsexual aims in a process that Freud sometimes compares and relates to repression or identification. This capacity transforms the instincts into new and nonsexual aims that often take artistic forms, according to Freud.

In his *Recommendations to Physicians Practicing Psycho-Analysis* (1912), Freud suggests the strained nature of the relationship between sublimation and "lay analysis" when he describes sublimation as a skill (a "high talent" and an "art"), but one better kept independent of psychoanalysis. He warns that "efforts invariably to make use of the analytic treatment to bring about sublimation of instinct are, though no doubt always laudable, far from being in every case advisable" (1989, 362). Freud seems to believe that sublimation can lead some patients to illness (as, say, repression also can become an illness), so that pressing a patient toward sublimation in analysis might actually worsen his condition. To be sure, Freud is not opposed to sublimation, but in this essay he emphasizes his opposition to the use of sublimation by the analyst as part of the psychoanalytic cure. Freud's description of sublimation as an "art" better left alone by the analyst serves to set this "talent" apart from the theory, practice, and space of psychoanalysis. The latter practice is defined as "scientific" insofar as it motivates patients to engage in an analysis of their symptoms rather than incite them to sublimate their cause. Indeed, sublimation can be argued to function for Freud as a limit or a border that defines the proper space of "lay analysis." For Freud, psychoanalysis is a practice independent from both the professional field of medicine, as well as from the "arts." But Freud's warning also remains as evidence that, for him, sublimation also was at some level a tempting tool of analysis.

From this perspective, Kristeva clearly does something different from Freud, actively blurring the boundaries between sublimation and "lay analysis" (or between fiction writing and psychoanalysis), also suggesting a further difference between a Kristevan and a Freudian form of cultural analysis. In a later interview, Kristeva confirms her therapeutic use of fiction writing when discussing the cathartic uses of imaginative writing. There, she goes so far as to say that aesthetics has inspired her mode of therapy: "There is evidence of [the passage of words into the body and vice versa] in the therapeutic role of writing and of aesthetics in general, in the use of art as a therapeutic medium in psychoanalysis. It may be a limited use, but it exists and has inspired therapy to a significant degree," she writes (1991a, 220–21). Indeed, Kristeva appears to mean something slightly different from Freud by "lay analysis," something perhaps more like the *work* of art or even aesthetics. Insofar as she describes modern and poetic fiction writing as a means and an opportunity to sublimate "our" crises and malaises, Kristeva appears to underscore a similarity between analysis and art (or sublimation) that Freud sought to minimize, and she also suggests a mode of cultural analysis based on our own sublimation of our crises, that is a form of auto-analysis. From both of these perspectives, Kristeva's use of the term "lay" can be interpreted to mean a mode of analysis located outside the "scientific," "proper," and "professional" borders of Freudian psychoanalysis, and a mode based on what I will call a negative aesthetics.

A Negative Aesthetics

Drawing in part from the aesthetic pedagogy of Friedrich Schiller, Miglena Nikolchina has persuasively argued that Kristeva returns value to the aesthetic practice at the end of the twentieth century, a century when the figure of the artist has become a ruin, and when the therapeutic dimension of the work of art has all but disappeared. Indeed, she calls Kristeva's technique a "problematized rescuing of aesthetics" (64). Nikolchina means by this problematized rescue that Kristeva performs two important inversions in her theory. The first inversion is the aestheticization of the subject. According to Nikolchina, Kristeva places the work of art before the artist in her theory. In other words, unlike a more traditional psychoanalytic approach (like that of Freud in his interpretation of Leonardo da Vinci's works), Kristeva does not interpret the work of art as a symptom of the psyche of the artist so much as a necessary *work* that builds and lays the foundation for the psyche of the subject, thereby aestheticizing the self (Nikolchina, 65). The second inversion is closely related to the first. If traditional psychoanalytic commentary draws from theoretical insight in order to apply it to works of art, Nikolchina's account of Kristeva's theory as a "quest" containing "the history and the tale of the mother, of her absence . . . and of her power" suggests the opposite might be true in the case of Kristeva's psychoanalytic method and theory. In other words, that Kristevan psychoanalytic commentary first draws insight from works of art, and then applies it to theoretical production (18).

Kristeva, then, might be said to simultaneously aestheticize her theory as much as the subject of her theory. And this aestheticization is "problematic" in two distinct ways. It is problematic in that this aestheticization represents an inversion, or a "negative" mode, of the role of art, which becomes a point of departure for lay analysis rather than a limit or a border setting psychoanalysis apart from art. But this aestheticization is also problematic in that Kristeva's redemption of aesthetics is not a utopian rescue modeled after Romantic poets like Schiller. Instead, Kristeva's aestheticization is "negative" in that it describes the *work* of art as a descent into an order and an experience that is contradictory, a zero-degree, confident and yet negative, act of signification, both historical and ahistorical, both temporal and timeless.

Negative Sublimation

Given my description of Kristeva's "negative aesthetics," it might appear as somewhat surprising that she appears to revert back to Freud's distinction between psychoanalysis and fiction writing (or art) when asked by her interviewers in 1985 whether she will "write something novelistic." While she leaves the door open for a future incursion into novel writing, she also tells her interviewers that she has no current plans to write novels (1996b, 34). Kristeva adds that her theory, criticism, and psychoanalysis give her "enough balance," and that they spare her "the need for novelistic writing" (1996b, 201–02). Given Kristeva's "negative aesthetics" and her statements about the modern novel in the interviews, it is safe to assume that what she means here by "valid creative work," or by "the need for novelistic writing," is the value of narrative construction (poetically inflected) as a first working-through of the lessons of the unconscious, the death drive, and the Chora, or a first transformation (or sublimation) of what remains perhaps in a more pure negative form in the poetry of Nerval and Mallarmé, for example. Indeed, Kristeva's comments about modern narrative suggest that fiction performs a problematic form of analysis, a form of "sublimation" that is "negative" in that it returns a minimum of balance (just "enough balance") to a subject who comes to stand between the crises, malaises, and loss troubling the unconscious, and their expression in a similarly disturbed narrative language.

In other words, Kristeva answers her interviewer that psychoanalytic interpretation does for her what writing fiction does for novelists: it gives her a balance that she describes as an intermediary position in between "certain subjective elements" and the "life story of the other person" (1985, 201–02). She further describes this balance as "enough" in the sense that it is a limit, a minimum, just a hint, a tipping point if you will, that allows a "back and forth" movement between self and other, between the mother tongue and artistic expression (1996b, 201). I call this tipping point a "negative mode of sublimation" in that it does not so much divert, defuse, or deflect the disturbing instinct at its origin as it instead meets it, encounters it, and turns its instability into the defining characteristic of Kristeva's psychoanalytic interpretation. Insofar as Kristeva finds that her own theory already provides her with this precarious balance, her comments suggest that the theory she writes is, in fact, a mode of fiction.

Beyond Freudian Sublimation

In an interview from 1990, published shortly after the publication of her first novel, *The Samurai*, Kristeva tells her interviewer that writing "this type of fiction eases . . . an *awakening* of the unconscious that ventures *beyond sublimation* and revitalizes the potential of interpretation" (1996b, 251–52, my emphasis). Kristeva's narratives describe a mode of writing that uncovers (or reveals) an aspect within the self that resonates with the pain, the perversity, and the death drive of all people, and even of social collectives; a link with others that is negative in its denial of life. Nevertheless, the narratives also represent a positive wager that both self and other, analyst and analysand, writer and reader can tolerate the intensity of the transferential experiences at their core. Kristeva's narratives suggest that writing can be a transferential experience beyond Freudian sublimation, an experience that can take the writer (but also the reader) beyond a process that diverts, defuses, attracts, or deflects the sexual instincts to nonsexual aims. In other words, for Kristeva writing can be an experience that lies beyond a process that returns stability to the subject, beyond the Freudian sublimation that acts like a pressure valve when it lets off some of the steam that threatens to explode the subject. Writing for Kristeva can be an experience that goes beyond a process that turns the drives into expressions that are more acceptable to the cultural establishment. Instead, the "negative sublimation" that is Kristeva's writing is both a challenge to the self and a challenge to the cultural establishment. In other words, the "negative sublimation" of Kristeva's writing rides the instincts, experiences the disturbing and contradictory feelings produced by the drives, and wagers that such an experience will have, in fact, a revitalizing effect, not just on the writer and the reader, the analysand and the analyst, but also on the individual and the social collective.

In what could be described as a study of the aesthetic logic behind this process of "negative sublimation," Nikolchina goes back to Kristeva's early work (*Séméiotiké*, 1969, and *Revolution in Poetic Language*, 1974) and finds in it a process of reduplication, or a mirroring of inverse opposites, that Nikolchina also identifies with Kristeva's semanalysis and polylogue. It is significant that Nikolchina traces back Kristeva's reduplicating method and technique not only to the 1964 school of formalist and linguistics-based theory of Jurii Lotman (52), but also to the "work" of fiction, and more specifically to the novels of Marguerite Duras, which Kristeva studies in *Desire in Language* (36), and also in *Black Sun*. Nikolchina's account of Kristeva's method and technique suggests that reduplication is a lesson contained by the aesthetic experience that is, in turn, drawn from the maternal experience or from the lost maternal body. It is a lesson learned from exposure to a "negative" force (or energy) also contained in the female libido that is "negative" in two complementary ways. On the one hand, the lesson is "negative" in that it disavows the void (or absence) that is the maternal experience and sets the subject in a quest of union with the maternal, like a moth is drawn to light. On the other hand, the lesson is also "negative" in that it sends the same subject in the opposite direction. The subject moves away from the maternal absence and toward language or toward a symbolic presence. The subject does this through what Nikolchina describes as parables of union with the father, or "parables of exile," that are identical to the "quests for the mother" in their impossibility (45). By revealing the double impossibility of both the poetic quest and the narrative parable, this "negativity," or reduplication, reversibility or instability, at the center of the Kristevan writing method (and of her psychoanalytic technique) points to a new trajectory for the subject, a trajectory that Kristeva describes as an awakening "beyond sublimation," that "revitalizes the potential of interpretation," and which her recent commentators have insisted is both political and ethical (see Beardsworth, 132–33; Bové, 29).

Kristeva's 1994 study of Marcel Proust is a good source for insight into this awakening that she describes as a point of reversibility and instability, or as a "two sided sensoriality," and a "chiasmatic reversibility" (1996i, 247). In an example of her aestheticization of the subject, Kristeva compares the writing of Proust to Freud's metaphor for the multilayered processes of the cognitive apparatus (1996i, 231).[7] Indeed, Kristeva uses "the mystic writing pad" to illustrate or make visible what I would describe as the "negative sublimation" of Proustian writing. On the one hand, she compares Proust's style (the surface of his writing) to the surface of the writing pad. These two surfaces receive the stimulus of the "language" of sensation; they are receptive to the inner layer of the death drive; but they are also an invisible armature and a first defense against the death drive. "Its traces can be registered such that they imitate motor activity and eventually turn into judgments," writes Kristeva (1996i, 231). On the other hand, she compares Proust's characters and narrators to the celluloid screen of the writing pad, insofar as they reshape and reconstruct this stimulus into figures and voices. Kristeva's fiction can be said to occupy the same point of reversibility, or negativity, as the style of Proust. This "negative" position beyond sublimation is perhaps best represented by the similarly troubled content, form, and narrative voice of her novels, all of which take the reader in a turbulent and politicized journey through the unconscious and toward an ethics based on what Kristeva calls a "negative diagnosis."

A Negative Diagnosis

Kristeva tells Jonathan Rée in a 1992 televised interview that she doesn't think ours is the time for providential militancy or advice. It is "the time (Kristeva insists) for a negative diagnosis" (1998a). Stephanie Delacour, the anti-heroine of Kristeva's detective novels, lives in this time: an untimely point in an uncanny existence. Like us, Stephanie is "homeless" in that she is both exiled from, and overdetermined by the absence of what I called earlier our "mother tongue": the disavowals and negations of a disturbing archaic experience, the disavowals and negations that are also the source and origin of our *noir* fiction and of our similarly negative cultural production. This uncanny place of absence is Stephanie's home, but unlike us she doesn't disavow or repress its turbulence. Instead, Kristeva's ur-detective even helps to bring about an existential orphanhood for her self by analyzing perversely, by writing turbulently, by traveling through her unconscious, by interrogating herself, and by identifying with both the matricides and parricides that crowd her world. Stephanie does what is necessary to survive during a time that the characters describe as "the nontime that is beginning" and the "time of analysis" (2006b, 109). Rather than act out, Stephanie bears witness to the violence of the society she inhabits, and delays her actions (2006b, 159). Most importantly, she suspends the mastery of judgment. In this attitude, Stephanie is an anti-hero for our time.

Similarly, Kristeva's fiction writing "doesn't . . . narrate or novelize but remains perhaps more a quest, an enigma" (2006b, 237). Her novels are similar invitations to a disturbing quest, to a turbulent journey, to an inquiry and a self-interrogation about the troubled origins of the self and society. "The reader is invited yet again to put himself on a journey, to suffer the turbulence, the mutations, no longer of history but of the species," as she puts it (2005c, 636). Her novels interrogate the illusion of the stable self by putting it on a strange voyage "that unfolds identities, that goes back in time and doubles back through different spaces" (2006b, 237). Indeed, as my brief introductory synopsis of her novels suggests, Kristeva's *romans noirs* engage with, and speculate about, the causes of current political events, the reasons for present and past history. They respond to, and repeat, an invitation that comes from a dark point of origin, an invitation that for Kristeva is incarnate in our memory of our missing parents who remind us to hold ourselves up while refusing to rid ourselves of our so-called corruption (2006b, 237). And their ironic tone and experimental style insist on presenting obstacles to the reader who wants to find in them solutions for the future.

In other words, like Stephanie, Kristeva performs a "negative diagnosis" in her fiction insofar as her detective novels do not offer solutions to the crimes perpetrated. Instead, they are examples of a disturbed and disturbing mode of writing and analysis (what I call a negative mode of sublimation), that only goes so far as to call attention to an obscure point of origin: a negative of diagnosis insofar as it is the opposite of determining the nature and cause of a disease or the analysis of the nature of something. This "negative diagnosis" nevertheless sets the conditions of possibility for a rebirth or for a renewal of psychoanalysis, which Kristeva has also called for elsewhere in her writings.

Like critics of psychoanalysis since Deleuze and Guattari's *Anti-Oedipus* (1972), Kristeva has taken issue with a type of normative psychoanalysis that interprets Freud's description of the Oedipus complex as an imposition of norms and laws, and she has challenged a society that delegates to the so-called sciences of psy the task of working out and solving our conflicts and crises (2002c, 22–23). Following what she calls French women psychoanalysts, Kristeva has called for a revitalization (rather than a categorical rejection) of the Oedipus complex and for the redefinition of Oedipus as a practice of interrogation where desire and death are continuously questioned (2002c, 74). She has also called for a more nuanced analysis of madness, psychosis, and perversion—for an analysis that does not idealize these states and maintains them in relation to what she calls a flexible prohibition (2002c, 23). She has called for a mode of psychoanalysis that listens to the new maladies of the patient's soul, rather than to the masters, or to their schools (be they Freudian or Lacanian 2002c, 78), as well as for a mode of psychoanalysis that limits itself to demanding self-interrogation and creativity from its patients (2002c, 115–16). Finally, she has called for a mode of psychoanalysis that is sensitive to changes in the social environment, while simultaneously vigorously refraining from working out or solving the problems of society (2002c, 57–58). I would call this a Kristevan (or *noir*) mode of psychoanalysis.

And yet, the "negative diagnosis" of Kristeva's fiction even goes beyond her *noir* psychoanalysis. Kristeva's fiction reveals what perhaps amounts to a blind spot in her psychoanalytic theory and what might be the source of renewal, if we follow her psychoanalytic theory. Parricide repeats and returns to Kristeva's fiction, despite her theoretical insistence on the central importance of a symbolic matricide that is beyond representation, despite her nuanced attempt to bring meaning and signification back to a pre-Oedipal, or trans-Oedipal mother tongue of bodily sensation through the disturbed style and disturbing, artificial language of her novels.[8] What could be the meaning of this returning parricide, of this obsession with the murder of the father, that reads like the wish fulfillment of a dream, if it isn't the unsaid, the blind spot, the obscure point that comes back in her fiction to trouble and renew Kristeva's psychoanalytic theory? Indeed, parricide might be the pretext and the point of origin that gives way to her *noir* (or negative) analysis, and perhaps it is Kristeva's mode of professional *père*-version, her seduction by the sacred, or by what she elsewhere calls the "dark eros" of *homo religiosis* (2006). In other words, the parricide in her fiction is a sign of Kristeva's openness to a point of negativity that she calls both the "dark eros" and the sacred in her theory. By allowing parricide to return in her fiction, and by representing it again and again, Kristeva dramatizes her openness to repeat, but also to work through, that point of negativity.

Paradoxically, then, the blind spot in Kristeva's fiction also could be interpreted to be the model for a Kristevan *noir* psychoanalysis. In other words, her parricidal novels contain the point of an interrogation, the point of what I am calling here a negativity, which is distinctly different from the point of certitude and truth that is often the beginning and end of our contemporary cultural analyses, with their dead certainties, and their so-called culture wars. Her novels contain a process that is different from the reduction that simplifies our complex life experience into fashionable but misleading (and ultimately self-defeating) truths or academic trends. The motility of this process is the opposite of all-too-real, bite-sized, jaw-busting, "affirmative" nuggets such as "French theory," "multiculturalism," "feminism," and "globalization." The reversibility and turbulence of her *noir* detective fiction is analogous to the transference and countertransference in *noir* psychoanalysis. Kristeva calls this point the reflexive moment of "possession" or the moment of "grace." "The capture of this 'without self' in a formula and in a rhythm, is akin in its effects to the moment of grace of analytic interpretation, when I am in osmosis with the unconscious discourse of the patient, detached from my self and from my reasoning self, possessing him at the moment he possesses me," she writes (2005c, 642). From this point of negativity that Kristeva also calls a moment of grace, psychoanalysis resists the requests of the analysand for a positive response, or for a response that takes her in a specific direction. Only the "insolent openness" of a "negative diagnosis" can give a measure of serenity to the analysand. Kristeva writes, "she is satisfied with her repeated free associations, with searching again for her lost time and desire, only in this way does she appease them" (2005c, 654). But from this moment of grace, "the professional perversion of the analyst" (1996i, 247) is also revealed. And in the practice of writing *noir* detective fiction, the analyst can listen to the silence of our "mother tongue." She can perform an act of "negative sublimation," of liberation of the death drive, and of confrontation with the resentment it generates (2006). She can journey through the unconscious, and she can translate its language. The Kristevan psychoanalyst writes *romans noirs* in the hope of turning her darkest illusions into the "abracadabra" questions of *noir* or negative psychoanalysis (2004a, 411).

In the end, Kristeva's *noir* fiction and psychoanalysis return us to our original questions. *Why* a novel? I have suggested here that Kristeva writes novels in the hope of renewing her psychoanalytic practice, and that she hopes to do this by putting her death drive in the service of the *work* of art. The work of art, or the work of detective fiction in Kristeva's case, performs a negative sublimation that prevents acting out and instead sets the conditions of possibility for Kristeva's engagement with her analysand in the transference/countertransference of analysis. *Why* psychoanalysis? If writing, or the *work* of detective fiction, prepares the ground for the psychoanalytic session, then the *work* of psychoanalysis (its negative diagnosis, its speculative, open-ended interpretation, and its disturbing process of transference/countertransference) extends this safe ground and sets the conditions of possibility for the repetition of an endless cycle of writing and analysis. And, finally, *What* kind of psychoanalysis? The Kristevan kind, the kind that accompanies the *work* of art, the kind that similarly forgives the negativity of the death drive and continuously allows us to rewrite, to represent again, our darkest fantasies and illusions. In the words of Freud, the work of psychoanalysis must be an art that focuses all the light on an obscure point.

Notes

1. By *noir* I mean to suggest a form of analysis that focuses on the source of what I have elsewhere described as a noir anxiety visually represented by the genre of film noir: a primordial ambiguity and difference (that I call negativity in this essay) that lies at the origins of both individual and social identity (Oliver and Trigo, xxxi–xxxv).

2. All translations are my own, unless otherwise stated.

3. Brooksbank (6) and Kristeva (1992a, 173) report the debated demise of psychoanalysis, while Margaroni (2008, 34–36) eloquently and succinctly summarizes the contemporary arguments against psychoanalysis by feminist, postmodern, and postcolonial theory. Kristeva suggests that the cause of the loss of interest in the psyche by our contemporary culture is to be found partly in the self-destructive tendencies of dogmatic psychoanalysts and sectarian analytical societies, but also in the "inflated growth" of the media and the neurosciences in our sometimes secular sometimes fundamentalist Western culture (1996b, 167, 168, 173). Kristeva also challenges a normative vision of psychoanalysis (or "a normative therapy") that aims to "cure" the patient of his so-called abnormalities or to make him "successful" at work by imposing norms and laws instead of questioning desire and death, and she refers to it as "a sort of decline of psychoanalysis" (2002c, 103, 120–21).

4. What I am calling here Kristeva's negative aesthetics also points to the negative dialectics that Adorno theorized, as it does to his critique of an "affirmative" mode of psychoanalysis. Adorno writes that psychoanalytic monographs that suggest that "art should deal affirmatively with the negativity of experience" fall short of the productive opacity of the aesthetic experience (8). For Adorno art is a mode of identification with the negativity of the social situation, namely the disasters and catastrophes brought about by the Second World War (21). I am grateful to Ewa Ziarek for pointing out the resonance between Kristeva's negative aesthetics and Adorno's aesthetic theory and negative dialectics.

5. By emphasizing the *work* of art I mean to suggest a parallel between the processes of condensation and displacement that Freud identified in the dream *work*, a process of working through the unconscious drives, and a similar *work* or process that can be found in art and that is theorized by aesthetic theory.

6. Nikolchina has persuasively described this double motion as "a parabolic movement" of a subject who is always in-process in that it is in-between the effort to both approximate and escape from the lost maternal territory, according to Kristeva (74).

7. The reader will recall that Freud divides the writing pad into two layers: the surface that receives the stimulus and the piece of celluloid that covers this surface and acts like a screen. He describes the psychic apparatus as made of two analogous layers: the unconscious and the perceptual-conscious system (1981, 22–23).

8. Even in a novel like *Possessions*, focused on the death of a mother, the victim dies by decapitation, and Kristeva's detective (while skeptical of the possibility) cannot help but wonder if her obsession with such images confirms that women "can feel passion only for a guilty phallus," where the word "guilty" in French (*coupable*) is highlighted to call attention to the double sense of a phallus that is also open to the cut, to decollation, and to castration (1996h, 20).

7

Fiction, Analysis, Possession, and Violence in Kristeva's Mirror of Writing

John Lechte

"So for whom does one write? Like everyone else, for one's parents, for or against them."

—Julia Kristeva, *Murder in Byzantium*

Introduction

With what are we dealing when we turn to examine Julia Kristeva's fiction? This is the question to be addressed in what follows. As we shall see, it is a question that opens up various lines of inquiry and association, particularly as concerns the nature of fiction in general, the nature of violence, and the crossover between fiction, violence, analysis, and psychoanalysis.

The point, as I will attempt to show, is that the assumption that we can clearly distinguish Kristeva's fictional texts from her nonfictional scholarship is not as straightforward as it might at first appear.

Fiction

Fiction is produced, as they say, by "the imagination." But this, as we know, is only half the story—firstly, because fiction—however much it is immersed in phantasy—can contain a truth of the unconscious. Thus, Lacan, in his doctoral study of "Aimée," refers to Aimée's efforts at writing fiction, which would reveal the patient's "mental state at the time of their composition" (Lacan 1975, 177).

The obvious here is that a certain censorship is foiled because the psyche kids itself that what it allows under the guise of fiction is not really true (when of course, it is).

Historically, modern fiction emerges as a genre at the crossroads between the true and the false. Montesquieu, as (fictional) editor, in the introduction to his *Lettres persanes* (1973 [1721]) writes: "I have selected these first letters in order to test public taste: I have a great many more in my portfolio that I could subsequently follow up with." Where and when were these letters written? "The Persians who write here were boarding with me; we lived together. As they regarded me as someone from another world they hid nothing from me. In fact, people transplanted from so far away could no longer keep any secrets. They showed me the majority of their letters and I copied them" (1973, 47–48). And the editor continues: "I am merely the translator: all my efforts have been geared to have the work conform to our customs" (48). The point of the fiction—in large part—is that Montesquieu is not the author.

To remain in the eighteenth-century context (crucial in the evolution of the novel), we find in the first preface to Rousseau's *Julie, ou La Nouvelle Héloïse* (1964 [1762]) the following words: "Although I only have the title of Editor, I cannot hide the fact that I have myself worked on this book. Have I done everything and is the entire correspondence a fiction? People of society, what does it matter? It is certainly a fiction for you" (1964, 5). Are the letters, then, fiction or nonfiction?—the "Second Preface" asks. Before answering this question, the fictional Rousseau repeats in the dialogue of the "Second Preface" that he is only the editor (26). Not satisfied with Rousseau's answer the interlocutor points out that Rousseau has his name as author on the book—that the book is *by* Jean-Jacques Rousseau. Still, "Rousseau" is evasive as to whether he is truly the author. The interlocutor continues by pointing out that if the work is fiction, Rousseau has written a bad book. But if the letter writers had really existed it is a totally captivating work (29).

According to Rousseau's logic, whether or not the letters are fictional depends on the circumstances. For those who are, or have been, in love, the letters are not fiction: they are a true expression of love. For those in high society and those who do not know true love, the letters are fiction. Thus it is not just a matter of the text but also one of the identity context of the reader.

For eighteenth-century writers, the question of fiction was always at the forefront of reading. It was always a matter of deciding whether a text was fiction or nonfiction, especially given that, by today's standards, the format of the text (collection of letters, historical document, etc.) was predominantly nonfictional. This is say that the substance of the text had to be evaluated and analyzed in order that its truth or falsity could be established. Fiction, therefore, was contingent upon the specific conditions of the text—which included, as we have seen with Rousseau, the conditions of reading. It is also worth noting for future reference that truth or falsity here pertains to the object (the world) and not to the subject-psyche, as will become the case with a more Romantic inflexion.

In modernity, by contrast to the Enlightenment approach, a prior, analytical, distinction is made between fiction and nonfiction. This implies that some effort is required if the classification in question is to be ignored. This further implies that writers can say the truth knowing that, due to the classification, many will see this truth as fiction, much like the purloined letter, which is "invisible" to the police because it is exposed for all to see in the letter rack. For the police mind, a stolen object can only be hidden by being concealed in a particular way: out of the sight of probing eyes. It cannot be hidden by being exposed to view. But of course, as with the purloined letter, the expectations of a text's recipient can always be thwarted in the game of specular oscillation, illustrated not only by the child's game of even and odd, but also by the Dupin's claim to superiority. In other words, a text such as Poe's "The Purloined Letter" teaches us that the prior classification of texts into fiction and nonfiction is misleading; for one can always reveal the truth in the guise of fiction and one can also conceal the truth in the guise of nonfiction. As Lacan indicates, Freud showed his awareness of the issue with the joke about the two Jews, one of whom asks the other the following question: "Why do you tell me you are going to Cracow so that I'll think you're going to Lemberg, when you really are going to Cracow?" Thus, the eighteenth century's approach to texts might have been right: it is always a matter of examining each text on its merits in order to determine its status.

The issue of fiction emerges also with the theme—popular in the 1970s—of the death of the author. In terms of author-intention theory, the text is a mirror of the writer's intentions, which are linked to biography. Here, it is evident that the text can never be a place for hiding. For, the theory says, the author must be there somewhere. The author is the secret of the text. In Umberto Eco's terms, we have the potential for a paranoid reading: "The paranoiac is not the person who notices that 'while' and 'crocodile' curiously appear in the same context: the paranoiac is the person who begins to wonder about the mysterious motives that induced me to bring these two particular words together. The paranoiac sees beneath my example a secret, to which I allude" (Eco 1992, 48). The paranoiac, above all, cannot treat the text as "innocent" but sees malevolence potentially at every turn, so that censorship becomes the paranoiac's default position. Society, after all, needs to be protected. If this is the social face of paranoia, what of its psychoanalytical form?

The Paranoid Critical Method—or: Fiction as Delirium

When, in 1932, Lacan (1975) presented his thesis on paranoia and its relation to the personality through a case study of Aimée, he had already been touched by

Salvador Dalí's "paranoid critical method." According to the painter, the method at issue was based on the capacity for things to reveal multiple significations—almost to the point of madness. Instead remaining in a state of mystery, the paranoid-critical method made the multiple significations of images only too visible. Things—objects—and also words thus become the giant pun to which Dalí's paintings bear testimony. In Dalí's terms, the paranoid-critical method revealed the being of the image as at least double: "It is by a clearly paranoid process that it was possible to obtain a double image: that is, the representation of an object without the least figurative or anatomical modification."[1] Although hallucination is no doubt involved, as Roudinesco says, paranoia, for Dalí, pluralizes interpretive possibilities, Dalí's wager being that the plural dimension is "in" reality; it is not just a delirious relation to reality—hence the emphasis on a scrupulous realism and Dalí's rejection of abstract painting. True, such a paranoid relation can only be assumed with difficulty by an individual subject in a nondelirious state; for to pluralize meaning is to challenge univocal identity and the imaginary disposition upon which this identity relies. Indeed, the pluralization of meaning can doubtless disturb identities as much as the complete erasure of meaning.

At stake, though, is less the plurivocity of meaning as grasped by the critic, and more the fact that a paranoid disposition—reinforced by a certain delirium—can reveal things hitherto invisible. Dalí's point, supposedly confirmed by Lacan's thesis, is that the "normal" state of the personality is, to a certain extent, a paranoid state. Meaning surfaces in all kinds of ways. A certain delirium binds the subject to its meaning. When things go awry we are thus dealing with an excess, and not a paucity, of meaning, as may occur in forms of psychosis.

Fiction and Interpretation

For her part, Julia Kristeva writes: "faced with the fundamental choice 'to be or not to be,' the exact statement of my position would be this: to propose or not to propose theoretical fictions in order to expand the limits of the signifiable and push back the frontiers of ghosts, visions, experiences of possessions. . . . An endless enterprise, in fact . . ." (Kristeva 1996e, 116). To propose "fictions" means to propose interpretations that have effects, not because of their irrefutable truth value, but because they work *as though* their truth value were irrefutable for both analysand and analyst alike. These are fictions, too, because they are, like the symptom, purely contingent, uniquely pertinent to a given situation. Put another way: the Imaginary is at work here to the extent that a conviction of truth underlies the contingent nature of the fiction—a conviction of truth that works as an image (which is continuous with the real) and not as simulacrum (which is discontinuous with the real).

Importantly, Kristeva argues (making a point that will resurface in our later analysis of Kristevan fiction), failure to maintain the border between fiction and nonfiction is the mark of the borderline patient whose discourse frequently flows between fiction and nonfiction without this being signaled. This leads into another sense of "possession." In Dostoyevsky's *Devils*, Kristeva tells us, the characters are "possessed" to the extent that "they have lost any reference to absolute and divine truth" (1996e, 114). Then, our author reminds us that Dostoyevsky borrowed a famous passage from St. Luke, where "Christ chased the devils from the possessed" (114). "Possession," then arrives in a discourse without any unifying or organizing principle—the signifier, One, in Lacanian theory. The possessed often have no name because they make a claim to all names. Thus:

> The possessed person of the Gospels very much recalls borderline cases: he speaks disjointedly, is unaware of contraries (he lives in tombs), hesitates regarding inside and outside, his and the other's, the forbidden and the permitted (therefore, he does not wear clothes), and so on. Christ frees him by asking him: "What is your name?" The unfortunate man then admits that his "name is Legion," meaning: "My name is opposed to the Name." (114)

As we now know in light of Bakhtin, Dostoyevsky finally produced a "polyphonic" fictional text, one that, unlike Tolstoy's, did not have not a single center, but a plurality of centers of enunciation. To find truth in fiction may be a way of bringing to a halt the proliferation of these centers; but it also risks a fall into possession of a different kind: one that sees all fiction as harboring a secret and all true discourse as being fictional in an unceasing fluidity of borders between fiction and nonfiction.

Kristeva's Fiction

Kristeva's novel, *Possessions* (1998c), is not obviously of the possessed, but, on the contrary, of the "name." Not of fluidity and borderline discourse but, precisely, of the "logical landscape of Paris" (1998c, 211). In fact, although the narrative begins with the decapitation of Gloria Harrison in Santa Varvara, the text is far from bodily and is instead excessively cerebral—in the French style. Reflection upon reflection (including, of course, a comparison between France and elsewhere in favor of France) implies that the narrator knows the inner workings of all that has been and is unfolding—or, at least she is aware, on the rare occasions when this is appropriate, of when she is in a certain state of ignorance.

If this novel itself could speak it would say that its author is the last one to be possessed, the last one to write in delirium, the last one to adopt a surrealist persona. And, finally, the novel would say, the author is the last one to write a polyphonic novel à la Dostoyevsky. In Roland Barthes's terminology, Kristeva's fiction is very much a fiction of pleasure and not one of bliss—of *jouissance*.

On this basis, we need to consider the genre so important for Kristeva's fiction: the detective novel. Here, we note that Edgar Allan Poe is said to be its earliest practitioner publishing, in 1845, "The Purloined Letter," "The Murders in the Rue Morgue," together with other works. For his part, Sherlock Holmes is thought to have been born circa 1858, which would make him two years younger than Freud. Both Holmes and Freud share a passion for analysis. And thus, for Juliana de Nooy (2003), there is an overlap between Kristeva's fiction and psychoanalytic theory:

> That a psychoanalyst should write a detective novel should hardly surprise us. Historically, the two practices flourished at around the same time. Poe's stories foreshadowed psychoanalytical developments and Conan Doyle and Freud were strict contemporaries. Both psychoanalysis and detective fiction promote an interpretative practice that is attentive to clues, to the uncanny, and to the pathological. Both seek truth through the rehearsal of past events. And both are concerned with cases. The case studies are the point of overlap between Kristeva's fiction and theory . . . (2003, 114)

But what is being said here? Perhaps de Nooy is jumping the gun. For, if we are to believe a passage in Kristeva's novel, *Murder in Byzantium* (2006b), Byzantium gives us the first detective story: Byzantium, she writes, "is a detective story written long before Agatha Christie, Patricia Cornwell, and other Mary Higgins Clarks came on the scene! Byzantium is a maze of legends and half-knowledge, a dead end with no way out," "a fake Occident hung out to dry" (2006b, 84). If Byzantium is the true detective story, Bulgaria is part of the former Byzantium Empire. Byzantium gives it a characteristically Christian Orthodox stamp, where the Holy Spirit proceeds from the Father (*Filioque*) but not from the son (*per Filium*) as in Catholicism. Or rather, this is the question:

> Does the Holy Spirit proceed from the Father and the Son or from the Father by way of the Son? This was the question [the novel tells us,] a crucial one in the history of the world, that now stymied a contemporary citizen of Santa Varvara but led inevitably to divorce. (Kristeva 2006b, 91)

The very division between East and West is in good part located here.

Inspired by the work of Marie-José Mondzain on iconoclasm (seventh to eighth century of our era) (see Mondzain 1996), Kristeva refers to the origin of "icon" in the notion of "economy": the distribution of the Holy Spirit in the Trinity. The detective story, as a quintessential exploration in analysis, suddenly takes a profoundly ontological turn. From the play of conventions of a popular genre, the foundation of the division into East and West is recalled. Thus, still in the novel we read:

> The image was not sign but sense. Sebastian knew the arguments of the ancients by heart: not *pros ti* but *skhésis*. Bizarre how this *skhésis* first designated intimacy for the Byzantine fathers, a tone of affect, and the love and grace of the incarnation. For the profane, the intimacy in question is that of man and woman, what is called sexual commerce, but you understand that in this kind of incarnation, the one Sebastian observes on the walls of Byzantium, the term designates the passion between two men, God the father and his Son. However, the Byzantine side of all this doesn't end here because the same Father-Son Incarnation that the spectator is asked to contemplate in the Christ image—referred to as its *economy*, the word having, you know, the same root as the word *icon*—the same economy, or if you like the same icon, will be supposed to be active in any profane image no matter what the model. (173. Kristeva's emphasis)

Invoked here, almost word for word, is Mondzain's thesis. But it is also Kristeva's thesis to the extent that she is, in good part, a Byzantine figure. Christ as economy and icon, then, gives direct access to God. The Christ-image is thus an absolute transparency. This is indeed the argument of the iconodules in the iconoclastic controversy. To turn the image of Christ into an idol is at the same time to turn it into a thing and thereby to deny its status as an image. An earlier passage clarifies what is at stake: "The image that Sebastian saw before him was the incarnation itself because for the people of Boyana to be the image of someone or something meant nothing less than being in a living relationship with that person or thing" (2006b, 172).

As if driven by a fear of becoming too conventionally fictional, Kristeva often allows academic discourse to take over, with the provision of materials such as a map of the first crusade (2006b, 93) and the Byzantine Empire (125), reproductions of Byzantine paintings (171, 174–75), and photographs of Byzantine churches (178–79). Kristeva's own scholarly work is echoed here. For she previously referred to Mondzain and the distinction between *pros ti*[2] and *skhésis* in *Visions capitales* (1998d, 60–61). If *skhésis* is the indissoluble bond between the image and what it represents—or, better: if the true image is constituted through such a bond—it is never possible to worship an image in itself. For an image in itself does not exist. This is the real message of the iconodules as presented by Mondzain. In a different way—as I have tried to explain elsewhere[3]—it is also Sartre's message against those who treat the image as a thing and so commit the error of the "illusion of immanence"—the illusion that the image of Christ is a reality quite separate from Christ himself. In other words, on this mistaken understanding, immanent in the image are two elements even if they are not initially perceived as such: one element is the image as such and the other is what the image represents. Even if the simulacrum has shed the element of representation, it still echoes the illusion of immanence by implying that the only *thing* that exists is the image.

Evoked here, then, is the society of the spectacle as the society of the simulacrum. However, before rushing in to claim that sections of the novel itself are simulacra of academic discourse, we should recall that a simulacrum refers only to itself; it has no referent, whereas, clearly, *Murder in Byzantium* presents the reader with actual documents and authentic scholarly discourse on the icon. Conventionally, the text is a novel (it bears this designation); but substantively, it is, in good part, an actual scholarly text. In other words, it is truth in the guise of fiction recalling Lacan's quip that the real perfection of deception is that, against every expectation, the illusionist *actually* shows the audience how the trick is done, just as the purloined letter is all the more securely hidden from a police officer's gaze if it is available for all to see. To a large extent, therefore, Kristeva's fiction is a purloined letter: scholarship for all to see, if only one is prepared to accept what one sees.

Analysis

In light of the discussion of the icon in Kristeva's novel, it is pertinent to ask whether an image can be analyzed. Those who argue that it can be inevitably treat the image as being fundamentally opaque rather than as a direct passage to the thing itself. They forget that an opaque image is not an image but a thing. Kristeva herself oscillates between the kind of transparency evoked by the notion of transubstantiation and the image as object in the society of the spectacle. The Byzantine period, too, pivots around this oscillation between the opacity and transparency of the image. The issue is important to the extent that Byzantium represents an important point in Kristeva's own analysis. As a Bulgarian, she identifies with this oscillation—the oscillation between God the Father as central and the model, and Christ the Son as the transparent/opaque image.

To understand Freud and psychoanalysis in this vein—to come to grips with analysis in the most profound sense—entails a certain sensitivity to aspects of theology, including the theology of Judaism. Orthodoxy, though, or Byzantium, is the break with Jewish culture, even if it is also centered on the Father. In some sense, the Father and analysis go together: Father in Judaism—Father in Byzantium, the era of the first detective story! The Father and not the Son (icon: intermediary) is the driver of analysis. Just why the Father is a key principle for Kristeva is best shown in her study of melancholia—a condition in desperate need of analysis. A gap between father and son that would allow the emergence of the symbolic only occurs with difficulty, with suffering—with, in the extreme case, melancholia. Forgiveness becomes the counterpart of suffering and the only vehicle for analysis:

> *Forgiveness:* giving in addition, banking on what is there in order to revive, to give the depressed patient (the stranger withdrawn into his wound) a new start, and give him the possibility of a new encounter. The solemnity of that forgiveness is best displayed in the conception Dostoyevsky elaborates in connection with the meaning of melancholia: between suffering and acting out, aesthetic activity constitutes forgiveness. This is where one notices the imprint of Dostoyevsky's orthodox Christianity, which thoroughly imbues his work. (Kristeva 1989, 189–90, Kristeva's emphasis)

Analysis gains access to forgiveness (and to the Father) when it is manifest in aesthetic productions: "*Forgiveness is aesthetic*" (1989, 206, Kristeva's emphasis). "Forgiveness at the outset constitutes a will, postulate, or scheme: *meaning exists*" (206, Kristeva's emphasis). Finally, forgiveness and the loving Father of "individual prehistory" are inextricably linked. Indeed, forgiveness enables identification with "a loving father, an imaginary father" (207).

Analysis and Detective Fiction

As we saw through the remarks of Juliana de Nooy, detective fiction and psychoanalysis have a similar structure. Like the detective in search for the clues that will enable a solution to the murder, the psychoanalyst searches for clues to the original trauma. In any case, analysis in both cases means that the detective/analyst always arrives after the event: just as the detective cannot prevent murder, so the analyst cannot prevent trauma, the task being to help the analysand deal with the trauma, to reconfigure it in such a way that it can be integrated into the secondary processes that constitute the symbolic order.

Analysis, therefore, is always retrospective: the significant time is always time past and not time future. This time is also equivalent to a specific régime of signs. Thus, in the opening to the detective novel by Umberto Eco, *The Name of the Rose* (1994), William helps to establish the whereabouts of a missing horse, Brunellus. It is winter with snow on the ground. William thus deduces (engages in analysis) the gait and appearance of the horse from the trail it has left—a procedure quite foreign to the monks of the early fourteenth century. The monks are amazed—including his protégé, Adso—at the demonstration by William of Baskerville of his skills of analysis and thus deduction (Eco 1994, 21–26). These are the skills, of course, of every good detective.

If we accept Foucault's version of the nineteenth-century episteme, it is clear that while the world is no longer a system of signs as it was in the Renaissance, language now emerges in its sovereign autonomy. Freud, the contemporary of Saussure and Mallarmé, brings language to the center of analysis. Analysis goes with language and signs as creative synthesis.

Analysis can be compared with synthesis—with a particular meaning of synthesis as a form of emergence. Synthesis in this sense is the event as it happens; it is in the present as oriented toward the future. If analysis is tied to the way the detective story unfolds, synthesis is this unfolding itself.

Kristeva herself is not, in *Murder in Byzantium* (and probably not in all her novels), simply engaging in analysis in relation to a murder. In this sense she is neither William of Baskerville, nor Dupin, nor even Freud. Indeed, numerous stages of the narrative offer the reader material for analysis, so that he or she is in the position of analyst.

Instead, Kristeva's fictional fiction which we introduced a moment ago, invites the reader to follow a circuitous route of the narrator's musings—musings identical to those found in Kristeva's academic work—on a range of topics from the society of the spectacle and French and American culture to the history of art and theology. The genre of analysis—the detective novel—thus provides the opportunity to present material of a synthesis. Such material can include references to Kristeva's own nonfictional persona,[4] material evocative of Kristeva's biography. But, of course, for those not *au fait* with the *oeuvre*, Kristeva's novels are no doubt pure fiction—just as Rousseau wagered that for *les gens du monde*, *Julie, ou La nouvelle Héloïse* would be pure fiction.

Violence

Have we now arrived at a point where we can conclude that in a certain important sense violence never really happens in this fiction, peppered as it is with scholarly and literary references to Kristeva's own scholarship and the scholarship of others? That violence is reported—coldly—as it is in the media there can be no doubt. But there is certainly no violence *of* the text; it is not semiotic in this sense. It does not do violence to language, as Mallarmé was accused of doing. Rather, it sticks to convention.

What can violence be in a text in any case? Will it not always be a matter of working at the level which Kristeva in her textual theory has called the *pheno*-text (transparent and denotative), as opposed to the semiotically driven *geno*-text (based in affect)?

No doubt a certain violence is manifest in every event. Clichés (predictability) shield us from the violence of an event. As a symbolic entity, language itself shields us from violence—from trauma. With regard to Kristeva's fiction, there are two levels of event: the first is what I will call the clichéd, pseudo-events of Kristeva's detective novels; the second is the event of these novels themselves: the level of their *énonciation* (Benveniste).The event of these novels exudes a certain predictability: the violence is entirely displaced.

Finitude/Murder

To be born is to be mortal. This principle of finitude governs Kristeva's approach to a range of things, from analysis itself, through sexuality to the practice of art as a gesture toward the infinite (read: immortality). In this context, it is significant that the murderer in *Murder in Byzantium* is represented by the number eight: the number evoking infinity as well as by the Chinese evocation, in the figure of *wuxian*, of the sign for the infinite. Here, let it be understood that infinity is not to be confused with a so-called empirical infinity deriving from a series with a starting point—a point of origin. For, in effect, this is another version of finitude. Indeed, an empirical infinity is not only empirically impossible (one could never experience it); it is also a logical impossibility in the sense that a beginning only is so in relation to an end. Violence, then, is the essential agent and mark of finitude. Violence is an entity of beginning and end.

There is, perhaps, another twist. It is evident in the question of the connection between "the murderer" in the aforementioned novel and the infinite itself. Surely, we are in fact dealing with a fairly banal version of finitude? Perhaps this is not the case if every murder can plausibly be said to evoke the original murder of the Father and the constitution of the symbolic. On this basis murder would be the destruction of finitude itself. (But as Jean-Luc Nancy has said in this reading of Bataille, existence (finitude) cannot be sacrificed [Nancy, 1991, 20–38].)

In the novel, the finite in its most banal form is put in touch with the infinite: "Today Number Eight decided to kill because he was feeling an irresistible urge to vomit" (147). The detective novel, like psychoanalysis, thus dwells at the threshold of finitude and the infinite.

The Dead Father

> "Everyone has a mother tongue. I got mine from my father."
>
> —Stephanie Delacour in *The Old Man and the Wolves*

Following Maria Margaroni's remarkable analysis of the implication of Kristeva's reworking of the Oedipus myth around the idea of the Father of Individual prehistory—a loving father of agape, not the harsh father of the law as represented by the superego (Margaroni and Lechte 2004, 34–62)—we can perhaps better appreciate how the themes of violence and death, writing and the image coalesce in Kristeva's *oeuvre*. There is, though, the complication that Kristeva is the daughter of a father committed to the Orthodox faith. As the analyst herself had explained in her nonfiction some years before the publication of *Murder in Byzantium*, this implies that the daughter/son can never, in terms of theology, assume the father's position:

> God is threefold in Orthodoxy, but not in the same way as in Catholicism: the Holy Spirit proceeds from the Father *through* the Son for the Orthodox (*per filium*), the Holy Spirit proceeds from the Father *and* from the Son for the Catholics (*filioque*). While this "and" puts the Father and Son on an equal footing and prefigures the autonomy and independence of the person (that of the Son, as well as that of the believer, which opens the way to Western individualism and personalism), the Orthodox "through" suggests a delicious but deadly annihilation of the Son and of the believer. (Kristeva 2000b, 138–39. Kristeva's emphasis)

Again, according to the analyst, the risk in Orthodoxy is that in never being able to measure up to the father, the Oedipal crisis is never fully resolved and depression is a risk: "In psychoanalytic terms, one might say that Orthodox experience valorizes the pre-oedipal, narcissistic, depressive stages of personality" (Kristeva 2000b, 149). In Orthodoxy, too, lack of filial rivalry with the father suggests that agapic love—the love of the Father of "individual prehistory"—can assume more or less uninhibited expression.

"No one believes in myths these days, and that includes me" (Kristeva 1994, 176), says Stephanie imitating her father and the Old Man. The death of the father, giving rise to the "name-of-the-father" and the symbolic order, at the same time supposedly inaugurates the separation (Orthodoxy aside) of the speaking being from the mother. To foreclude the name-of-the-father, Lacan claimed, is to enter the world of depression and psychosis—a world, Kristeva has shown, where it becomes difficult if not impossible to believe in the meaning of words.

Through a separation that is inevitably a complex configuration, a style emerges that marks a mode of being-in-the-world. What can we say about Kristeva's style in light of the myth of the dead father? The implication is that it is necessary to be aware of whether or not the Oedipus myth is any longer operational. The failure of the myth is also the failure of the Law and the erasure of the border between good and evil. The failure of the Law (the father principle) can also lead to a blurring of the boundary between self and other and in this sense Kristeva is neither Bataille nor Artaud, for whom continuity was also a key state of being, a lifting of repression that opened up another avenue of communication.

Kristeva is neither Bataille nor Artaud, even if their works expand symbolic and imaginary capacities. Instead, her style leans toward austerity exuding a certain discipline—not the *geno-* but the *pheno*-text is always in evidence, as we have said. Perhaps, then, the crimes of fiction are a return to the original crime: the crime of the killing of the father as the inauguration of the symbolic, the condition of possibility of articulated language. Whatever the case, there is always a certain transparency in Kristeva's style—her way of showing respect for the Law? The semiotic, which is a threat to the Law, is not in evidence in her detective fiction. There is little disturbance or disruption, little evidence of the drives or the body in the text—rather, the opposite. It is as though detective fiction, for Kristeva, would be a kind of celebration of the Law, even though the subject matter deals with crime. The "revolution in poetic language" has, one suspects, well and truly had its day.

We know of Kristeva's leaning toward minimalist realism since her analysis of Holbein's painting of *The Body of the Dead Christ in the Tomb* (Kristeva 1989, 106–38). Here, the image (and the text) must remain essentially transparent at the risk of becoming one more simulacrum in the "society of the spectacle." The image becomes a vehicle to the thing itself (*skhésis*). Copy and prototype are inseparable: they are indeed in a "transductive" relation (Simondon), where one element presupposes the other and only exists *as* its relation to the other element. This is why Holbein's picture is able to transport us into Christ's tomb. This *is* death in the tomb! There is perhaps no transcendence (only the material body), as Dostoyevsky feared. But what is it to write death? Is it to imply: no transcendence?

Without Catharsis . . . Writing as Death

Is it not true that the pale, white writing of Marguerite Duras's fiction—writing without catharsis, the "literature of our illness," Kristeva says—is also evident in Kristeva's own work? What some have seen as a refusal of the complexities of crime—riven as it often is by complex motives often infused with hatred and love in equal measure—might instead by viewed as an index of Kristeva's depressive disposition—on show for all to see like the purloined letter, if we only care to look. What is the mark of this depression? If we accept what Kristeva herself says, writing for the depressive person is a passage to silence—silence and sadness.

The irony is that even though they are constantly on the verge of not believing in language—in the symbolic, in fact—and of falling into "asymbolia" (Kristeva 1989, 42), the loss of affect or the "devitalization" of language can result in great productivity; for the depressive is not weighed down by the emotion that can stultify a more neurotic and anxious disposition. Kristeva even refers to "hyperactivity": "Such hyperactivity with signifiers reveals itself particularly by connecting distant semantic fields and recalls the puns of hypomaniacs" (1989, 59). And again: "Melancholy persons, with their despondent, secret insides, are potential exiles but also intellectuals capable of dazzling, albeit abstract, constructions" (64).

Thus, in light of this, we find that "Gloria was lying in a pool of blood with her head cut off" (Kristeva 1998c, 3). A simple statement referring to a horrendous event! Is not the blood of language entirely squeezed out of this line? Does not catharsis fail to arise? Where is the horror, really? Whereas a line from Bataille's *Story of the Eye* (1986) has us reaching for the guard rails to steady ourselves when faced with Simone's experience: "The utterly intoxicated girl kept wrenching the big cock in and out with her buttocks, atop the body whose muscles were cracking in our formidable strangleholds" (1986, 65). Is this not the point? Kristeva's detective fiction is far from being cathartic. Even de Beauvoir's writing—at least in passages—has a rhythm of the semiotic that is absent in Kristeva's writing. For example:

> Everything will begin again. I will tell myself, "It's just that I was feeling depressed." The facts that nail me to this bed, I will explain away as depression. No! I've denied enough, fled enough, lied enough. Once, one single time and forever, I want to make truth triumph. Death has won; death is now the only truth. A single move and that truth will become eternal. (de Beauvoir 1957, 702)

Such a use of repetition (cf., "enough") is foreign to Kristeva's text. Another example in de Beauvoir's text is the following: "Sounds rose from the garden—steps, voices. But they did not disturb the silence. I could see, and I was blind; I could hear, and I was deaf" (702–03). Or again: "Leather! real, thick, supple leather! You could almost smell it through the shop window. . . . Real silk, real wool, flannel suits, poplin shirts!" (1957, 103).

Gloria Harrison was Stephanie's friend, and yet the description of her decapitation is entirely clinical. The detective is detective first of all and only secondarily, friend. Or, more broadly: Kristeva's fiction, we have said more than once, is first of all scholarly and academic and only secondarily, fiction. *Visions capitales* (1998d)—the book of Kristeva's *parti pris* of drawings of the head from the Louvre collection—is transported into the detective novel and not the reverse. *Visions capitales* with its myriad of heads depicted both attached and detached from bodies. The story of Herodias, wife of Herod, who tells her daughter, Salome, to ask for the head of John the Baptist as a reward for her dancing, appears in both the academic *Visions* (1998d, 72–79) and in the novel *Possessions* (1998c, 5–7). Even if the novel was published before the academic treatise, the approach in both remains academic—to the point where the narrator in *Possessions* becomes self-conscious about her clinical detachment and offers the following defense:

> I admit my pictorial reminiscences might strike some readers as literary and irrelevant, perhaps to the point of obscenity. But what use is art if it can't help us look death in the face? My purpose in remembering museum encounters with painters and sculptors is to be able to draw on them when I'm confronted with macabre experiences. Such ordeals aren't at all rare in Santa Varvara, and here more than anywhere I need art to help me see my way, to retain my common sense, and, if you'll forgive the expression, to keep my head. (1998c, 9)

Writing, Affect, Possession

It is time no doubt to conclude this interpretive thread lest it get out of hand and turn into pure speculation. It does, however, seem worth making two final points. The first concerns Kristeva's relation to writing; the second, is the status of possession in her work.

1. Writing and Affect

As compared to the relation Kristeva says her analysand, Didier, has to his art—Didier being an exemplary case of "new maladies of the soul"—Kristeva's writing seems to bear some similarities. With Didier, the analyst says, there is no affective link to what the content of his art evokes. His imaginary has broken down, which is increasingly the case in the "society of the spectacle." The point to be made in relation to Kristeva's work, however, is that being incapable of feeling means that violence in images ceases to be experienced as violence or to be shocking. There is no image-narrative of the passions in play. As the analyst explains:

> [Didier] brought me some pictures of his artwork—a combination of collages and paintings—and described them to me one at a time. I was struck by the violence of this pictorial "discourse," a violence that sharply contrasted with the neutrality, extreme politeness, and abstract discourse that had characterized his previous dealings with me. (Kristeva 1995, 18–19)

It is, to be sure, a big step to claim that the analyst herself manifests some of the traits attributed to her analysand—an analysand deemed to be emblematic of the consumer of images in the society of the spectacle (10). But, in light of a reading of Kristeva's fiction it is, I suggest, difficult not to draw such a conclusion. In effect, Kristeva's "academic" fiction begins to evoke Duras's "malady of grief" (Kristeva 1989a), where there is no "music" in letters. Could Kristeva be unwittingly writing about her own case when she says:

> Duras' writing does not analyze itself by seeking its sources in the music that lies under the words nor in the defeat of the narrative's logic. If there be a formal search, it is subordinate to confrontation with the silence of horror in oneself and in the world. Such a confrontation leads her to an aesthetics of *awkwardness* on the one hand, to a *noncathartic literature* on the other. (Kristeva 1989a, 225, Kristeva's emphasis)

Issues of formalism aside, the interpretation given here has been that, in effect, Kristeva's fiction is also based in an "aesthetics of awkwardness" and is "noncathartic" precisely because, as a writing exuding a formal academic style and content, it fails to unveil the recesses of affect one suspects must be there.

2. *Possession*

On the other hand, if "possession" concerns the fluidity or rigidity of borders, as Kristeva outlines it in "Name of Death or of Life"—the text referred to earlier—and if she is clearly an advocate of maintaining the rigidity of borders, fiction should not flow into nonfiction, just as phantasy should not intentionally feature in scientific, theoretical texts. Of course, it is acceptable and necessary to move from one domain to another, to be, at one moment, an actor writer of fiction, and at another moment, the "impresario," objective analyst, purveyor of the nonfictional text that may well have fiction as its object.[5] What is not acceptable is the "borderline" experience where fiction and nonfiction, the true and the false, phantasy and reality imperceptibly intertwine. But, we have seen, they do not really intertwine in Kristeva's fiction, except on a strictly formal basis, where what is proposed as fiction is substantively nonfiction. To use the more colloquial sense of possession, we could say that Kristeva is *possessed* by the field of scientific and theoretical (psychoanalytical) endeavor. That, we could almost say, *is* her life as presented by the public persona. Kristeva is really only a pseudo-borderline case. For, at all times, we see that there is almost always a barrier put up in her fiction—as with her nonfiction—to the play of affect, to the play of "music in letters," to the paranoid critical method's explosion of meaning. The surrealist endeavor, too, therefore, is not within Kristeva's fictional/artistic purview. And, in particular, Kristeva is not into the Dalían "paranoid-critical method," even if her mentor, Jacques Lacan, was. Moreover, the detective novel would not, strictly speaking, be within the purview of surrealism. For this genre is strictly nonphantasmatic, concerned only with the facts, and nothing but. . . . This is why it is the genre that best suits Kristeva in her fiction. Who, after all, can be sure that a detective novel is not a story of a real case but with the names changed? Many say, for instance, that Sherlock Holmes was none other than Sir Arthur Conan Doyle himself. Not to mention, of course, that the character, Sherlock Holmes, is the model of formality and constraint. No "music in letters" here.

Consequently, whether or not the academic Kristeva is all there is—whether there is a void at the heart of the person (see Kristeva's characterization of Duras), or whether there still remains a truly literary work—a "music in letters"—waiting to be liberated, only time will tell.

Notes

1. From Salvador Dalí, "L'âne pourri," in *Surréalisme en service de la révolution* 1 (July 1930), quoted in Roudinesco (1993, 55).

2. *Pros ti* is Aristotle's term in the *Categories* for a concrete relation: "the *pros ti*, literally the 'related-to something' " (Jansen 2007, 157). For Aristotle a relation is always between two clear elements; it is never one of absolute intimacy and transparency, as is the case with *skhésis*. In terms of *pros ti*, the father is related to the son. In terms of *skhésis*, one can see the father in the son.

3. See Lechte (2009, 84–88 and 2011).

4. See the reference to speaking about "New Maladies of the Soul" (Kristeva 2006b, 237).

5. In this regard, it is notable that in responding to certain questions—on culture and nation, for example—she invokes her "fiction" as readily as her academic work. Thus, when asked in an interview which cultures outside of the French she feels closest to, Kristeva quotes at length from *Possessions* (see Kristeva 1998, 78–79).

8

Byzantium, or Fiction as Inverted Theory

Miglena Nikolchina

When Julia Kristeva's first novel *The Samurai* appears in 1990, Kristeva is a prominent theoretician whose international standing is firmly established. The question why she should venture out of her habitual territory and turn to a different medium becomes, therefore, unavoidable. Throughout the years, and with each next novel, Kristeva offers a variety of reasons for her fictional turn. In an early interview apropos of *The Samurai* she refers to Sartre as the author of both *Being and Nothingness* and *Nausea* (Kristeva 1996g, 242). This is, of course, the obvious answer: it happens; this is what philosophers and scholars (and, going in the opposite direction, novelists) sometimes do. Simone de Beauvoir, whose *Mandarins* are vibrantly present in the very title of Kristeva's first novel, did it (notably, the protagonist of *The Samurai*, the young émigrée Olga, has the same name as the Russian woman to whom de Beauvoir dedicates *She Came to Stay*). Umberto Eco, a fellow semiotician, famously did it and keeps doing it. Bulgarian theoretician Tzvetan Stoyanov, a name to which I will return, also did it, although, perhaps unjustly, in his own country he is hardly remembered today as a novelist. Kristeva refers to Proust's notebooks where she came across the question, "Should I make this into a novel or into a philosophical study?" (Kristeva 1996g, 242).

It would seem, therefore, that turning now to fiction, now to theory is an occurrence that takes place in various times and locations. There is, however, something specific about the French theoretical scene ("the genius of the French people is rooted in the links they make between popular passions and the dynamics of intellectual tensions") and, as Kristeva specifies in a later interview apropos of *Murder in Byzantium*, about "the tendency, or school, in French philosophy which developed in the 60s, in which conceptual work is deeply involved with the personal and in which notions, or ideas, are sutured by style"

(Sutherland 2006). Yet it is precisely these links that Kristeva feels have been weakened and that, in the face of "the lewd and pervasive influence of television" (as she puts it in the earlier interview) and the society of the spectacle, as she prefers to call it in her later writing, dictate a sort of compromise with the "necessary anecdote demanded by the public" (Kristeva 1996g, 244).

Turning to fiction would thus seem to be simultaneously arbitrary ("should I make this into a novel or into a philosophical study"), the natural outgrowth of a (French) cultural configuration imbuing passion into concepts and conceptuality into rhetorical figures, and a sort of intellectual duty, a heroic response to the political exigency to bridge the gap between the life of thought and the popular demand for anecdote. Yet, there is more to it, as Kristeva's formidable self-reflexivity never fails to notice. "The core of the symbolic lies in the fundamental drives of the signifier, that is, in sensations, perceptions, and emotions. When we translate them, we leave the realm of ideas and enter the world of fiction . . ." (Kristeva 1996g, 243). This amazing sentence, which seems to imply that ideas do not translate sensations, perceptions, and emotions, but, rather, are directly driven by them, posits translation as the route to fiction. This route unfolds, notably, simultaneously in two registers or, perhaps, achieves a twofold effect in a single coup: it translates sensations and with this it leaves behind ideas. The ambition of this procedure is to "reach the sensory core of language by sifting through a network of memories and fantasies," and to bring forth a language that is immediately sensuous (Kristeva's ultimate examples for this achievement are Proust and Colette). Insofar as, however, the procedure amounts to detaching the sensations from the realm of ideas, it implies an analytic cut not unlike the one implied by Kristeva's theoretical methods.

In fact, the very logic of Kristeva's theoretical thinking imposes a movement from the conceptual to the fictional and from logic to poetry, that is, from theory to literature. There already *is* a narrative in Kristeva's theoretical writing. What her novels do is make it explicit. The discreet is revealed, the unsaid is articulated. The reversal is not simple insofar as it necessarily severs or, at best, occludes the links of the processes that have affected it, thus producing its own unsaid.

Trajectories of the Unsaid: From the Dome of Being to Crime Fiction

"There is a way of detaching oneself from the origin that is a form of matricide and that one avoids in distancing oneself in another language" (Kristeva and Rice 2002, 287). After her migrating to France in 1965 in the course of twenty-five years or so—in fact, until the collapse of the communist system in Europe—Bulgaria, Kristeva's country of origin, is hardly ever mentioned in her writing.

One notable exception is the painful—and rather unusual for her—confessional tone of "The Novel as Polylogue" where she states that she speaks "in French and about literature because of Yalta" (Kristeva 1980c, 161). By "Yalta" she means the division of Europe after World War Two, which was negotiated by the "Big Three" (Churchill, Roosevelt, and Stalin) at the Yalta conference in 1945 and which determined Bulgaria's fate as part of the communist Eastern Bloc.

Kristeva has sometimes been reprimanded for her reticence on her Bulgarian past: according to Gayatri Spivak, Kristeva's "own pre-history in Bulgaria is not even a shadow under the harsh light of the Parisian voice" (Spivak 1988, 161). And yet, it would be more accurate to say that the Bulgarian "shadow" has passed into the register of the "fundamental drives of the signifier" from where it emanates a mute narrative awaiting its "translation." As I have demonstrated elsewhere, Kristeva's theoretical preoccupations in her works from the 1970s and 1980s surreptitiously unfold a hushed story: the story of an irrecoverable lost territory, of an immortal sorrow, of a disconsolate wandering. The ciphers, which already include Byzantium, Orthodoxy, and Mediaeval murals and which mark the trajectory of this irredeemable sadness, envelop the map of the lost motherland. Although unnamed and invisible, this hidden icon emits powerful idealizing energies (see Nikolchina 2004, 45–61).

Now this lost territory had its proper theoretical dimensions and ramifications. Kristeva's early writing—from Σημειωτική (*Séméiotiké*) (1969) to *Polylogue* (1977)—is characterized by a broad interdisciplinarity, a taste for the exact sciences, a penchant for neologisms, and—in keeping with the claim that philosophy is the art of fabricating concepts, as Deleuze and Guattari would later put it—a profusion of newly formed or refunctionalized terms, many of which acquired wide circulation. Her tough terminological machinery addressing a plethora of literary and cultural issues through a multiplicity of schools and disciplines, while typical of the French but also of the international intellectual scene at the time, is nevertheless marked by an excessiveness whose precise lineage remains nameless. It includes, of course, the Russian formalists (criticized yet thoroughly read) and Bakhtin, whose integration into the French theoretical discussions owes a lot to the rightful or maybe wrongful, as sometimes has been claimed, mediation of Kristeva. Even more pertinent in this respect would be the figure of the legendary Tartu semiotician Yuri Lotman who edited, since 1964, a journal bearing the same title spelled in Greek as Kristeva's early book—Σημειωτική (*Séméiotiké*). However, it is little known in Bulgaria—and not at all elsewhere, I believe—that Kristeva's first book ever appeared in 1964 in Bulgaria before she left for France. Its title is *Characteristic Trends in Twentieth Century Western Literature*. In this book the twenty-three-year-old author discusses the "characteristic trends" in a manner characteristic of the time and place: on the surface, this is a critique of decadent Western literature and philosophy; in effect, this is a smart and seductive presentation of authors and books otherwise unavailable because of censorship. The book is slim and encyclopedically concise and yet striking in terms of both erudition and analytic incisiveness. It shares a lot of common ground with a number of contemporaneous Bulgarian authors, including earlier and later writing by Tzvetan Stoyanov, who was mentioned earlier as the author of both theoretical and fictional works. In Kristeva's first novel *The Samurai*, Stoyanov enters the stage as Olga's former boyfriend Dan. Although Bulgaria is as yet not named in the novel, Dan's appearance in it can be regarded as a sort of relay point: marking Kristeva's connection to the obscure Bulgarian intellectual scene and the henceforth growing visibility of Bulgaria in Kristeva's writing.

Dan, as described by Kristeva in *The Samurai*,

> knew practically every language and had read all the important works ever written in English, German, French, Russian, Spanish, and Italian, from the dim distant past up to the present. He was a glutton for culture and had absorbed all the great writers, philosophers, and poets. Like some representative of the Age of Enlightenment strayed into an obscure country and another age, he bestowed his erudition on the ignoramuses around him in the form of skeptical parables. To him Olga owed all she knew about Shakespeare and Cervantes, Browning and Emily Dickinson, Mallarmé and Faulkner (1992, 41)

The meeting does not go so well for Dan who is hoping to convince Olga to return to her native country. Dan's feeling is that Olga has moved to the "other side"—which would be true, if we speak of Tzvetan Stoyanov, not only in terms of Kristeva's defecting to France (and, as Dan points out, to an easy game of political protest as opposed to its deadly earnestness at home) but also in terms of theoretical debates around structuralism back in Bulgaria. What concerns me at this point, however, is, beyond such specifics, the phrase "glutton for culture [who] had absorbed all the great writers, philosophers, and poets." It could very well be applied to the voracity of Kristeva's own early project, already visible in her youthful Bulgarian book and most thoroughly exemplified in Σημειωτική (*Séméiotiké*) and *Revolution in Poetic Language* (both books are as yet not translated in their totality in English, precisely, I guess, because of their too-muchness). This voracity seems to share a common platform not only with Dan/Tzvetan Stoyanov but with various and sometimes conflicting trends in Bulgarian theoretical thinking at the time. Condemned to isolation by the communist regime, the friends and university colleagues whom Julia Kristeva had left behind assumed a stance that might be described as vertical catastrophism: as contemporary philosopher Boyan Manchev notes, the impossibility for Bulgarian thinkers to participate in the "horizontal" international debates sought resolution in an attempt to assume a meta-position and integrate vertically the summa of theoretical thought *tout court* (1999, 5–30).

The Bulgarian theoretical field was hence characterized by a sort of "domeness"—where the homonym of dome, *dom*, means "home" thus sending us in the direction of Heidegger's famous statement about language, which in this case would run as something like "Theory is the dome of being." The proper translation of dome in Bulgarian as *svod*, however, might refer, apart from the architectural structure, to the sky as firmament and to a library catalogue of catalogues. The dome-ness is for that matter a librarian firmament *alias* a heterogeneous congruence of authors, schools, disciplines, and any range of arts and sciences, which goes far beyond ideas of interdisciplinarity and whose receding horizons could be delineated only by the grand utopias of the totality of knowledge and languages. Last but, perhaps, not least, *svod* is related to *svat* and *svodnik*, matchmaker and go-between, which would pinpoint the propensity of dome-ness to bring together likely and unlikely theoretical bedfellows.

The mediation and the effort to assemble discourses is not a matter of simple addition, however, as one of Kristeva's Bulgarian peers—Radosvet Kolarov—has recently claimed through the concept of transmodality (see Kolarov 2009, 220–27).[1] The transmodal idea is an idea that passes from one discourse into another, from one discipline into another, and from one epoch into another. In the course of these transitions it acquires specific auras, which may coalesce or diffract and altogether make it unrecognizable. Its various reincarnations can even deny each other or, indeed, completely ignore each other. Going beyond these auras to unveil the sameness, however, which a ravenous theoretician is bound to do, would have the paradoxical effect of disclosing dynamics, process, metamorphosis, and singular points of torsion and inflexion. Kristeva's early work stands as the visible (French) articulation of this agenda.

In the context of communist repression the agenda was, ultimately, a defiant faith in the material power of thought. In Kristeva's work, the transmodal invariant of this faith takes the form of a program for finding a new universality in the perspective of the singular and the unique: from the "revolution in poetic language" to the "intimate revolution" in her more recent writing. But, we might note at this point, with a *différance*. Kristeva herself attributes this difference to her encounter with Freud whom she did not have in her communist suitcase. (Freud is, in fact, discussed in her Bulgarian book, so she probably means Freud's absence in terms of psychoanalytic practice.) Consequently, Kristeva's focus on the reverse of signifying practices, on the semiotic traversing of symbolic structures, on the subject-in-process and on the site of the production of subjectivity and signification evolves as an answer to a number of poststructuralist aporias concerning universality, identity, and linguisticality. In her early work Kristeva terms her method for exploring this underside of signification semanalysis, which amounts to describing "the signifying phenomenon, or signifying phenomena, while analyzing, criticizing, and dissolving 'phenomenon,' 'meaning,' and 'signifier'" (1980, vii).

This corrosive—as Kristeva herself defines it—procedure obviously runs counter to the procedure that fabricates new concepts: it dissolves them. If philosophy is the fabrication of concepts, what would be the discipline of dissolving them? Wouldn't Kristeva's theoretical project be overrun by an antitheoretical drive? Less dramatically put, the very logic of semanalysis as the decomposition of meaning and signifier calls for a metamorphosis into the narrative and the fictional, and, ultimately into the (intimate) revolutions of poetry. The fictional dimension of Kristeva's theoretical works, which she repeatedly highlights,[2] is therefore a spontaneous and inevitable product of the semanalytic dissolution of conceptuality and a logical result of her method.

If Kristeva's fictionality materializes in a reversal of the philosophical procedure that invents concepts, her novels cannot be made of the material that novels are usually made of. Nor are they similar to the philosophical novel as variously exemplified by authors like Voltaire or Thomas Mann where philosophical ideas are embodied and provided with a story. Some studies have claimed that Kristeva's novels are allegorical in the sense of Benjamin's analysis of the German *Trauerspiel* (see, e.g., Margaroni 2009, 107–24), yet it should be stressed that Benjamin discusses allegory as the life of irresistible decay and as the form that finds its perfection in ruin (1977, 178; see also Nikolchina 2004). If we can describe Kristeva's novels as allegorical, it is because, in them, allegory emerges effectively in the decay of concepts (as with the growing nails of a corpse, to use Benjamin's metaphor). As the site of conceptual dissolution, the body that ideas in Kristeva's novels gravitate toward tends to be a dead body; and the story they are granted tends toward carnage. Ergo, murder is their subject matter and their genre, crime fiction, whose nature is even stranger than it looks.

B&B

Inversion as the transmutation of semanalysis into fiction might be conceived in Lacan's terms, as a specular reversal and as a transformation in the imaginary. The imaginary acts as a barrier and causes discourse to be transmitted in an inverted form (Evans 1996, 92). One could also refer to Russian-Georgian philosopher Merab Mamardashvili. His elaboration of Marx's idea of the *verwandelte Form* puts a major emphasis on the erasure of causal links and structural connections in objects that have been effectively cut off—and hence function as a concealment of—the operations that produced them (Mamardashvili 1992) In Kristeva's case, where a message transmitted as theory returns as fiction, the inversion involves a turning around of the said and the unsaid, a change of guard, so to speak (with reference to Derrida's gloss of Hegel's *Aufhebung*) of mystery and articulation, which, not surprisingly, brings forth a further mystery.

This amounts to saying that crime and mystery in Kristeva's novels articulate the unsaid of her theory and, first of all, the silent reverse of her method as dissolution. What comes to the surface is propelled by the specific type of secret imbuing Kristeva's theoretical thinking. As already pointed out, this secret revolves around a muffled narrative of exile, of wandering and seeking for a lost object and a nameless territory, of matricide attenuated by migrating to another language. At one pertinent point Kristeva relates this silent story to the "mute sister of philosophy" (Kristeva 1989, 4). A murderous secret, a dark sorrow, a shadowy country, a restless search, and an asymbolic feminine subject: in the novels after *The Samurai* the hidden parable becomes explicit and the narrative finds its fictional buttress in Kristeva's protagonist Stephanie Delacour, a perennial foreigner and "a globetrotting investigative reporter-detective" (Kristeva 1992, 75)

Stephanie Delacour weaves together the multifaceted reversals that take place in Kristeva's fiction and in her theoretical writing contemporaneous with the novels. Up until the beginning of the nineties Kristeva is frequently criticized for focusing her research on male artists. It is claimed that her study of the semiotic and the maternal privileges male creativity. Critics, however, overlook the fact that Kristeva's theoretical figuration includes herself as relentless explorer of the matricidal alchemy of male artistic subjectivities. Fiction, on the other hand, allows this discreet fact to become visible: the theoretician jumps on stage as detective-reporter Stephanie Delacour. In the second half of the 1990s Kristeva adds a further and important twist to this change: the trilogy on "female genius" dedicated to three women excelling in different fields (Hannah Arendt, Melanie Klein, and Colette) focuses on female creativity. The appearance of twelfth-century Byzantine princess Anna Comnena—the first woman historiographer and, according to Kristeva's novel, the first woman intellectual in European history, author of the fifteen volumes of the *Alexiad*, dealing with the historical events of her own tempestuous times—as a pivotal figure in *Murder in Byzantium* is indicative of this shift toward a female object of scientific interest, veneration, and love. Kristeva's most recent book on Saint Teresa indicates that this interest continues to evolve.

Similar processes occur with respect to the "lost territory" of Kristeva's earlier *oeuvre*. Almost never mentioned before *The Samurai*, Kristeva's country of origin, Bulgaria, becomes more and more explicitly present in her subsequent writing. This growing presence of the lost object takes the form of a veritable return of the abject: Bulgaria is depicted as a typical waste product of the age of "Santa Varvara," Kristeva's fictional representation of the negative effects of globalization, of the society of the spectacle, the domination of images, corruption, fundamentalism, and terrorism, and, ultimately, of the decline of thinking. The controversial essay "Bulgaria, My Suffering" written in 1995 is emblematic: from the poverty of language ("this poor language of sensitive peasants and naïve thinkers") to the mafia bosses, everything concerning the country is placed under the category of gruesome tastelessness or, as one particularly upset commentator, Dusan I. Bjelic, notes, of shit: "Kristeva regards Bulgarians as political excreta, an abject of the polis' superego" (Bjelic Web).

Bulgaria does have, however, one saving grace: in the Middle Ages, it was, in terms of culture and religion, and, as we shall shortly see, in terms of royal marriages, part of the Byzantine civilization. In *Murder in Byzantium* the presence of Bulgaria is purged of its abject, "Santa Varvaran" aspects insofar as Bulgarian cultural history is closely intertwined with Byzantium. Bulgarian settings emerge, mostly as enticing landscapes and fascinating medieval relics, in the context of the novel's quest for the "true story" of the Byzantine princess Anna Comnena. An abject by-product of present-day Santa Varvara, which, since the fall of the Berlin Wall, "has expanded continuously,"[3] Bulgaria is also the material holder of traces from a sublime Byzantine past.

The inversion that brings forth a female subject-object dichotomy and a territory bifurcated between abjection and sublimity opens up two theoretically unspeakable realms, which, in Kristeva's novels, seek expression in two distinct styles, the journalistic and the poetic. The first one offers opinions on various issues as directly as can be. It is frequently blunt, self-confident, for the most part unsympathetic and judgmental; it leaves little space for doubt, ambiguity, or, indeed, dialogism and polyphony. It is passionate; it is frankly and openly biased. Sometimes this is the way the characters think; sometimes this is the way they talk: conversations in Kristeva's novels tend to turn into heated debates. It is worth noting that higher forms of journalism, of the type of *j'accuse*, of the political pamphlet, and of the controversial tract have been set apart as a separate genre in the Russian and Bulgarian literary tradition: it is called *publizistika*, complete with its history dating back to the biblical prophets and Roman satire, with its major representatives and its contemporary researchers. It is opposed to both regular journalism and theory: to the former, through its polemical engagement with ideas rather than events; to the latter, through its emotional appeal to common sense and persuasive power rather than argument. If Stephanie Delacour gave up on the charms of philosophy and became a reporter, one would assume that it was partially because of the guiles of *publizistika*.

The second realm comprises unique "moments of being" and, in its sensory richness, unpredictability, and stunning precision, verges on the impossible. It gives flesh to the singular thus incorporating the privileged concern of Kristeva's theory as experience rather than as an object of study. The two styles are tied to two divergent novelistic perspectives, one flat, external, and anecdotal; the other one all interiority. They both are free floating in the sense that they can be attached to different characters or speakers in Kristeva's novels. Yet it is also notable that in Kristeva's first novel *The Samurai* these two styles are rather evenly distributed between Olga Morena and Joëlle Cabarus, between regular script and italics, and between the social and the intimate. With the next novels they come to coexist in Stephanie Delacour, who, in *Murder in Byzantium*, finds her historical precedent in Anna Comnena's capacity to "describe events from the perspective of both a military strategist and a depressed psychologist" (2006b, 81).

Both styles thus find their native soil, so to speak, in the virtuality of Byzantium. On the one hand, Byzantium is the *publizistika* platform for direct polemical charges against Santa Varvara, as "the opposite of Byzantium" (ibid., 67) and as the stand for an alternative vision of Europe. In this aspect it tends to coincide—as a statement but also as a sort of cautionary tale—with contemporary France, this citadel of a dying civilization.[4] On the other hand, Byzantium is the sensuous cipher for the unnamable, a node of utopia and imagination, a different way of seeing and perceiving, a dream and a memory of things that never were, the hope of retrieving a lost territory or, rather, a lost time, a "future anterior."

Under this arch between present and future anterior the recent past, the past that came to be "because of Yalta," once again disappears. Its absence, however, produces a glitch.

The Wink of the Real: Anna Comnena and Vera M.

Anna Comnena's *Alexiad*, which serves as a frame of reference to Kristeva's story about her, is mostly concerned with politics, palace intrigues, military conflicts, and the idealized image of her father, the Byzantine emperor Alexius I. Anna was betrothed for political reasons while still a child; later, for political reasons, the betrothal was cancelled; she married somebody else and went into no end of effort to have her husband, rather than her younger brother, on the throne; she had several children, four of whom survived; she was ultimately and, in view of her conspiracies, mercifully sent to a monastery by her imperial brother where she wrote the *Alexiad*. What Kristeva inscribes in this frame is a fictional erotic encounter between Anna and a Western crusader who, as a result of this brief meeting, decides to give up on crusades and marry (not the princess, of course) in Bulgaria. His trajectory is a reversal of Kristeva's own biographical displacement and there are many marks in the novel indicating the connection.[5] So far as Anna Comnena is concerned, Kristeva's point is that what Anna's writing omits is the one important amorous experience of her life.

The imaginary meeting between Anna Comnena and the knight takes place while Anna is visiting her Bulgarian grandmother: one of the grandmothers of the Byzantine princess was, indeed, a Bulgarian princess. In fact, Kristeva claims in her novel that a Bulgarian historian, "a certain Vera M." (2006b, 123), found proof for this visit about which the *Alexiad* says nothing.

This fleeting intrusion of a contemporary Bulgarian reference deserves unraveling. Vera M. is Vera Mutafchieva, an important historian and novelist whose novel *I, Anna Comnena* appeared for the first time in 1991, shortly after the end of the communist regime, and who is also the author of *The Knight*, a novel about a crusader's adventures and death in Bulgaria. *I, Anna Comnena* is of particular interest here. It is structured as alternating narratives in the first person by Anna Comnena and a number of women who were close to her (her mother, her grandmothers, her maid). Unlike Kristeva who, apart from the fictional love episode, treats Anna Comnena's *Alexiad* with a fair degree of trust, Mutafchieva uses the fictional setting in order to present an entirely different perspective on Anna's biography, on the historical events of the time, on the protagonists in them, and indeed, on the bearing they had on Anna herself. Mutafchieva thus creates a split or, indeed, a chasm between the "official" narrative of the *Alexiad* and the "unofficial" narrative of the female narrators in her novel, a split not simply between the social and the intimate, the political and the personal, the "military strategist" and the "depressed psychologist" but between political and political, personal and personal, intimate and intimate. It is this chasm that really interests her, the impossibility of really saying "it," the historical truth, or the truth of one's life. Nothing and no one is spared in this undoing of the *Alexiad*, including Anna's idealized father, the Emperor Alexius, about whom Mutafchieva's Anna Comnena dryly notes: "I think my father must have had his spiritual backbone broken very early on in his life and then had grown up with this hidden handicap" (2008, 52). There is a brutality, an intellectual ruthlessness in Mutafchieva's effort to make her point, which is in sharp contrast to the dreamy and utopian quality of Kristeva's version. Toward the end of Mutafchieva's novel Anna observes that, for her, the words she writes down in the *Alexiad* have more value and reality than the world of political power, of intrigue, and conflicts that she inhabited and described. Yet these words—the *Alexiad*—say nothing about what she knows to be true concerning both the people and the events she writes about, or, indeed, about herself. So why do these words matter to her? And what would be the status of her writing, then? Anna concludes that "writing is not a reflection of being: it is a separate, parallel being. It has its own life, independent of its author" (ibid. 324).

Mutafchieva's novel reads like a powerful feminist statement: only, we should add that its strategy of rewriting, with a sharp and merciless eye, of an existing more or less sacrosanct historical and autobiographical account was applied also in other of Mutafchieva's novels where the protagonists were men. Her own father was an eminent "bourgeois" historian, repressed by the communist regime: there is no doubt that her sensitivity to the split between what one writes and what one thinks provides a wry commentary on the conditions of communist censorship and on her own personal and familial experience. Whatever the case, one year before her death and seventeen years after the first edition of *I, Anna Comnena* it became known that Mutafchieva was enrolled in 1969 as an informer to the dreaded Sixth Department of the communist secret services, the department spying on and repressing intellectuals.

In one of his discussions of the uncanny, Mladen Dolar notes that "in order for the mirror image to contain the object *a*, a wink or a nod is enough" (1991, 13). Imagine, he suggests, that you look at your image in the mirror and the image closes its eyes. In her analysis of *Murder in Byzantium*, discussing Kristeva's appeal for Byzantium to be integrated in the European "phantom," Maria Margaroni asks a number of times: What about the communist past of the region? We know: the icons, the Trinity, the crusades, Byzantine culture. What about recent communism? (Margaroni 2009). In the end, the communist past is not simply about streets less clean but also about tough choices that intellectuals had to make under conditions hostile to thinking. It is about the stakes for thought to continue to do its work. If today things with the global Santa Varvara stand as badly as Kristeva's novels claim, the implications of such choices might be the very unsaid that should keep haunting us.

Notes

1. It is impossible to trace here the transmodality of this very idea. One of the tracks could take us back to the 1960s and to Krassmir Mantchev's elaboration of Gustave Guillaume's concept of *idéogenèse*. See Mantchev 1967, 1998.

2. The temptation of "literary or para-literary fiction," which is resisted in the preface to *Desire in Language* (1980, ix), turns into an *inescapable* "share of fiction" in *Powers of Horror* (1982, 68). Later on her project is described as resembling "narrative fiction"; as, ultimately, close to literature and art in its ambition to "restore to illusion its full therapeutic and epistemological value" (Kristeva 1987c, 21) and its cathartic effect (Kristeva1989, 35).

3. "Today Philippopolis is a city like any city in Santa Varvara. . . . Since the fall of the Berlin wall Santa Varvara has expanded continuously" (Kristeva 2006b, 166). Philippopolis is the name given to the city by Philip of Macedon, the father of Alexander the Great. Using this name in this context rather than the modern name Plovdiv is indicative of the erasure of recent history subtending Kristeva's Byzantine utopia.

4. "Byzantium did not last, and France itself is fading" (Kristeva 2006b, 86).

5. In the novel, the crusader turns out to be the ancestor of Sebastian Chrest-Jones, a dark and obsessed murderous alter ego of Stephanie Delacour, who in her turn is

Kristeva's alter ego. Chrest/Krist sound like the Bulgarian word for "cross" (*krîst*), which forms the root of Kristeva's family name. It is believed, indeed, that this rather common family name goes back to the crusaders, the ones "marked with a cross," many of whom did stay behind and left their traces in a number of toponyms in Bulgaria. The initials of Chrest-Jones reverse Julia Kristeva's initials (CJ/JK); Krist-Eva could be seen as the feminine of Chrest-Jones, and so forth. The novel is full of similar labyrinths that involve elements more complicated than sounds and names.

9

The *Vital* Legacy of the Novel and Julia Kristeva's Fictional Revolt

Maria Margaroni

"What is intolerable about a woman writing?"

"... she wrote—in French and, on top of it, novels—"

—Julia Kristeva, "Aragon: *Blanche ou l'oubli*; or, 'The Farcical and Ferocious Quest for a Consciousness' "

Responses to Julia Kristeva's fiction so far (from *The Samurai* to her more recent *Murder in Byzantium*) have privileged Kristeva the theorist, seen paradoxically as either insufficiently or overwhelmingly present in the work of Kristeva the novelist. This is the reason why her fiction has mostly been approached as (a more or less effective) "exemplification" of her thought as a literary theorist and psychoanalyst (see, e.g., Chen). To the present, there has not been a thorough engagement with her fictional *oeuvre* in its own right. In response to the challenge this volume offers, my task in this essay is to interpret Kristeva's post-1990s turn to fiction for what it is: that is, a *revolt* that, more than complementary or supplementary to her work as a theorist, needs to be approached as critical of or even corrective to certain aspects of her theoretical work, especially her early writings on the avant-garde. My contention is that this critical/corrective function of her fiction can be appreciated when our focus shifts to the performative value of Kristeva's gesture. Thus, the question I am asking is: What does it mean for Kristeva the theorist *to write* (not an essay or a book but) in "the 'absolute' sense of the word," as she herself puts it in her analysis of Aragon's *Blanche ou l'oubli*? (2002a, 214). What does it mean for her to write *as a woman* and *as a foreigner*, the non-French wife of one of the most important contemporary French novelists? In sum, what performatively is the shock-effect of this re*volt* of hers, this turn to writing "in French—and, on top of it, novels" (2002a, 212)?

As I intend to demonstrate, Kristeva's fictional revolt consists in a) reclaiming the legacy of the novel, this "insufficiently miraculous genre" (2000, 117), against her earlier analyses of avant-garde writing and what she has come to call the "sacred Puritanism of the avant-garde" (2007,138);[1] b) her retheorization of the novel as "the writing of a woman" (2002a, 214) and her tentative conceptualization of a new artistic generation, an avant-garde in the feminine (2007, 142–43, 148–52). In my view, Kristeva's turn to fiction and her subsequent rethinking of the novel and the contemporary value of its legacy constitute a much-needed response to what until the 1990s had remained an open question in Kristeva: namely, her reluctance as a woman theorist of the avant-garde to discuss the production of female writers and artists. In a 1989 interview Françoise van Rossum-Guyon confronts Kristeva with the question: "Yet, as has often been pointed out to you, your analyses do not bear upon the work of female artists and writers, and you have often shown traces of a certain skepticism with regard to productions which purport to be specifically feminine" (2007, 130). In her response to this question Kristeva continues to discuss avant-garde writing as the product of the son's incestuous struggle against the phallic mother (2007, 132–33). Interestingly, however, a (nondepressive) avant-garde form of writing, the product of a woman/daughter, is no longer (as it used to be) an impossibility (see Kristeva 1986b, 156–58; and Kristeva 1989a). In the course of the interview Kristeva comes to talk about the work of a new generation of women writers that "does not resemble that of the avant-garde in the militant sense of the term," though it demonstrates the same concern with the "irreducible within the human being" (2007, 143). What distinguishes these young women writers, however, is a maternal commitment on their part to "reconcile the incommensurable with the community" (2007, 151). Taking my cue from this tentative delineation of an avant-garde in the feminine, I want to argue that what is at stake in Kristeva's fictional re*volt* is precisely the necessity and possibility of this reconciliation that involves the task of rethinking the relation between the avant-garde writer and the feminine. To this end, I shall attempt to read side by side two of Kristeva's seminal essays on the novel—each representative of a particular stage in her approach to avant-garde writing.

The Polylogue and the Innovator as "an anamnestic child"[2]

According to Leslie Hill, Kristeva's initial engagement with the novel needs to be appreciated in the context of her "concerted attempt to articulate the theoretical base of avant-garde literary practice in France in the early 1970s" (1990, 140). It is precisely in this light that Kristeva's review of Sollers's novel *H* acquires a seminal importance. As her opening remarks reveal, the essay entitled "The Novel as Polylogue" seeks to take up the challenge opened by the "jolt of May '68," making a concrete intervention in what Kristeva insists is "a historical turning point": "this whirlwind, this reversal, this confrontation of the old within the new" (1980c, 160). It is written as a response to the "illusion that the negative—death, violence—does not concern" us, "us, here, now, concretely, enclosed within a still-active bourgeoisie" (160, 161). Reading *H*, then, Kristeva invites her reader to "a negative vigil."[3] Her aim is to share the experience of being kept awake by the emergence of the heterogeneous that Sollers renders possible and subtly orchestrates (165). As she clarifies from the beginning of her analysis, this "heterogeneous object is of course a body that invites me to identify with it (woman, child, androgyne?) and immediately forbids any identification" (163). It carries with it echoes of the maternal territory that the "I" has lost, a territory Kristeva herself mourns in her opening remarks as she wonders about her "right to speak, in French" (161). Which is why the "I" is forbidden to "doze off" for, exposed to the work of this heterogeneous negative, it is called to witness its own dissolution: "infinite, repeated, multipliable" (161, 164). At the same time, it finds itself (not without discomfort) drifting to "the other side, where society constitutes itself by denying the murder it inflicts" on a body that is "not me, . . . a non-me in me, beside me, outside of me, where the me becomes lost" (163, 164).

It is the "dismembered score" resulting from the breathing of this body *within* language[4] as well as the simultaneous loss and return of the subject in its drifting to and fro an immemorial "before"[5] that Kristeva calls "the text," a term she is committed to in this early phase of her intellectual becoming[6] as the index to a signifying practice that she clearly privileges over other practices, such as narrative, metalanguage, and theoria.[7] In this light, it is important that Kristeva insists on the need *not* to approach avant-garde writing within conventional interpretive and generic frameworks. *H*, she argues, is neither poetry ("a pleasure of merging with a rediscovered hypostatized maternal body") nor a narrative ("the fulfillment of a request, the exchange of information," which involves "the subject of a family, clan, or state group"). It is, instead, the process of "playing these contradictions one against another; being neither" (174). If the body/text of Sollers's *H* is precisely a *polylogue*, this is because it is the infinite "collision between *semiotic operations* . . . and *symbolic operations*," a collision that, according to Kristeva, is experienced as "joy ripped with pain" (174, 184). This is why and despite its roots in dialectics, the polylogue (we are told) emphasizes music (180) and "asks for nothing—no deciphering, at any rate, no commentaries, no philosophical, theoretical, or political complement" (159). It is no wonder, then, that the reader it invokes and addresses is called to occupy the traditional position of the "feminine": "your role," Kristeva writes, "is tolerated only if it resembles that of women in Sade, Joyce and Bataille. . . . What is important is to listen to it, in your own way, indefinitely, and to disappear within the movement of this attentiveness" (166). Interestingly, "you" are advised not to "consider yourself either as the weaving or as the character against whom [the polylogue] is woven" (166). But who is this "character" haunting *H* whose murder is rehearsed again and again, every time "sociality [re]constitutes itself by killing, by throttling the outlay that keeps it alive" (168)? And who is the "*some One*" carrying out the operation of weaving (165)?

If Sollers's polylogue succeeds in producing a language that is adequate to the revolutionary moment that marks the confrontation of the old with the new; if, indeed, this language is experienced as the dissonant music of an affective, discursive, and social explosion,[8] this is because its rhythm is, as Kristeva demonstrates, materialist, transfinite, and transfamilial. In other words, the polylogue is a practice of/against limits. It unfolds as a "polemic with finitude [the finitude of the sentence, structure, and meaning], with pause, with totality" and with any symbolic thesis (180–81). Though it does not contest the inescapability of syntax and of that boundary that "shifts instinctual motility into logically structurable signifiers," it, at the same time, takes up the task of opening this boundary to its excess: "more-than-a-sentence, more-than-meaning, more-than-significance" (167, 168). "The problem," Kristeva writes, is not to elude the boundary (as artistic practices have traditionally attempted to do) but "to raise and transform" the moment of the emergence of a thesis, "to allow it to sing" (168). Such a process, she explains, can only be carried out by "a *materialist* who *speaks*," a subject, that is, who enunciates while not forgetting that he "has an unconscious that beats within him as rhythm-intonation-music" (183–84).

As she does not fail to remind us, the roles to be taken up in this experience of a materialism that "is able to utter itself" are "determined by sexual difference" (164, 184). For only a male subject can afford to risk both symbolic and semiotic supports; only "he" (a Mallarmé, a Sollers, a Joyce) can become the agent of "a practice where logical superego and fetishist oralization neutralize each other without mastery and without regression" (169). Finally, it is only the son-qua-"poet" who is able to engage in battle with both paternal and maternal authorities, pitting one against the other and, in doing so, shattering the procreative familial economy they set up. Kristeva makes clear that it is the figure of the Phallic Mother that lies at the heart of this economy: "The phallic mother," she writes, "has possession of our imaginaries because she controls the family, and the imaginary is familial" (191). This is why, according to her, no "language can sing unless it confronts the Phallic Mother" (191). As she herself acknowledges in her 1989 interview with Rossum-Guyon, it is precisely her foregrounding of the role of the phallic mother that constitutes her unique contribution to a theorization of avant-garde writing at the end of the nineteenth and twentieth centuries (2007, 130). Following her analysis in "The Novel as Polylogue," the avant-garde writer is primarily the mother's (rather than the father's) son because he continues to be nourished by the mother's *jouissance* and is, thus, able to "emerge from schizophrenic decorporealization" (1980c, 192). Hence the paradoxical position that the "poet"-son occupies as "some-One" who is neither "man" (for " 'man tends to bury himself under words because he still doesn't know how to let the words bury the words' ") nor "woman" (by definition hysterical, a "symptom of symbolic weakness . . . , index of a poorly controlled phallus") (196–97). Associated with the ambiguous, feminine phallicity of the ancient Greek god Dionysus, the avant-garde "poet"-son rejects both the Oedipal injunction to leave the mother "untouched, outside, opposite, against the law" and its Oresteian alternative that seeks to bring the mother—violently—under the Father's law (191). As Kristeva tells us, the avant-garde "poet"-son refuses to forget the mother while continuing to war against her, "leaving a trace of their conflict in the very language he uses" (196). Neither fusing with her, nor "trampling [her] underfoot," he wavers "between the cult of the mother and the playful, laughing, stripping away of its mystery" (192, 196). The avant-garde innovator, then, is "like an anamnestic child" (196), who ceaselessly retrieves the mother only to "swallow her, eat her, dissolve her" (191) or, as Kristeva puts it in her interview with Rossum-Guyon, possess her "as a man possesses the body of his sexual partner" (2007, 133). Which is why the male innovator's anamnestic confrontation with the mother is as triumphant as it is traumatic (1980c, 193). By contrast, Kristeva tells Rossum-Guyon, "[w]hen the author is a woman," such confrontation entails a graver psychotic risk given that "the woman-mother" remains "the ultimate guarantee of her proper sexual identity" (2007, 134).

It is due to the "poet's" incestuous and yet un-procreative relation to the mother[9] that, as Kristeva comes to suggest, "the wife of a 'poet,' of this particular poet, no longer exists."[10] It seems that the revolutionary force of the polylogue opens up a space where a new relationship may arise "out of sexual difference," one that is "diametrically opposed to familial, mothering, and domestic tranquility" (166, 197). Because this new relationship is the product of an explosion (Sollers compares it to "the big bang hypothesis"), the protagonists of the familial story find themselves moving further and further apart: " 'He?' 'She?' Each is split apart, twisted, infinitized, usurping the other's place, giving it back, an enemy, alone, incomprehensible, dissolved, harmonizing, making war again elsewhere, surer, truer" (197–98). As Kristeva explains, the task "he," the polylogizing "poet"-son, sets himself is to invent "a new meaning for love," one impregnated with "negativity, contradiction and conflict" (197). In other words, the innovator/"some One" is by definition a demystifier of love, a *thinker* who exposes (and rejoices in) its constitutive hatred (197). Hence Sollers's invocation of the "impossible couple" par excellence (see Kristeva 1987, 210), the enemy-lovers who survive in eternal sleep precisely through defying the law of the couple: "Romeo? Juliet? They are dissonant," Kristeva reminds us (1980c, 198).

Not surprisingly, this dissonance at the heart of the couple is a reflection of the "poet"-son's loving triumph over the archaic mother. Kristeva admits as much in her analysis of Shakespeare's *Romeo and Juliet*: "The beyond of the couple is a beyond of the mother. Those who believe they have reached it do not cease violating her in the language: they are creators of style, of music. . . ." (1987, 228). They also introduce a new historical time (*trans*finite, *trans*familial), which, in Kristeva's account, is the sole guarantee of the politics of the polylogue that "infuses our identity with a sense of struggle to have us desire social conflict and no longer separate the one from the other" (1980c, 204).

Between the shattered familial time ("the time of reproduction, generations, life and death, the linear-phallic time," 201) and the polyphonic rhythm of the polylogue, there is, however, a temporal modality that, inevitably, one loses sight of. This is what in *Tales of Love* Kristeva will call "the nontime of love," which she defines as "a sort of future perfect," "both instant and eternity, past and future" or, indeed, a form of "abreacted present" in terms of which the hope/promise of a *meeting* between lovers might be conceptualized: "Till tomorrow, forever, as ever, faithfully, eternally as before, as when it will have been, yours . . ." (1987b, 6).

Forgetting and the Writing of the Woman-Stranger

By contrast, in her 2002 chapter on Louis Aragon's *Blanche ou l'oubli* Kristeva foregrounds instead the author's "concern to link differences" (2002, 184). As Kristeva's analysis demonstrates, the links that lie at the heart of "the ethical problem posed by this novel" (213) involve the links between man and woman (beyond the war of the sexes but also beyond "the consensual illusion of the idyllic couple," 184); the links of the (male *or* female) writer with the forgotten, abjected feminine; the links between personal pronouns ("I" and "you" as "my" intimate, real or invented, feared or desired *correspondent*), as well as the links between the novel's narrator and the world or, as Aragon himself puts it, "The Unhappy Crowd" (Aragon, 565).[11] Ultimately, then, what Aragon's *Blanche* affirms, according to Kristeva, is the deeply felt concern over the need "to continue establishing connections at the heart of a livable community" (2002, 203).

As I intend to argue in the remainder of this essay, it is a similar concern that has motivated Kristeva's fictional re*volt*, her post-1990s turn to a genre largely ignored or disparaged by a militant avant-garde due to its representational legacy and its widely acknowledged popularity. Indeed, since 1990 Kristeva has not ceased expressing her dismay over the failure of all secular bonds—amorous, familial, national, political. As she emphasizes in her speech in the context of the Holberg prize award ceremony (2005d),[12] this failure has led to the rise of religious fundamentalism we are currently witnessing and to the culture of death cultivated by religion, politics, and the media alike. In Kristeva's account, it is primarily our "bond to life that is suffering" today (2005e, 430). If, she writes, "peace is in crisis—in Gaza, Jerusalem, Paris, New York . . . , this is because we lack a discourse of life at the beginning of the third millennium" (2005e, 425). After Hannah Arendt, she continues, we seem to have no discourse on the meaning, let alone on the *love* of life (2005e, 426). This is precisely, according to Kristeva, where the value of the novel lies—hence the need to reclaim and renew what for her is its *vital* legacy. "The novel," she reminds us, "since its emergence in the Middle Ages," has defined itself "as a narrative of amorous life" (2005b, 427). It has functioned as the space where life could unfold as love, in other words as the desire for a multiplicity of connections. Because amorous life is the "hearth" of any *vital* imaginary (2005e, 432), the novel for Kristeva has the potential to open up a new configuration of politics: "[t]he need for connection," she writes in *Intimate Revolt*, "might establish another politics, some day" (2002a, 223).

It is in this light that we need to approach Kristeva's increasing interest after the 1990s in the distinct nature of the novel as the instillation of life (in all its enfleshed passion and its singularity) within a shareable narrative. It is also in this light that we need to appreciate her growing concern with the cultural, ritualized act of storytelling and its therapeutic function; the intimate sharing of the word (through the reading and writing of fiction or in the course of an analytic session) that opens trauma to history and binds addresser and addressee into an ephemeral, perhaps, but impassioned community. Examples of this concern abound—I could mention her defense of narration in her critical biography of Hannah Arendt (the first volume of her "Female Genius" trilogy); her very reclamation in this trilogy of the philosophical value of *biography*, in other words, of this form of life that does not fear to question itself in its unfolding as narrative; her sparse but very significant comments on installation as the incarnation (through visual and tactile narration) of human experience (especially, her reading in *La haine et le pardon* of Annette Messager's *Casino*);[13] what is more, her committed rethinking of the value of free-association in the process of analysis and Freud's understanding of it.[14]

This is the wider context, I would argue, in which we need to reflect on Kristeva's turn, in volumes 1 and 2 of *The Powers and Limits of Psychoanalysis*, to Louis Aragon, the political activist and writer of novels at a time when (as he himself admits) the Dadaist and surrealist avant-garde was clearly dismissive of the genre, considering it nothing more than "one of the forms of literary ambition, indeed of a certain *arrivisme*" (Aragon, 403–04).[15] *Blanche ou l'oubli* unfolds consciously as an "apologia" on behalf of the novel, though it may borrow the guise of the "antinovel"; the novel, in other words, that sets out to interrogate its established conventions and practices.[16] "Contemporary man," Aragon writes, "needs the novel. Despite what its critics say." As his narrator goes on to explain, this is because "the novel has become the *I* which organizes the we," a "changeable we, that fades if the novel ceases to exist" (153).

In her own analysis of Aragon's *Blanche ou l'oubli*, Kristeva posits the novel as one of the remaining sites of revolt against the all-encompassing Empire of the Spectacle. "Can the novel now rival television?" she asks (2002, 218). As her committed engagement with the genre suggests, her conviction (or, perhaps, her hope) is that it can, given its ability to preserve a space of thought for each individual subject while, at the same time, reaching "the maximum number of people" (Kristeva 1996i, 241). Indeed, it is the popularity of the novel (an anathema for a militant avant-garde now dated)[17] that Kristeva attempts to reclaim as a response to the personal and collective crisis we are currently facing: "I liken the era in which we live to the fall of the Roman Empire, but without the promise of a new religion," she tells Alain Nicolas and adds: "I look to the novel to offer an imaginary that might correspond to this reality without accommodating the culture of the spectacle. This brings up the question: how can we write a critical, incarnate, sensory narrative that could be transmitted to the masses, a goal that has been the traditional vocation of the novel?" (1996i, 241). Faced with the mass appeal of the spectacle, an appeal based on unreflective immersion, Kristeva turns to Victor Hugo, Stéphane Mallarmé, and Céline in order to reconceptualize the popularity of the novel as a form of affective and sensory contagiousness: "When a state of enthusiasm is attained through immediate access to an undecidable experience that appears to be less concerned with formal problems, it serves as *a magnet of joy, anguish, and pain*," she tells Elisabeth Bélorgey (Kristeva 1996g, 244; my emphasis). According to Kristeva, it is this sympathetic attraction of another's feelings that accounts for the communicability of the novel and the childlike pleasure it can offer.[18] Interestingly, in his defense of the genre, Aragon invokes, in his turn, a similar form of pleasure. The force of the novel, he argues, lies in its ability to revive the inquisitive and hard-to-satisfy child within us (482). This is why it constitutes an important site of resistance against any figure of "adult" authority that, having internalized a system of answers, is no longer capable of doubting. Likewise, in *Intimate Revolt* Kristeva foregrounds the significant contribution of the novel (especially, of those more popular versions of the genre, such as the detective novel) to "keep[ing] the possibility of questioning alive." Hence her insistence in the introduction to this volume that the novel offers "a minimal variant of revolt" (2002a, 4–5).

What attracts Kristeva to Aragon's passionate vindication of the novel in *Blanche ou l'oubli* is not simply his concern with articulating a new semantics of the genre but, more importantly, his conscious attempt to carry out this task through rethinking the writer's eroticized relation with the maternal/feminine. As we have seen, it is precisely this relation that Kristeva has posited at the heart of her 1970s theory of avant-garde writing, a theory I have tried to elucidate with close reference to Kristeva's seminal essay on Sollers's *H*. In contrast to Sollers's anamnestic innovator, however, the "some One" addressing us in Aragon's novel is a senile linguist trying to come to terms with the growing realization that words are tombs to a referent forever lost and human beings no more than speaking machines "turning in the void" (Aragon, 155). This void, as Aragon calls the human experience of forgetting, haunts the narrator from the very opening of the novel and renders impossible the task he has set himself, that is, the retrieval in writing of what Kristeva tells us is "the ultimate referent" in the Aragonian imaginary, namely, woman (2002, 192). What we witness in the course of the novel, instead, is the reluctant betrayal of woman, the inevitable realization on the part of the "poet"-son (who was, as we have seen, triumphant in Sollers) that the object of his love and rage, the source of his *jouissance* and music is and will remain *elsewhere*. Her presence no longer vibrates in the son's writing as the rhythmic breathing of an eroticized, possessed, and, in the final analysis, abjected body but gets lost in a name that is (as all names are) a misnomer and fails to capture her: *Blanche*—or, in other words, the fading of presence, the whiting out of the material feminine body, the impossibility of remembering.

If (in Kristeva's reading) Aragon's *Blanche ou l'oubli* opens new possibilities for avant-garde writing and introduces an alternative, more feminine-inflected future for the novel, this is due to the fact that, in this novel, the avant-garde "poet"-son has to come to terms with his own senility, in other words, with the human inevitability of forgetting. What is more, he needs to accept and internalize his guilt with regard to the "silent and silenced female passion" that his musicated writing (infused with this passion) nevertheless obscures (2002, 194). He, the demystifier of bourgeois love, is also forced to see through his own pretensions to love which turns out to be a barely disguised arrogance toward a femininity that ends up being contained through being mimetically usurped. This is how Kristeva articulates the unconscious logic that drives the "poet"-son's incestuous game with the maternal/feminine, a logic that Aragon consciously sets out to expose:

> In effect, if "I" [the "poet"-son] am at once mother and the one who possesses her and cancels her out in image-language, all other women can only be foreigners to this inherent complicity. Yet "I" prefer the one who remains truly foreign, "I" choose the true foreigner, a woman who in any case comes from far away, remains distant, and whom "I" keep at a distance. The foreigner protects me, she is the

> proof that I am sovereign in the incestuous solitude of my game; in this sense I love her. (2002, 216)

Whereas in her reading of Sollers's *H* Kristeva never comes to question the othering of the "poet"-son's wife who is "the foreigner" kept out of the love-hate game between mother and son, in her analysis of Aragon's novel she foregrounds precisely the function and fate of the *other* woman:

> As if the imaginary and above all the novelistic confrontation with the primordial model, the archaic idol, could only be pursued provided another woman, any other woman, be kept foreign, made an eternal foreigner. The foreigner being the one who, by definition, has no access to the maternal language, or very little access, or never full access: a foreigner to the mother-son mystery that the writer has precisely set out to reveal for better or worse. Long live foreigners, in short, since they do not touch the essential, since they leave the writer alone with the essential. (2002, 216)

In Aragon's novel, "Blanche" turns out to be the maternal, eroticized phantasm the narrator himself has constructed, a phantasm behind which, as he comes to realize, his wife (whose real name is never shared with us) stifles (547–50). It is because the novel's ultimate gesture (through the narrator's own desire for atonement) is to acknowledge the pain, the frustration, the humiliation of the *other* woman that the wave of avant-garde "deconstructive rage" carrying through (as we have seen) Sollers's *H* "takes on" in Aragon "the tonality of tenderness" (2002, 183). As Kristeva puts it, "we perceive . . . a serenity beyond melancholy, a certain appeasement, finally, that confers something feminine upon the Aragonian imaginary" (2002, 183). Thus, the novel as Aragon retheorizes it refuses to posit itself as "a defense against the feminine" (2002, 183) and unfolds, instead, as a *signaling to* the feminine,[19] a feminine that is neither expelled nor usurped but allowed its own space. Interestingly, this *elsewhere* of the feminine in Aragon is the space of another writing, the *other* woman's writing that gradually takes over the novel so that the narrator comes to experience it (*and* himself) as "the book of *one* woman" (Aragon, 546–47).[20]

As Kristeva notes, one of the strengths of Aragon's self-reflexive novel is that it shifts the emphasis from the "poet"-son's struggle against the archaic mother to "the very peculiar jealousy" *he* experiences when he finds out that his wife (meant to remain, as we have seen, an outsider to this intimate struggle) *also* writes (2002, 215): "And yet she wrote words," the narrator tells us, "for weeks, months, words that were evidently not useful in the way words usually are" (Aragon, 398). This is why he comes to conclude that "what Blanche wrote . . . was precisely what she did not want or could not tell me, in other words, she wrote *against me*" (396).[21] Taking her cue from what, she acknowledges, is Aragon's "courage to unveil" this "more radical" form of jealousy that can erupt between man and woman (the "poet"-son and his wife) (2002, 215), Kristeva asks: "What is intolerable about a woman writing?" And she goes on to argue:

> That a woman too is confronting this ungraspable, archaic feminine that all imaginaries want to apprehend, appropriating this mystery, this strangeness that the (male) imaginary strives to capture: this destabilizes the (male) writer. . . . If a woman writes (especially his own wife), this means that a male writer is not the holder of the feminine enigma, that the male writer is not the real woman, the Bovary finally unveiled and rendered to herself, but that another woman—a stranger—pretends to explore, to steal the dark continent of the lost maternal. (2002, 215–16)

Significantly, in *Blanche ou l'oubli* the narrator is forced to confront this truth through the intervention of another woman-stranger, namely, Marie-Noire, the rebel-daughter who avenges the mother, spoils the son's solitary pleasure, and beats him in his own game. Initially, Marie-Noire (as her name suggests) is presented as the inverse side of maternal, idealized Blanche. Young, beautiful, yet unsophisticated and flat (the stereotype of the bimbo), she is introduced as a character within the narrator's unfolding narrative, one he invents to help him retrace and understand Blanche, who, we are told, has abandoned him. As the novel develops, however, Marie-Noire comes to usurp the authorial position to such an extent that the narrator no longer knows who has invented whom: "I thought I was imagining Marie-Noire, and, look, she is the one imagining me. She is imagining everything. The world. The totality of life" (Aragon, 135). What is more, she too begins to write and, in writing, she seduces the narrator's memories of Blanche elsewhere: "Marie-Noire, you are crossing the line. It is I who remembers Blanche. It is through me that you have what you know about her. The only thing I have asked from you is your female intuition that can understand another woman . . . ," the narrator complains. To which Marie-Noire replies:

> Is this what you think? Yet, whenever I seduce you further than you desire, you shout that what I'm saying is not convincingly true. Deep down Blanche, for you, needs to remain a mystery . . . the inexplicable. For you, woman is what cannot be explained. If woman could be explained, then what would happen to you men? You could

> be wrong, right? How convenient—is it not?—the invocation of the eternal feminine! (Aragon, 372)

Because of the challenge the woman-stranger constitutes in the male narrator's monologic invention of the feminine, the threat of murder (a murder taken for granted and repetitively staged as an eroticized game in Sollers) haunts Aragon's novel from the very beginning. Marie-Noire is, indeed, strangled at the end of the narrative at precisely the moment when she is ready to define her own "elsewhere" as the other-directed future of motherhood.[22] Faced with the news of her murder, the narrator does not hesitate to assume her murderer's guilt, having already acknowledged the compulsive attraction of this act:

> The experience of vertigo over a woman who you suddenly feel absent, other, a stranger. . . . If a madman who resembles me, one day, years and years later, in his attempt to understand someone called Blanche or someone other, were able to stifle her in his arms, to strangle her with his own two hands, to dig with his fingers within her flesh, her heart or her soul, believe me, oh!, yes, believe me, I will pity him as much as my own self. (Aragon, 520)

According to Kristeva, if the drama of the woman-stranger we witness in Aragon permits us to retheorize the novel as "the writing of a woman," this is due to Aragon's tender address to the feminine other (including *his own* feminine other) (2002, 214). In fact, it is Aragon's concern with the very question of *address*, the desperate yet passionate correspondence between an "I" and a fleeting though indispensable "you," that seems to lay the foundations for a feminine future for the novel.[23] What recommends this future (which, I will argue, Kristeva, in her turn, *is* in the process of inventing) is that it promises to help us reconceptualize the "human problem" no longer in terms of "self-knowledge" but as the difficulty and necessity of seeing and understanding others (Aragon, 530). Such future, Kristeva (following Aragon) seems to suggest, owes itself to "the unhappy crowd."[24] What is more, it cannot but hold an alternative fate for the woman-stranger who will "not always, not necessarily" (she insists) "allow herself to be strangled" (2002, 216). If this future appears all-too-tentative, this may have something to do with what for Aragon remains the anomalous nature of the novel, its loathing of norms or rules, its staking in impossibility (Aragon, 522–23, 527–28). To me, however, this future in the feminine that Kristeva attempts to claim *in the name of* the novel sounds more like a bet she, Kristeva the theorist, makes against herself, perhaps, and against her readers: "what if . . . ?" she ponders playfully in her analysis of Aragon. *What if* the woman-stranger "becomes a psychoanalyst and in addition continues writing (in the absolute sense)?" (2002, 217).

A *Vital* Theory *for* the Novel: The Circle of Cor(ps)respondence and the Diagonal

As I tried to emphasize in the previous section, the significance of Kristeva's analysis of Aragon's *Blanche ou l'oubli* lies in her insistence that the writer's reconfigured relation to the feminine goes hand in hand with his commitment to rethink the problem of personal as well as communal links—"beyond the annihilation that acts intrinsically in vision and in words and that makes us what we are: namely, forgetful beings, strangers, stranglers" (2002, 184). According to Kristeva, Aragon's *apologia* on behalf of the novel unfolds on a hypothesis that we cannot afford to ignore: "And what if this feminine (the other's or mine), were simply the last barricade, recasting the virtuosity of devastation into a bitter dignity, violence into tenderness, so that a connection could still be possible?" she asks (184). If, in her own return to the amorous legacy of the novel, she seems determined to pursue this hypothesis, this is not merely out of a conviction (which she shares with Aragon) that a rethinking of the novel from the position of the feminine might raise its contemporary stakes, (re)constituting it as "the modern version of the link" (184). It is also because a more feminine-inflected theory of the novel might contribute to what, in her view, is a major task for us today: namely, the task of conceptualizing and rendering possible a link that remains "*free* in its polyphony and disabused of its game" (184; emphasis added).

At issue, then, in Kristeva's fictional re*volt* is, on the one hand, the reconfiguration of links that are self-reflexive (indeed, self-questioning; links "disabused of [their] game," as she puts it) and that do not constrain or imprison because they do not exclude the possibility of other links. On the other hand, at stake is precisely the cohesion and viability of the social contract and, hence, our ability to "maintain the link beyond [and despite] the impossibility of the link" (2002, 184). At stake, in other words, is our bond with what denies, resists, cancels, and escapes all bonds—be it the unrepresentable affect or act, the secret that breaks the chain of communication, "la chose sexuelle" (as Kristeva calls the sexual drive whose carrier wave is the death drive) (2005d, 20), "elle" (what we have discussed as the abjected maternal/feminine),[25] or, indeed, the singular and unshareable vulnerability of each one of us.

In one of her clinical accounts Kristeva describes the case of a bulimic patient who is rid of her symptoms when, through the narrativization of the violence taking her psyche apart, she learns how to "be tender with . . . her instinctual being" (2000c, 64). It is significant (and the psychoanalyst draws our attention to this fact) that the poetry the patient wrote before the beginning of the treatment proves to be useless in her struggle against the deadly symptoms. As Kristeva explains, "[t]he poetic writing, tangled in itself, phobic, and apparently protective, was a powerless mausoleum in the face of the destructive attacks" (64). What the patient needs is a push "outside, to the cultural or historical"—which is what the narrative of free association offers her (62). "Is language the tenderness of the *parlêtre*?" Kristeva wonders. "*Tender to the parlêtre* through free association? Beyond hallucination and cruelty, isn't language (*or better yet, narrative*) within therapy a reconciliation between word-presentation and thing-presentation that makes us perceive—unconsciously—that *meaning communicated to someone else* shelters us (temporarily) from death?"(2002c, 64).[26]

It is important to note at this point that if, for Kristeva, the narrative imaginary is vital for us today, this is because the life it helps us tend to is one "that coexists with the violence of desire" (2005e, 430). It is no surprise, therefore, that in the most recent volume of *The Powers and Limits of Psychoanalysis* she moves on to oppose "the narrative of cruelty (echoing Artaud's theatre of cruelty)" that unfolds in the context of analysis and in what she calls "le roman du Sujet"[27] to Paul Ricoeur's hermeneutic account of narrative, which, in her view, reduces analysis "to a simple dialogue between two psyches" (2002a, 26) and has "propelled the medicalization of the analytic cure" (2005b, 284). In response to this reduction, Kristeva proceeds to counter Ricoeur's theorization of narrative as intersubjectivity with the Proustian understanding of the novel as transubstantiation. From a Proustian perspective, she insists, narrative is "this delicate art of putting flesh into words" (2005b, 314). Irrespective of the context of the act of storytelling (be it the analyst's couch, a novel, or an installation), narrative is a renewal of our bonds with enfleshed being, a process of incarnation through which the event of discourse comes to be inextricable "from the passion of the live body: its flesh, its perceptions, its (familial, social, historical) connections and dis-connections" (2005c, 617–18).[28] This is why narrative, according to Kristeva, constitutes one of the last vestiges of a site of intimacy that she seeks to reclaim, namely, experience—a concept that (it needs to be reminded) she was very cautious about in the 1970s (see 1984, 195–234). In her discussion of installation at the opening of her *Sense and Non-Sense of Revolt* Kristeva writes:

> In an installation, the entire body is called to participate through its senses—sight, of course, but also hearing, touch, sometimes smell. As if instead of creating an object, these artists seek to situate us in a space at the border of the sacred and ask us not to contemplate images but to commune with beings, an unquestionably tentative and sometimes unvarnished communion but a call nonetheless. And seeing these young artists' installations . . . I got the impression that . . . they were communicating this: the ultimate goal of art is perhaps what was once celebrated as incarnation. I mean by that the desire to make one feel—through abstraction, form, color, volume, sensation—a real experience. (11)

This need for a real experience, which Kristeva places at the heart of the Society of the Spectacle and which she sees as inextricable from narration, demands (as she emphasizes) a turn away from the privileging of the concept of the text. As she puts it, it is important to go "beyond the notion of text—the elaboration of which I have contributed to, along with so many others—which has become a form of dogma in the best universities in France, as well as in the United States and other, more exotic places. In its stead, I will introduce the notion of experience, which includes the pleasure principle as well as the rebirth of meaning for the other" (2000c, 8).

It is because both of these aspects of experience are mobilized in narrative that Kristeva sees in it the promise of reviving the mystical body of the ethical community Immanuel Kant envisaged.[29] Palpitating with desire, drives, affect, sensations, narrative as incarnate being (i.e., experience) is the carrier of "an unsettling strangeness" (2000c, 66), the mystical index of an "elsewhere" that remains unrepresentable yet does not cease to be shareable among subjects who change and are reborn in their attempt to tend to(ward) it. This is why Kristeva, *contra* Ricoeur, insists that the community formed by analysts and analysands is not based on "the complacent communication of ego to ego . . . but [on] an altered subject's relationship to another being" (2000c, 67). As she goes on to explain,

> [t]here is a piling up of otherness: the addressee is an other-being; 'I' is an other-being; these others are altered by contemplating each other. Far from being absolutized as the summit of a pyramid from which the other gazes at me with an implacable and severe eye, the problematic of psychoanalytical alterity opens a space of interlocking alterities. Only this interlocking of alterities can give subjectivity an infinite dimension, a dimension of creativity. (2000c, 67)

Is this space of interlocking alterities a promising refiguration for what we seem to be lacking today, namely, a conscience of belonging, a culture of staying-with?[30] I would argue it is, because it reclaims the value of connection *contra* the fetishization of difference in our terror-haunted societies but also *contra* any (political, philosophical, aesthetic or, indeed, amorous) idylls of communality. In her discussion of *Murder in Byzantium*, one of her most recent novels, Kristeva describes this connection as the intimacy shared by "subjects in transverberation," in other words, subjects who are "diffracted into a mosaic of confessions, associations, inadvertent actions or speech" (2005c, 610) and whose sense of belonging remains attuned to what Stephanie (the fictional protagonist in her detective novels) calls "se voyager" (617).[31] If the shape traced by the interlocking intimacy of these travelers is a circle, this does not resemble the "wheel of smiles" that Kristeva reads into Leonardo da Vinci's *The Virgin and Child with St. Anne and John the Baptist*. It is not a utopian dream returning from "the imaginary prehistory of the individual," a circle formed by a series of mirror-effects: that is, the return of the son's into the mother's gaze, the reflection of her love into his love.[32] It needs, rather, to be rethought as the circle of co-response that interests Kristeva in her account of Paul Celan's correspondence with his wife, Gisèle (2005a, 577–88). This is the circle traced by an amorous bond, a gesture that "embraces the bodies" of the correspondents and relieves the fragmentation experienced by the subject of/to the "poetic explosion" (2005a, 579, 581). This is why it retraces community outside containment or persecuting enclosure (581): community, then, as precisely a *cor(ps)respondence*, that is, as the embodied act of address ("to no-one, to nothing," Kristeva emphasizes, 586) and the patient waiting for (or the attentive listening to) a response (579).[33]

What recommends Kristeva's refiguration of community, however, needs to be sought outside the circle of loving address and love-full response or transference/countertransference in analytic terms. This is, in fact, where the true significance of the novel lies, for the secret it shares with us is no other than the "Freudian discovery": namely, the recognition that all love is destined to fail (2005f, 477). Indeed, if, as Freud contends, finding a love object is, in reality, the *re*finding of a phantasmatic object forever lost (1975, 88), then the subject is inevitably caught in the vicissitudes of an unfulfillable desire for (re)possession. Art, literature, and especially the novel, according to Kristeva, have taken up the task to trace the doomed destinies of love and to work through the suffering resulting from the absence of an *enduring* love object. The novel, then, confronts us with the "unbearability of love" as well as with love's (heroic or pathetic) attempts to disguise, evade, or deny its failures (2005f, 477).

Yet, in Kristeva's account, the unbearability and unendurability of love that the novel echoes in "composing and recomposing the laws and figures of the amorous adventure" are no "cause for desolation" but a chance for the creation of new bonds (2005f, 477). In her analysis of *Murder in Byzantium* Kristeva conceptualizes the opening of the circle of *co(rps)-response* in the figure of a diagonal that traverses the intimate, connecting it with sites and stakes *beyond*, "philosophical, ethical, political" (2005c, 616). The diagonal, then, stands for whatever introduces an attitude of detachment from the amorous link. It cuts through the circle formed by interlocking alterities in order to open it up to what Kristeva discusses as Colette's atheist conviction: namely, the belief that there is no "absolute object" and, hence, there is no amorous bond and no dogma or Truth that can be placed beyond questioning or irony (2005b, 338). "It is this traversal, this diagonal," Kristeva argues, "that constitutes the true flesh of the novel of the subject" (2005c, 616). As she explains responding to a question by

Pierre-Louis Fort, the novel of the subject continues to focus on "stories of the Ego." These, however, are in this context "played and played out, put in perspective, detached, endlessly reduplicated" (2005c, 619). In other words, the novel of the subject literally *plays* "the card of the Ego . . . like a card in a game" that can be staked and lost (2005c, 619–20). The diagonal line in Kristeva's figuration emerges as the possibility of this loss cutting across "the circle of confinement of the self for itself" (2005c, 617). It is, therefore, the image of what Kristeva calls "dépassionnement,"[34] that is, the traversal of passion, the necessary checking of the fervor of devotion through questioning and self-questioning, the insufflation of irony into the very heart of the Ego and its desire for an absolute, ideal form of communion. Irony, Kristeva tells us, does not involve an attitude of "rejection" but one of "distant participation: inside and outside, the outside of the inside" (2005c, 622). In *Murder in Byzantium*, the diagonality of irony is thrown into relief through the protagonist-narrator's dispassionate attitude that keeps her in critical (though tender) complicity with "the Unhappy Crowd." In Aragon's *Blanche ou l'oubli* it (re)traces itself in the *other* woman's writing, which cuts through the phantasmatic bond between mother-and-son and reinvests the amorous force of the feminine "elsewhere."

"What, then, remains of our loves?" Kristeva asks (2005f, 471). Laughter, she will go on to reply—be it the laughter of *tender* irony or the laughter owed to Aragon's "unhappy crowd," a laughter that will mark the possibility of "a humanity-to-come" (2005f, 476). This humanity (which, like the world, needs to be invented)[35] will assume the task of remaining lucid both in the fragile experience of its strangeness as well as in the most passionate of its bonds. "There is an illusion that I, on my part, would like to preserve," Kristeva writes at the end of "Que reste-t-il de nos amours?," "that of a humanity capable of laughing at love the moment it is joyous with love" (2005f, 478). It is not hard to see why for her the novel, this Aragonian anomaly in the feminine, is the vital, shareable, and self-questioning site for the unfolding of such an illusion.

Notes

1. All translations from this text are mine.
2. Kristeva 1980c, 196.
3. Kristeva writes: "The 'author,' as I perceive him through my reading *H*, keeps me awake during my negative vigil" (165).
4. Kristeva writes: "A breathing movement thus coincides with the attitude of the speaking subject and the fluctuating range of denotation. The next breathing movement introduces the speaking subject's new attitude and a new sphere of denotation. The human body and meaning, inseparable as they are, thus fashion a dismembered score" (1980c, 169).

5. "For this polylogical 'I' speaks of a *before:* before logic, before language, before being," Kristeva writes (1980c, 188–89).

6. See the following passage from "The Novel as Polylogue": "This heterogeneous object is a body, because it is a *text.* I have written down this much abused word and insist upon it so that you might understand how much risk there is in a text, how much nonidentity, nonauthenticity, impossibility, and corrosiveness it holds for those who chose to see themselves within it" (163).

7. See chapter 13 entitled "Four Signifying Practices" in Kristeva 1984, 90–106.

8. Kristeva concludes her essay thus: "This is all possible because *someone* refashioned his 'I' and his language into a music adequate to the continuing, splintering times. But also and at the same time, this is possible because *H* has gone beyond the *One* in order to be written, and thus calls on every 'one' to venture out into the explosion that surrounds us, moves through us, refashions us and that sooner or later we shall have to hear . . ." (1980c, 207–08).

9. Kristeva writes: "The procreator, an unconscious genetrix, who accomplishes the Phallic Mother's desire, is thus the antonym of the 'actor,' of the 'poet' " (1980c, 199).

10. See Kristeva 1980c, 166. One cannot miss the irony of Kristeva's self-reflexive invocation of the wife of "this particular poet" who willingly submits to (and is dissolved in) the eruptive rhythm of the polylogue.

11. In English in the original.

12. All passages quoted from this volume are my own translations.

13. See Kristeva 2005, "Au *Casino*, ou Comment une femme joue la condition humaine" in *La haine et le pardon*, 527–37.

14. See especially her very important chapter on "The Metamorphoses of 'Language' in the Freudian Discovery (Freudian Models of Language)" in *Sense and Non-Sense*, 32–64.

15. All translations from this text are mine.

16. See the introduction by Giorgios Spanos, the translator of the novel in Greek, in Aragon, 13.

17. In "Quelle avant-garde aujourd'hui?" Kristeva argues that the "sacred Puritanism of the avant-garde which dominated for a century, from roughly 1860 to 1960 . . . in the world of the spectacle, is swept aside and [proves to be] totally inefficacious." In Kristeva 2007, 138.

18. In this context, Kristeva draws a distinction between two different currents in postwar literature: on the one hand, the more avant-garde "neutral writing" of which the writings of Samuel Beckett can be considered typical; on the other hand, what she calls a "Plutonian" current, which, she argues, "is more similar to *contagious writing*, the postmodern, communicable writing I mentioned earlier while discussing the 'popular' novel." See *Julia Kristeva Interviews*, edited by Ross Guberman (New York: Columbia University Press), 245–46.

19. In the conclusion of her essay Kristeva writes: "Rather, I leave you with this because this scattered novel investigates the major questions of being and its nihilation. . . . Because it is inflected and ends with gentleness, without expelling the feminine, and because, beyond the incompatibility and the antics, it signals to the feminine." See Kristeva 2002, 218–19.

20. I am also citing Kristeva's comment on this passage: "Could one conclude by saying that the novel is the apotheosis of the humiliated woman from whom the narrator asks forgiveness, seeing himself as nothing other than a book, the 'book of one woman'?" (2002, 199).

21. Kristeva comments: "Blanche does not write against him, as the narcissistic husband supposes for an instant in order to protect himself. She writes *elsewhere*, exploring her own elsewhere, where he is not . . ." (2002, 215).

22. Marie-Noire chooses to give birth alone, abandoning, in her turn, both the narrator (frustrated, in *medias res* of his narrative) and her boyfriend.

23. See Aragon, 54, 390, 395, 432–33, 437, 441, 462, 550. It is also interesting that Aragon situates his novel within the neglected tradition of the epistolary novel. See, for example, 544.

24. Aragon concludes his novel thus: "Till now novelists have contented themselves with producing a parody of the world. Now we need to invent it. TO THE UNHAPPY CROWD" (565).

25. Kristeva 2002, 214–19. See also Kristeva 2000c, 65 and Kristeva 2005d, 20.

26. My emphasis on lines 2–5.

27. That is, the novel of the Subject, which she opposes to the novel of the Ego. See 2005c, 610.

28. In *Thérèse mon amour*, her fictional biography of Saint Teresa of Avila, Kristeva's narrator, Sylvia Leclercq, refers to fiction as "la représentation narrative sensible" (i.e., sensible or sense-based narrative representation; 2008a, 114).

29. See Kristeva's brief but important references to the Kantian *corpus mysticum* in 2005b, 409, 610.

30. In her interview with Arnaud Spire, Kristeva argues that "Left-wing movements lack a culture of 'staying with,' . . . which should be thought of not as the culture of neoliberalism and management, but as the culture of care and modernization" (2003a, 23).

31. This is an ungrammatical form that is difficult to translate. It makes "to travel" a reflexive verb, suggesting that the action denoted by the verb involves the self and returns to the self.

32. See Kristeva's "The Wheel of Smiles" in *New Maladies of the Soul* (1995, 154, 155, 158). The "circle" is another figuration in Kristeva's work of what throughout this essay has been denoted through a variety of congruent terms, such as: "link," "bond," "connection," "community," "interlocking intimacy."

33. In the same vein, Aragon's narrator acknowledges the need "I have for an interlocutor. This tragedy of *you*. I take myself to be another who is listening to me. I speak to the wall. Or do I predict that there will be a *you*? The correspondent." See Aragon, 53.

34. In "La passion selon la maternité" Kristeva discusses maternity as the paradigm of what appears to be "the impossible": that is, the coexistence of an impassioned relatedness to the other with the serene freedom of detachment. See 2005b, 175–97.

35. See note 24.

Works Cited

Adorno, Theodor. 1997. *Aesthetic Theory*. Edited by Gretel Adorno and Rolf Tiedemann. Translated by Robert Hullot-Kentor. Minneapolis: University of Minnesota Press.

Adriaens, Mark. 1981. "Ideology and Literary Production: Kristeva's Poetics." In *Semiotics and Dialectics: Ideology and the Text*, edited by Peter Zima, 179–220. Amsterdam: Benjamins.

Agoston-Nikolova, E. 1999. "The World Is Vast: Bulgarian Exile Writers between Two Cultures." *Studies in Slavic Literature and Poetics* 34: 3–10.

Anderson, Pamela Sue. 2000. "Writing on Exiles and Excess: Toward a New Form of Subjectivity." In *Self, Same, Other: Re-Visioning the Subject in Literature and Theology*, 106–24. Sheffield, UK: Sheffield Academic Press.

Anonymous. 1994. "*The Old Man and the Wolves*." *Publishers Weekly* 241 (43): 52.

———. 2005. "*Murder in Byzantium*." *Publishers Weekly* 252 (48): 35.

Aragon, Louis. 1987. *Μπλανς ή η Λησμονιά*. Μετ. Γιώργος Σπανός. Αθήνα: Εξάντας.

Arendt, Hannah. (1958) 1998. *The Human Condition*. Chicago: University of Chicago Press.

———. 1989. *Lectures on Kant's Political Philosophy*. Edited by Ronald Beiner. Chicago: University of Chicago Press.

Atack, Margaret. 1997. "The Silence of the Mandarins: Writing the Intellectual and May 68 in *Les Samouraïs*." *Paragraph: The Journal of the Modern Critical Theory Group* 20 (3): 240–57.

Bastiaenen, Etienne. 1990. "Génération Samouraïs." *La Revue nouvelle* 46 (10): 90–91.

Bataille, Georges. 1986. *Story of the Eye*. Translated by Joachim Neugroschal. Harmondsworth, England: Penguin Books.

Beardsworth, Sara. 2004. "Kristeva's Idea of Sublimation." *The Southern Journal of Philosophy* 42 (Supplement: Spindel Conference 2003 on "Julia Kristeva's Ethical and Political Thought," edited by Sara Beardsworth and Mary Beth Mader): 122–36.

Benjamin, Walter. 1977. *The Origin of German Tragic Drama*. Trans. J. Osborne. London: NLB.

Berglund, Briggite. 2000. "Desire and Devices: On Women Detectives in Fiction." In *The Art of Detective Fiction*, edited by Warren Chernaik, Martin Swales, and Robert Vilain, 138–15. New York: St. Martin's Press.

Birley, Anthony R. 2005. *The Roman Government of Britain*. New York: Oxford University Press.

Bjelic, Dusan I. 2004. "The Balkans and the 'History of Shit.'" *Eurozine* http://www.eurozine.com/articles/2004-06-11-bjelic-en.html. Accessed March 22, 2011.

Bodin, Helena. 2009. "Seeking Byzantium on the Borders of Narration, Identity, Space and Time in Julia Kristeva's Novel *Murder in Byzantium*." *Nordlit: Tidsskrift i litteratur og kultur* 24: 31–43.

"Bogomil." *Encyclopedia Britannica Online*. Encyclopedia Britannica, 2011. http://www.britannica.com/EBchecked/topic/71461/Bogomils. Accessed May 16, 2011.

Boiadjiev, Tzotcho. 1992. "Dialogichnijat printsip na istoriko-kulturnoto isledvane." [The Dialogical Principle of Historic Cultural Research]. In *Avgustin i Dekart* [St. Augustine and Descartes]. 91–119. Sofia: Sofia University Press.

Bové, Carol Mastrangelo. 2006. *Language and Politics in Julia Kristeva: Literature, Art, Therapy*. Albany: State University of New York Press.

Brooksbank Jones, Anny. 1993. "Julia Kristeva and Her Old Man, Between Optimism and Despair." *Textual Practice* 7 (1): 1–12.

Butler, Judith. 1989. "The Body Politics of Julia Kristeva." *Hypatia* 3 (3): 104–18.

———. 1993. "The Body Politics of Julia Kristeva." In *Ethics, Politics, and Difference in Julia Kristeva's Writing*, edited by Kelly Oliver, 164–78. New York and London: Routledge.

Cairns, Francis. 1980. *Tibullus: A Hellenistic Poet at Rome*. Cambridge, UK: Cambridge University Press.

Cavarero, Adriana. 2000. *Relating Narratives: Storytelling and Selfhood*. New York: Routledge.

Chen, Szu-Chin Hestia. 2008. *French Feminist Theory Exemplified Through the Novels of Julia Kristeva; The Bridge from Psychoanalytic Theory to Literary Production*. Lewiston: The Edwin Mellen Press.

Colette. (1922) 2006. *Claudine's House*. Translated by Andrew Brown. London: Hesperus Press.

Crownfield, David, ed. 1992. *Body/Text in Julia Kristeva: Religion, Women and Psychoanalysis*. Albany: State University of New York Press.

Davis, Colin. 2002. "Psychoanalysis, Detection, and Fiction: Julia Kristeva's Detective Novels." *Contemporary French and Francophone Studies* 6 (2): 294–306.

———. 2003. *After Poststructuralism: Reading, Stories, Theory*. New York: Routledge.

de Beauvoir, Simone. 1957. *The Mandarins*. Translated by Leonard M. Friedman. London: Collins.

de Lauretis, Teresa. 1989. "The Female Body and Heterosexual Presumption." *Semiotica* 67: 259–79.

de Nooy, Juliana. 1998. "How to Keep Your Head When Everyone Else Is Losing Theirs: Translating *Possession* into Revolt in Kristeva." In *After the Revolution, On Kristeva*, edited by John Lechte and Mary Zournazi, 47–61. Woolloomooloo, Australia: Artspace Visual Arts Centre.

———. 2003. "How to Keep Your Head When All About You Are Losing Theirs: Translating Possession into Revolt in Kristeva." In *The Kristeva Critical Reader*, edited by John Lechte and Mary Zournazi, 113–29. Edinburgh: Edinburgh University Press.

de Sherbinin, Julie W. 1997. *Chekhov and Russian Religious Culture: The Poetics of the Marian Paradigm*. Evanston: Northwestern University Press.

Debord, Guy. (1967) 1992. *La Société du spectacle*. Paris: Gallimard.

———. 1994. *The Society of the Spectacle*. Translated by Donald Nicholson-Smith, New York: Zone Books.

Dolar, Mladen. 1991. "I shall be with you on your wedding night." *October* 58: 5–23.

Donadey, Anne. 1993. "Julia Kristeva, *Le Vieil homme et les loups*." *The French Review* 67 (1): 157.

Dubois, Richard. 1990. "*Les Samouraïs*. Par Julia Kristeva." *Relations* 562: 188–89.

———. 1991. *General Psychological Theory: Papers on Metapsychology*. New York: Touchstone.

Eco, Umberto. 1992. *Interpretation and Overinterpretation*. Edited by Stefan Collini. Cambridge: Cambridge University Press.

———. 1994. *The Name of the Rose*. Translated by William Weaver. San Diego, New York, and London: Harvest Books.

Edelstein, Marilyn. 1992. "Metaphor, Meta-Narrative, and Mater-Narrative in Kristeva's 'Stabat Mater.'" In *Body/Text in Julia Kristeva*, edited by David Crownfield, 27–52. Albany: State University of New York Press.

Edmundson, Mark. 1998. "*Possessions*." *New York Times Book Review*, April 5: 35.

Enjolras, Laurence. 1998. "*Possessions*." *The French Review* 71: 676–67.

Enterline, Lynn. 2006. *The Rhetoric of the Body from Ovid to Shakespeare*. Cambridge, UK: Cambridge University Press.

Evans, Dylan. 1996. *An Introductory Dictionary of Lacanian Psychoanalysis*. London: Routledge.

F., C. 1991. "*Le vieil homme et les loups*." *Lire* 193: 108.

Feldherr, Andrew. 2010. *Playing Gods: Ovid's Metamorphoses and the Politics of Fiction*. New York: Columbia University Press.

Fletcher, John, and Andrew E. Benjamin, eds. 1990. *Abjection, Melancholia and Love: The Work of Julia Kristeva*. London: Routledge.

Fraser, Nancy. 1990. "The Uses and Abuses of French Discourse Theories for Feminist Politics." *boundary 2* 17 (2): 82–101.

Freud, Sigmund. 1966. "Femininity." In *The Complete Introductory Lectures on Psychoanalysis,* translated by James Strachey, 576–99. New York: W.W. Norton & Company.

———. 1975. *Three Essays on the Theory of Sexuality*. Translated by James Strachey. New York: Basic Books.

———. 1981. "A Note Upon the 'Mystic Writing-Pad.'" In *The Standard Edition of the Complete Psychological Works of Sigmund Freud*, Vol. XIX, translated by James Strachey, 227–32. London: The Hogarth Press.

———. 1989. *The Freud Reader*. Edited by Peter Gay. New York: W.W. Norton and Company.

———. 2005. *Civilization and Its Discontents*. Translated by James Strachey. New York: W.W. Norton & Company.

Gehr, Richard. 1990. "A Man and a Woman." *The Village Voice*, December 11: S31.

Girard, René. 1979. *Violence and the Sacred*. Translated by Patrick Gregory. Baltimore: The Johns Hopkins University Press.

———. 1987. *Things Hidden Since the Foundation of the World*. Translated by Stephen Bann and Michael Metteer. Palo Alto, CA: Stanford University Press.

———. 1989. *The Scapegoat*. Translated by Yvonne Freccero. Baltimore: The Johns Hopkins University Press.

———. 2001. *I See Satan Fall Like Lightning*. Translated by James G. Williams. Maryknoll, NY: Orbis Books.

———. 2011. *Sacrifice*. Translated by Matthew Pattillo and David Dawson. East Lansing, MI: Michigan State University Press.

Gleize, Mélanie. 2005. "En Croisade contre les croisés: *Meurtre à Byzance* de Julia Kristeva." *Spirale* 201: 48–49.

Greaney, Michael. 2008. "Violence and the Sacred in the Fiction of Julia Kristeva." *Theology and Sexuality* 14 (3): 293–304.

Hernández Martín, Jorge. 1995. *Readers and Labyrinths: Detective Fiction in Borges, Bustos Domecq, and Eco*. New York: Garland Publishing.

Herrin, Judith. 2007. *Byzantium: The Surprising Life of a Medieval Empire*. Princeton and Oxford: Princeton University Press.

Hill, Leslie. 1990. "Julia Kristeva: Theorizing the Avant-Garde?" In *Abjection, Melancholia, and Love: The Work of Julia Kristeva*, edited by John Fletcher and Andrew Benjamin, 137–56. London and New York: Routledge.

Hite, Molly. 2007. "Yeah, Baby." *The Women's Review of Books* 24 (1): 26–27.

Holquist, Michael. 1971. "Whodunit and Other Questions: Metaphysical Detective Stories in Post-War Fiction." *New Literary History* 3 (1): 135–56.

Hood, Roger. 2002. *The Death Penalty: A Worldwide Perspective*. Oxford: Oxford University Press.

Hooper, Brad. 1998. "*Possessions*." *Booklist* 94 (12): 982.

Howard, Maureen. 1992. "*The Samurai*." *Yale Review* 81 (2): 134.

Hughes-Hallet, Lucy. 1992. "Egghead Out of Her Shell; Julia Kristeva, Once the Darling of the Paris Avant-Garde, Explains Why She Now Thinks Individuals Are More Interesting Than Isms." *The Independent*, February 9: 26.

Irons, Glenwood, ed. 1995. *Feminism in Women's Detective Fiction*. Toronto: University of Toronto Press.

Irvine, Ann. 1994. "*The Old Man and the Wolves*." *Library Journal* 119 (21): 132.

———. 1998. "*Possessions*." *Library Journal* 123 (2): 111.

Jansen, Ludger. 2007. "Aristotle's Categories." *Topoi* 26: 153–58.

Jones, Kaylie. 1993. "Psychoanalyst's First Attempt at a Novel Inspires a Yawn of Boredom." *The Los Angeles Times*, March 1: E3.

Judt, Tony. 1992. "*The Samurai* by Julia Kristeva." *Book World* XXII (45): 6.

Keltner, Stacy. 2011. *Kristeva: Thresholds*. London: Polity Press.

Kerr, Tom. 1989. "A Postmodern Novel?" *Paragraph: The Journal of the Modern Critical Theory Group* 12 (1): 97–101.

Kirkby, Joan. 1998. "Julia Kristeva: A Politics of the Inner Life?" In *After the Revolution, On Kristeva*, edited by John Lechte and Mary Zournazi, 109–23. Woolloomooloo, Australia: Artspace Visual Arts Centre.

Kolarov, Radosvet. 2009. *Povtorenie i sutvorenie: Poetika na avtotekstualnosta* (*Repetition and Creation: Poetics of Autotextuality*). Sofia: Prosveta.

Kolocotroni, Vassiliki. 1993. "A Little Inner Mythology: Kristeva as Novelist." *New Formations* 21: 146–58.

Kraver, Geraldine. 1997. "Revolution Through Poetic Language: Bilingualism in Latina Poetry from La Frontera." *Literature, interpretation, theory: LIT* 8 (2): 193–206.

Kristeva, Julia. 1969. *Séméiotiké: Recherches pour une sémanalyse*. Paris: Seuil.

———. 1972. "La Joie de Giotto." *Peinture* 2/3: 35–51.

———. 1975. "Maternité selon Giovanni Bellini." *Peinture* 10/11: 11–37.

———. 1977. *Polylogue*. Paris: Seuil.

———. 1980. *Desire in Language: A Semiotic Approach to Literature and Art*. Edited by Leon S. Roudiez and translated by T. Gora, A. Jardine, and L. S. Roudiez. New York: Columbia University Press.

———. 1980a. "Giotto's Joy." In *Desire in Language: A Semiotic Approach to Literature and Art*, edited by Leon S. Roudiez and translated by T. Gora, A. Jardine, and L. S. Roudiez, 210–36. New York: Columbia University Press.

———. 1980b. "Motherhood According to Bellini." In *Desire in Language: A Semiotic Approach to Literature and Art*, edited by Leon S. Roudiez and translated by T. Gora, A. Jardine, and L.S. Roudiez. 237–70. New York: Columbia University Press.

———. 1980c. "The Novel as Polylogue." In *Desire in Language: A Semiotic Approach to Literature and Art*, edited by Leon S. Roudiez and translated by Thomas Gora, Alice Jardine, and Leon S. Roudiez, 157–209. New York: Columbia University Press.

———. 1982. *Powers of Horror: An Essay on Abjection*. Translated by Leon S. Roudiez. New York: Columbia University Press.

———. 1983. "Stabat Mater." In *Histoires d'amour*, 295–327. Paris: Denoël.

———. 1984. *Revolution in Poetic Language*. Translated by Margaret Waller. New York: Columbia University Press.

———. 1986b. "About Chinese Women." In *The Kristeva Reader*, edited by Toril Moi and translated by Sean Hand, 138–59. Oxford: Blackwell.

———. 1986c. "Stabat Mater." In *The Kristeva Reader*, edited by Toril Moi, 160–86. New York: Columbia University Press.

———. 1986d. "Women's Time." In *The Kristeva Reader*, edited by Toril Moi, 188–213. New York: Columbia University Press.

———. 1987. "Romeo and Juliet: Love-Hatred in the Couple." In *Tales of Love*, translated by Leon S. Roudiez, 209–33. New York: Columbia University Press.

———. 1987a. "Stabat Mater." In *Tales of Love*, translated by Leon S. Roudiez, 234–63. New York: Columbia University Press.

———. 1987b. *Tales of Love*. Translated by Leon S. Roudiez. New York: Columbia University Press.

———. 1987c. *In the Beginning Was Love*. Trans. Arthur Goldhammer. New York: Columbia University Press.

———. 1989. *Black Sun: Depression and Melancholia*. Translated by Leon S. Roudiez. New York: Columbia University Press.

———. 1989a. "The Malady of Grief: Duras." In *Black Sun: Depression and Melancholia*, translated by Leon S. Roudiez, 219–59. New York: Columbia University Press.

———. 1990. *Les Samouraïs*. Paris: Fayard.

———. 1990a. *Les Samouraïs*. Paris: Gallimard.

———. 1991. *Le vieil homme et les loups*. Paris: Fayard.

———. 1991a. *Strangers to Ourselves*. Translated by Leon S. Roudiez. New York: Columbia University Press.

———. 1992. *The Samurai*. Translated by Barbara Bray. New York: Columbia University Press.

———. 1992a. "Roman noir et temps présent." Interview with Bernard Sichère. *L'Infini* 37: 75–86.

———. 1993. *Les Nouvelles maladies de l'âme*. Paris: Fayard.

———. 1993a. *Proust and the Sense of Time*. Translated by Stephen Bann. New York: Columbia University Press.

———. 1994. *The Old Man and the Wolves*. Translated by Barbara Bray. New York: Columbia University Press.

———. 1994a. *The Samurai*. Translated by Barbara Bray. New York: Columbia University Press.

———. 1995. *New Maladies of the Soul*. Translated by Ross Guberman. New York: Columbia University Press.

———. 1996. "A Conversation with Julia Kristeva." Interview with Ina Lipkowitz and Andrea Loselle. In *Julia Kristeva Interviews*, edited by Ross Guberman, 18–34. New York: Columbia University Press.

———. 1996a. "Avant-Garde Practice." Interview with Vassiliki Kolocotroni. In *Julia Kristeva Interviews*, edited by Ross Guberman, 211–25. New York: Columbia University Press.

———. 1996b. "Intertextuality and Literary Interpretation." Interview with Margaret Waller. In *Julia Kristeva Interviews*, edited by Ross Guberman, 188–203. New York: Columbia University Press.

———. 1996c. "Interview: *The Old Man and the Wolves*." Interview with Bernard Sichère. In *Julia Kristeva Interviews*, edited by Ross Guberman, 162–75. New York: Columbia University Press.

———. 1996d. *Julia Kristeva Interviews*. Edited by Ross Guberman. New York: Columbia University Press.

———. 1996e. "Name of Death or of Life." In *Writing and Psychoanalysis: A Reader*, edited by John Lechte, 103–16. London and New York: Arnold.

———. 1996f. "On New Maladies of the Soul." Interview with Catherine Francblin. In *Julia Kristeva Interviews*, edited by Ross Guberman, 85–91. New York: Columbia University Press.

———. 1996g. "On *The Samurai*." Interview with Elisabeth Bélorgey. In *Julia Kristeva Interviews*, edited by Ross Guberman, 242–53. New York: Columbia University Press.

———. 1996h. *Possessions*. Paris: Fayard.

———. 1996i. "Proust: 'A Search for Our Time.'" Interview with Alain Nicolas. In *Julia Kristeva Interviews*, edited by Ross Guberman, 235–41. New York: Columbia University Press.

———. 1996j. *Sens et non-sens de la révolte: pouvoirs et limites de la psychanalyse, I*. Paris: Fayard.

———. 1996k. *Time and Sense: Proust and the Experience of Literature*. Translated by Ross Guberman. New York: Columbia University Press.

———. 1997. *La Révolte intime: pouvoirs et limites de la psychanalyse, II*. Paris: Fayard.
———. 1997a. *New Maladies of the Soul*. Translated by Ross Guberman. New York: Columbia University Press.
———. 1998. *Contre la dépression nationale: Julia Kristeva*. Interview with Philippe Petit. Paris: Les éditions textuels.
———. 1998a. "Julia Kristeva interviewed by Jonathan Rée." Director Alex Marengo. Producer Patricia Llewallyn. *Wall to Wall Television, Films for the Humanities and Sciences*. Talking Liberties Series. London, UK: Channel 4.
———. 1998b. *L'Avenir d'une révolte*. Paris: Calmann-Lévy.
———. 1998c. *Possessions*. Translated by Barbara Bray. New York: Columbia University Press.
———. 1998d. *Visions capitales*. Paris: Editions de la Réunion des Musées Nationaux.
———. 2000. "Aragon, Defiance, and Deception: A Precursor?" In *The Sense and Non-Sense of Revolt: The Powers and Limits of Psychoanalysis I*, translated by Jeanine Herman, 107–48. New York: Columbia University Press.
———. 2000a. "Bulgaria, My Suffering." In *Crisis of the ~~European~~ Subject*, translated by Susan Fairfield, 163–83. New York: Other Press.
———. 2000b. *Crisis of the ~~European~~ Subject*. Translated by Susan Fairfield. New York: Other Press.
———. 2000c. *The Sense and Non-Sense of Revolt: The Powers and Limits of Psychoanalysis I*. Translated by Jeanine Herman. New York: Columbia University Press.
———. 2001. *Hannah Arendt*. Translated by Ross Guberman. New York: Columbia University Press.
———. 2002. "Aragon: *Blanche ou l'oubli*; or, 'The Farcical and Ferocious Quest for a Consciousness.'" In *Intimate Revolt: The Powers and Limits of Psychoanalysis II*, translated by Jeanine Herman, 181–219. New York: Columbia University Press.
———. 2002a. *Intimate Revolt. The Powers and Limits of Psychoanalysis II*. Translated by Jeanine Herman. New York: Columbia University Press.
———. 2002b. *Le génie féminin: Colette*. Saint-Armand-Montrond: Fayard.
———. 2002c. *Revolt, She Said*. Translated by Brian O'Keefe. Los Angeles: Semiotext(e).
———. 2002d. "The Future of Revolt." In *Intimate Revolt: The Powers and Limits of Psychoanalysis II*, Translated by Jeanine Herman. New York: Columbia University Press.
———. 2002e. *The Portable Kristeva*. Edited by Kelly Oliver. New York: Columbia University Press.
———. 2003. *Hannah Arendt*. Translated by Ross Guberman. New York: Columbia University Press.
———. 2003a. "The Future of a Defeat: An Interview with Arnaud Spire." *Parallax* 27: 21–26.
———. 2004. *Colette*. Translated by Jane Marie Todd. New York: Columbia University Press.
———. 2004a. *Meurtre à Byzance*. Paris: Fayard.
———. 2004b. *Thinking About Liberty in Dark Times: The Holberg Prize Seminar*. Bergen: University of Bergen.

———. 2005. "Au Casino, ou Comment une femme joue la condition humaine." In *La haine et le pardon: Pouvoirs et limites de la psychanalyse III*, 527–37. Paris: Fayard.

———. 2005a. "Celanie." In *La haine et le pardon: Pouvoirs et limites de la psychanalyse III*, 577–88. Paris: Fayard.

———. 2005b. *La haine et le pardon: Pouvoirs et limites de la psychanalyse III*. Paris: Fayard.

———. 2005c. "*Meurtre à Byzance*, ou Pourquoi 'je me voyage' en roman." In *La haine et le pardon: Pouvoirs et limites de la psychanalyse III*, 609–55. Paris: Fayard.

———. 2005d. "Penser la liberté en temps de détresse." In *La haine et le pardon: Pouvoirs et limites de la psychanalyse III*, 15–27. Paris: Fayard.

———. 2005e. "Peut-on faire la paix?" In *La haine et le pardon: Pouvoirs et limites de la psychanalyse III*, 419–33. Paris: Fayard.

———. 2005f. "Que reste-t-il de nos amours?" In *La haine et le pardon: Pouvoirs et limites de la psychanalyse III*, 471–78. Paris: Fayard.

———. 2006. "A Father Is Beaten to Death." Presentation at "The Dead Father" International Symposium, Columbia University, New York, April 29–30, 2006.

———. 2006a. "Crossing the Borders: An Interview with Julia Kristeva by Birgitte Huitfeldt Midttun." *Hypatia: A Journal of Feminist Philosophy* 21 (4): 164–77.

———. 2006b. *Murder in Byzantium*. Translated by C. Jon Delogu. New York: Columbia University Press.

———. 2006c. "Thinking in Dark Times." In *Profession 2006*, 13–21. New York: Modern Language Association of America.

———. 2007. "Quelle avant-garde aujourd'hui?" In *Seule Une Femme*, 129–52. Paris: Editions de l'Aube.

———. 2008. "Decollations." Translated by Caroline Arruda. In *Psychoanalysis, Aesthetics, and Politics in the Work of Julia Kristeva*, edited by Kelly Oliver and Stacy Keltner, 29–45. Albany: State University of New York Press.

———. 2008a. *Thérèse mon amour*. Paris: Fayard.

———. 2009. *This Incredible Need to Believe*. New York: Columbia University Press.

———. 2010. *Hatred and Forgiveness*. Translated by Jeanine Herman. New York: Columbia University Press.

———. 2012. *The Severed Head: Capital Visions*. Translated by Jody Gladding. New York: Columbia University Press.

———, and Alison Rice. 2002. "Forgiveness: An Interview." *PMLA* 117 (2): xx–xx.

Lacan, Jacques. 1975. *De la psychose paranoïaque dans ses rapports avec la personnalité* suivi de *premiers écrits sur la paranoia*. Paris: Seuil.

———. 1977. "The Agency of the Letter." In *Ecrits: A Selection*, translated by Alan Sheridan, 146–78. New York: W.W. Norton.

———. 1981. *The Four Fundamental Concepts of Psycho-Analysis*. Edited by Jacques Alain-Miller and translated by Alan Sheridan. New York: W.W. Norton & Co.

———. 1988. "Seminar on 'The Purloined Letter.'" Translated by Jeffrey Mehlman. In *Purloined Poe: Derrida, Lacan, and Psychoanalytic Reading*, edited by John P. Muller and William J. Richardson, 28–54. Baltimore: The Johns Hopkins University Press.

Laplanche, J. and J.-B. Pontalis. 1973. *The Language of Psychoanalysis*. Translated by Donald Nicholson-Smith. New York: W.W. Norton and Co.

Lechte, John. 1990. *Julia Kristeva*. London and New York: Routledge.

———. 2009. "Julia Kristeva and the Trajectory of the Image." In *Psychoanalysis, Aesthetics, and Politics in the Work of Kristeva*, edited by Kelly Oliver and Stacy Keltner, 79–95. Albany: State University of New York Press.

———. 2011. "Some Fallacies and Truths Concerning the Image in Old and New Media." *Journal of Visual Culture* 10 (3): 354–71.

———, and Mary Zournazi, eds. 1998. *After the Revolution; On Kristeva*. Woolloomooloo: Artspace Visual Arts Centre.

———, and Mary Zournazi, eds. 2003. *The Kristeva Critical Reader*. Edinburgh: Edinburgh University Press.

Levenson, Michael. 1994. "The Critic as Novelist." *The Wilson Quarterly* 18 (1): 116–24.

Mamardashvili, Merab. 1992. "Prevrashtenye formy (o neobhodymosti iratsional'nyh vyrazheniy)" (Inverted Forms: On the Necessity of Irrational Expressions). In *Kak ia ponimaiu filosofii* (*My Understanding of Philosophy*), 269–82. Moscow: Progress.

Manchev, Boyan. 1999. "Interpretatsii na ideologiata, ideologia na interpretatsiata. Vîrhu polemikite v bîlgarskoto literaturoznanie." [Interpretation of Ideology, Ideologies of Interpretation: On the Debates in Bulgarian Literary Theory.] *Literaturna misîl* 1: 5–30.

Mantchev. Krassimir. 1967. "La hiérarchie sémantique des verbes français contemporains." *Cahiers de lexicologie* 10: 31–46.

———. 1998. *Sémiotique et Narratologie*. Sofia: Presses Universitaires "St. Kliment Ohridski."

Margaroni, Maria. 2009. "Julia Kristeva's Chiasmatic Journeys: From Byzantium to the Phantom of Europe and the End of the World." In *Psychoanalysis, Aesthetics, and Politics in the Work of Julia Kristeva*, edited by Kelly Oliver and Stacy Keltner, 107–24. Albany: State University of New York Press.

Margaroni, Maria, and John Lechte. 2004. *Julia Kristeva: Live Theory*. London: Continuum.

McAfee, Noelle. 2003. *Julia Kristeva*. London: Routledge.

Merivale, Patricia, and Susan Elizabeth Sweeney, eds. 1999. *Detecting Texts: The Metaphysical Detective Story from Poe to Postmodernism*. Philadelphia: University of Pennsylvania Press.

Merleau-Ponty, Maurice. 1969. *The Visible and the Invisible*. Translated by Alphonso Lingis. Evanston, IL: Northwestern University Press.

Mermier, Guy R. 2000. *France Past and Present*. New York: Peter Lang.

Messet, Peter. 2000. "Authority, Social Anxiety and the Body in Crime Fiction: Patricia Cornwell's *Unnatural Exposure*." In *The Art of Detective Fiction*, edited by Warren Chernaik, Martin Swales, and Robert Vilain, 124–37. New York: St. Martin's Press.

Michael, E. M. 1968. "Introduction." In *The Poems of Tibullus*, 7–31. Bloomington, IN: Indiana University Press.

Mondzain, Marie-José. 1996. *Image, icône, économie. Les sources byzantines de la'imaginaire contemporain*. Paris: Seuil.

———. 2004. *Image, Icon Economy: The Byzantine Origins of the Contemporary Imaginary*. Translated by Rico Franses. Stanford: Stanford University Press.

Montesquieu. (1721) 1973. *Lettres persanes*. Paris: Gallimard.

Muller, John P., and William J. Richardson. 1988. *The Purloined Poe: Lacan, Derrida, and Psychoanalytic Reading*. Baltimore: The Johns Hopkins University Press.

Mutafchieva, Vera. 2008. *I, Anna Comnena: The Knight.* (Az, Anna Comnina. Ritsariat.) Plovdiv: Janet-45.

Nancy, Jean-Luc. 1991. "The Unsacrificeable." Translated by Richard Livingston. *Yale French Studies* 79: 20–38.

Nikolchina, Miglena. 2004. *Matricide in Language; Writing Theory in Kristeva and Woolf.* New York: Other Press.

Nilsson, Ingela. 2005. "*Meurtre à Byzance*: Byzantine Murders in Modern Literature." *Byzantine and Modern Greek Studies* 29 (2): 235–38.

O'Grady, Kathleen. 2002. "The Tower and the Chalice: Julia Kristeva and the Story of Santa Barbara." *Feminist Theology: The Journal of the Britain and Ireland School of Feminist Theology* 29: 40–60.

Oliver, Kelly. 1993a. *Reading Kristeva: Unraveling the Double-Bind.* Bloomington: Indiana University Press.

———, ed. 1993b. *Ethics, Politics and Difference in Julia Kristeva's Writing.* New York: Routledge.

———, ed. 2002. *The Portable Kristeva.* New York: Columbia University Press.

———. 2003. *The Colonization of Psychic Space: A Psychoanalytic Social Theory of Oppression.* Minneapolis: University of Minnesota Press.

———. 2005. "Revolt and Forgiveness." In *Revolt, Affect, Collectivity: The Unstable Boundaries of Kristeva's Polis*, edited by Tina Chanter and Ewa Plonowska Ziarek, 77–92. Albany: State University of New York Press.

———, and Benigno Trigo. 2003. *Noir Anxiety.* Minneapolis: University of Minnesota Press.

———, and Stacy Keltner, eds. 2009. *Psychoanalysis, Aesthetics, and Politics in the Work of Julia Kristeva.* Albany: State University of New York Press.

Olivier, Jean-Michel. 1989. "*Les Samouraïs*, Julia Kristeva." *Revue de Belles-Lettres* 112 (3–4): 154–57.

Ovid. 2004. *Metamorphoses: A New Translation by Charles Martin.* New York: W.W. Norton & Company.

Payne, Michael. 1993. *Reading Theory: An Introduction to Lacan, Derrida and Kristeva.* Hoboken, NJ: Wiley-Blackwell.

Poe, Edgar Allan. 1970. *Great Short Works of Edgar Allan Poe.* Edited by G. R. Thompson. New York: Harper and Row.

Putnam, Michael C. J. 1979. *Tibullus: A Commentary.* Norman: University of Oklahoma Press.

Raoul, Valerie. 2001. "L'autre langue fécondatrice : 'l'étrangeité' en soi dans *Instruments de ténèbres* de Nancy Huston et *Possessions* de Julia Kristeva." In *La Francophonie sans frontière: une nouvelle cartographie de l'imaginaire au féminin*, edited by Lucie Lequin and Catherine Mavrikakis, 445–53. Paris: L'Harmattan.

Reineke, Martha J. 1997. *Sacrificed Lives: Kristeva on Women and Violence.* Bloomington: Indiana University Press.

Renard, Paul. 1992. "Des Mandarins aux *Samouraïs*, ou de l'engagement existentialiste à l'individualisme post-moderne." *Roman 20–50* 13: 111–24.

Rose, Jacqueline. 1986. "Julia Kristeva—Take Two." In *Sexuality in the Field of Vision*, 151–60. London: Verso.

———. 2007. *The Last Resistance.* London: Verso.

Roudinesco, Elisabeth. 1993. *Jacques Lacan: Esquisse d'une vie, histoire d'un système de pensée*. Paris: Fayard.

Rousseau, Jean-Jacques. (1762) 1964. *Julie, ou La nouvelle Héloïse. Ouvres complètes de Jean-Jacques Rousseau, II.* Paris: Gallimard.

Rubin, Merle. 2006. "Book Review: Detectable Trouble in Erudite Mystery." *The Los Angeles Times*, February 28: E.8.

Rus, Laura Bianca. 2010. "Remapping the European Cultural Memory: The Case of Julia Kristeva's *Murder in Byzantium*." *Atlantis* 35 (1): 15–24.

———. 2010. "The Ethical and Political Function of Revolt in Julia Kristeva's Novels." PhD dissertation, University of British Columbia.

Rzepka, Charles J. 2005. *Detective Fiction*. London: Polity Press.

Sage, Lorna. 1992. "*The Samurai*." *Times Literary Supplement* 4679: 20.

Savigneau, Josyane. 1990. "Quand les Samouraïs répondent aux Mandarins." *Le Monde*, March 9: 19–20.

Schaub, Michael. 2011. "Brutal And Perfect 'Third Reich': Bolaño's Final Gift." http://www.npr.org/2011/11/17/142358687/brutal-and-perfect-third-reich-bolanos-final-gift.

Schwager, Raymund. 2000. *Must There Be Scapegoats?* New York: Herder & Herder.

Shields, J. G. 2007. *The Extreme Right in France: From Pétain to Le Pen*. New York: Routledge.

Showalter, Elaine. 1990. "A Paragon and Her Position." *Times Literary Supplement* 4565: 1038.

Simon, Rita J., and Dagny A. Blaskovich. 2002. *A Comparative Analysis of Capital Punishment*. Lanham: Lexington Books.

Sirvent, Michel. 1999. "Reader-Investigators in the Post-Nouveau Roman: Lahougue, Peeters, and Perec." In *Detecting Texts: The Metaphysical Detective Story from Poe to Postmodernism*, edited by Patricia Merivale and Susan Elizabeth Sweeney, 157–78. Philadelphia: University of Pennsylvania Press.

Sjoholm, Cecilia. 2005. *Kristeva and the Political*. London: Routledge.

Smith, Anna. 1996. *Julia Kristeva; Readings of Exile and Estrangement*. London and New York: Macmillan.

———. 1997. "A Reversible Space: The Essence of Ambassadorship." *Paragraph: The Journal of the Modern Critical Theory Group* 20 (3): 209–20.

Smith, Anne-Marie. 1998. *Julia Kristeva: Speaking the Unspeakable*. New York and Sterling, VA: Pluto Press.

Solodow, Joseph B. 2002. *The World of Ovid's Metamorphoses*. Chapel Hill: The University of North Carolina Press.

Spanos, William V. 1972. "The Detective and the Boundary: Some Notes on the Postmodern Literary Imagination." *boundary 2* (1): 146–68.

Spivak, Gayatri Chakravorty. 1988. *In Other Worlds: Essays in Cultural Politics*. New York: Routledge.

Steinberg, Sybil. 1992. "Fiction: *The Samurai* by Julia Kristeva." *Publishers Weekly* 239 (39): 65–66.

Steiner, Wendy. 1992. "The Bulldozer of Desire." *The New York Times*, November 15: n.p.

Sutherland, John. 2006. "Why Is a Critic Ashamed of Being Fashionable." *The Guardian*. March 12. http://www.guardian.co.uk/education/2006/mar/14/highereducation.research1.

Swartley, Willard M. 2000. *Violence Renounced: Rene Girard, Biblical Studies, and Peacemaking.* Telford, PA: Pandora Press.

Thorne, Matt. 2006. "Killing in Theory and Practice: *Murder in Byzantium* by Julia Kristeva, Translated by C. Jon Delogu." *The Independent*, April 7: n.p.

Tibullus. 1968. Poems. Ed. E. M. Michael. Bloomington, IN: Indiana University Press.

———. 2012. *Elegies: With Parallel Latin Text.* Trans A. M. Foster. New York: Oxford University Press.

Tidmarsh, Angela. 1998. "Kristeva's Literary Interpretative Clinic." In *After the Revolution, On Kristeva*, edited by John Lechte and Mary Zournazi, 133–49. Woolloomooloo, Australia: Artspace Visual Arts Centre.

Todorov, Tzvetan. 1978. *The Poetics of Prose.* Translated by Richard Howard. Ithaca: Cornell University Press.

Walsh, Lisa. 2009. "Symptomatic Reading: Kristeva on Duras." In *Psychoanalysis, Aesthetics, and Politics in the Work of Julia Kristeva*, edited by Kelly Oliver and S. K. Kramer, 143–62. Albany: State University of New York Press.

West, Patrick. 2008. "Theoretical Allegory/Allegorical Theory: (Post)Colonial Spatializations in Jante Frame's *The Carpathians* and Julia Kristeva's *The Old Man and the Wolves.*" *Journal of New Zealand Literature* 26: 73–96.

White, Allon. 1977. "*L'Eclatement du sujet*": *The Theoretical Work of Julia Kristeva.* University of Birmingham Center for Contemporary Studies. Stenciled Occasional Paper no. 49.

Whitford, Margaret. 1994. "Review of Julia Kristeva, *The Samurai: A Novel* and Luce Irigaray, *Sexes and Genealogies.*" *Women's History Review* 4 (1): 139–41.

Wiseman, Mary Bittner. 1993. "Renaissance Painting and Psychoanalysis: Julia Kristeva and the Function of the Mother." In *Ethics, Politics, and Difference in Julia Kristeva's Writing*, edited by Kelly Oliver, 92–115. New York and London: Routledge.

Wood, Michael. 1995. "Time of the Assassin." *London Review of Books* 17 (2): 17–18.

Ziarek, Ewa Plonowska, and Tina Chanter, eds. 2005. *Revolt, Affect, Collectivity: The Unstable Boundaries of Kristeva's Polis.* Albany: State University of New York Press.

Zipp, Yvonne. 2006. "Page Turners; Murder and Intrigue Span the Globe, from Byzantium to Burundi. Who's Guilty? Reviewer Yvonne Zipp Is on the Case." *The Christian Science Monitor*, February 24: 13.

Contributors

Carol Mastrangelo Bové is Senior Lecturer in English at the University of Pittsburgh and Professor of French Emerita at Westminster College, Pennsylvania. She is the author of *Language and Politics in Julia Kristeva: Literature, Art, Therapy* (2006). She also has numerous publications on psychoanalytic writing and translation including, for example, "The Thimble and the Needle: Translating La Maison de Claudine," *Palimpsestes* 24 (2012): 131–47 and "Literary Translation and the Undergraduate Curriculum: A Forum," in the *Association of Departments of Foreign Languages Bulletin* 41 (2) (2009): 22–25. She has translated works by Claude Richard, Serge Doubrovsky, Hélène Cixous, and Luce Irigaray.

S. K. Keltner is Associate Professor of History and Philosophy at Kennesaw University, Kennesaw, Georgia. She is the author of *Kristeva: Thresholds* (2011). She is coeditor with Kelly Oliver of *Psychoanalysis, Aesthetics, and Politics in the Work of Julia Kristeva* (2009).

John Lechte is Professor of Sociology at Macquarie University, Australia. He is the author of a number of books on Julia Kristeva, including (with Maria Margaroni) *Julia Kristeva: Live Theory* (2004); *Julia Kristeva* (1990); and coeditor with Mary Zournazi of *The Kristeva Critical Reader* (2003) and *After the Revolution, On Kristeva* (1998). He has recently published *The Ontology and Genealogy of the Western Image and Its Digital Future* (2012).

Maria Margaroni is Associate Professor in Continental Philosophy, Literary Theory and Feminist Thought at the University of Cyprus. She is coauthor (with John Lechte) of *Julia Kristeva: Live Theory* (2004). Other publications include: *Intimate Transfers*, with Effie Yiannopoulou, special issue of *The European Journal of English Studies* (2005); *Metaphoricity and the Politics of Mobility*, with Effie Yiannopoulou (2006); *Violence and the Sacred*, special issue of *Philosophy Today* (2012).

MIGLENA NIKOLCHINA is a professor in the Department of Theory and History of Literature, Sofia University, Bulgaria. She is the author of several books including *Lost Unicorns of the Velvet Revolution: Heterotopias of the Seminar* (2013) and *Matricide in Language: Writing Theory in Kristeva and Woolf* (2004).

MARTHA REINEKE is Professor of Religion at the University of Northern Iowa in Cedar Falls, Iowa. She explores intersections in the work of René Girard and Julia Kristeva in such works as *Sacrificed Lives: Kristeva on Women and Violence* (1997); "Sacrifice and Sexual Difference: Insights and Challenges in the work of René Girard," in *For René Girard: Essays in Friendship and in Truth*, edited by Sandor Goodhart, Jorgen Jorgensen, Tom Ryba, and James G. Williams (2009); and "After the Scapegoat: René Girard's Apocalyptic Vision and the Legacy of Mimetic Theory, *Philosophy Today* 56 (2) (Summer 2012): 141–53.

FRANCES L. RESTUCCIA is Professor of English at Boston College, Boston, Massachusetts. She is the author of *James Joyce and the Law of the Father* (1989); *Melancholics in Love: Representing Women's Depression and Domestic Abuse* (2000); *Amorous Acts: Lacanian Ethics in Modernism, Film, and Queer Theory* (2006); and *The Blue Box: Kristevan/Lacanian Readings of Contemporary Film* (2012). She contributed a chapter to *Revolt, Affect, Collectivity: The Unstable Boundaries of Kristeva's Polis* (edited by Eva Ziarek and Tina Chanter) and another to *Psychoanalysis, Aesthetics, and Politics in the Work of Kristeva* (edited by Kelly Oliver). An essay on *Don Quixote*, love, and messianism in Agamben appeared in *Philosophy Today* (2012).

BENIGNO TRIGO is Professor of Spanish American Literature at Vanderbilt University, Nashville. Tennessee. He is interested in the intersection of the maternal body and writing and is the author of *Subjects of Crisis: Race and Gender as Disease in Latin America* (2000); and *Remembering Maternal Bodies* (2002). He is also the author of "Noir Analysis: How Kristeva's Detective Novels Renew Psychoanalysis," *Cultural Critique* 80 (Winter 2012): 27–55. And he is coauthor (with Kelly Oliver) of *Noir Anxiety: Race, Sex and Maternity in Film Noir* (2002).

EWA PLONOWSKA ZIAREK is Professor of Comparative Literature at the University of Buffalo, State University of New York, Buffalo, New York. She is the author of several books including most recently *Feminist Aesthetics and the Politics of Modernism* (2012); *An Ethics of Dissensus: Postmodernity, Feminism and the Politics of Radical Democracy* (2001); and she is the editor with Tina Chanter of *Revolt, Affect, Collectivity: The Unstable Boundaries of Kristeva's Polis* (2005).

Index

9/11. *See* September 11, 2001 attacks
abject, 2, 15, 20, 25–27, 42, 45, 54–55, 69, 97–99, 149–50, 160, 163, 167, 177–79
About Chinese Women, 25
Adorno, Theodor, 124
aesthetics, 18, 22, 41, 43, 76, 113–14, 116–20, 124, 133, 140, 169
affect, 17, 35, 37, 40, 42, 58, 60, 64, 78, 82, 97–101, 107, 131, 135, 138–41, 158, 162, 167, 169
Agamben, Giorgio, 81
agape, 72, 136. *See also* compassion; empathy
AIDS, 5
Al Qaeda, 8. *See also* September 11, 2001 attacks
allegory, 6, 13, 16, 31, 57, 89–90, 92; Benjaminian, 26, 148, 186
analysand, 23, 42, 57, 73–74, 118–19, 123, 128, 133, 139–40, 169. *See also* psychoanalysis
analyst, 1, 3, 5–6, 12, 14, 23, 41–43, 51, 57, 73–74, 108–9, 113, 115–16, 118–19, 121, 123–24, 128, 130, 133–34, 136, 139–40, 155, 166–69. *See also* psychoanalysis
anamnesis, 5, 93, 156, 459, 163
androgyny, 51, 53, 157
animal, 6, 26, 52–53, 55, 58, 60, 63, 73, 91. *See also* wolves
Anzaldúa, Gloria, 27
Aragon, Louis, 155, 160–67, 171–73; *Blanche ou l'oubli*, 155, 160–67, 171, 173
Arendt, Hannah, 73–74, 101, 108–9, 149, 161
Artaud, Antonin, 137, 168
Auschwitz, 12. *See also* Holocaust
avant-garde, 155–57, 159–64, 172. *See also* Dada; Surrealism

Bakhtin, Mikhail, 18, 47, 129, 145
Barthes, Roland, 26, 113, 130
Bataille, Georges, 76, 135, 137–38, 158
Beauvoir, Simone de, 10, 15–16, 103, 138, 143; *The Mandarins,* 10, 15–16, 143
Beckett, Samuel, 172
being, 12, 33, 37, 40, 49, 58–60, 62, 66–67, 70, 73–75, 83, 85, 88–89, 91–92, 98, 101, 106–8, 128, 136–37, 143–44, 147, 150, 152, 167–69, 172
Bellini, Vincenzo, 45, 47–49, 51–52. *See also* "Motherhood According to Bellini"
Berlin Wall, 6, 19, 24, 52, 150, 153. *See also* Cold War
betrayal, 3–4, 14–15, 17, 24–25, 163
bilingualism, 13–14
binary oppositions, 19, 99
Black Sun, 25–26, 119, 179
body, 6, 12–13, 26–27, 33, 36, 39–40, 46, 49–50, 53, 62–64, 69, 73–78, 83–85, 89–90, 96–97, 99–100, 104–5, 116, 119, 122, 129, 137–39, 148, 157, 159, 163, 168–69, 170–72. *See also* flesh
Bogomil heresy, the, 100, 103, 105–6, 109. *See also* heresy
Bolaño, Roberto, 18
Borges, Jorge Luis, 109

Brown, Dan, 26
Bulgaria, 3, 6, 19, 23–25, 55, 95–98, 102–5, 107–9, 130, 132, 143–47, 149–52, 154; Bulgarian language, 4
Butler, Judith, 12, 26, 45, 49, 53, 96
Byzantium, 8, 16, 22, 24, 33, 39–40, 48, 79–80, 83–87, 89–92, 95–96, 98, 100–4, 106–9, 130–33, 143, 145, 149–53

capital, 98
capital punishment, 7
capitalism, 52
castration, 15, 80, 91, 124
Céline, Louis-Ferdinand, 162
censorship, 126–27, 146, 153
Cézanne, Paul, 48
Chen, Szu-Chin Hestia, 1, 11, 17–18, 27, 155
Chirac, Jacques, 5, 7
chora, 118
Christie, Agatha, 26, 130
cinema, 32, 36–38, 42, 84, 92, 123
Clark, Mary Higgins, 130
"Cohabitation" (French politics), 5
Cold War, 6, 19
Colette, 51–85, 144, 149, 170
Communism, 5, 9, 14, 19, 24, 54, 144–47, 152–53
Comnena, Anna, 79, 87, 90, 100, 103–5, 107–8, 149–53; *The Alexiad*, 87, 103–4, 108–9, 149, 151–52
compassion, 13, 22, 57, 67, 71–73, 75, 106. *See also* agape; empathy
Cornwell, Patricia, 130
countertransference, 3, 74, 122–23, 170
crime, 6–8, 12, 14–15, 23–24, 31, 33–40, 42, 59, 61–62, 67, 80–81, 83–84, 87–88, 90–92, 96–101, 103–5, 108, 121, 137
crime fiction, 37, 144, 148. *See also* detective fiction

Da Vinci, Leonardo, 48–49, 117, 170
Da Vinci Code, The, 26
Dada, 161. *See also* avant-garde; Surrealism
Dalí, Salvador, 128, 141
Dante, 49
"dark continent," 8, 15, 165
De Lauretis, Teresa, 12, 26
death, 6–8, 12–13, 21–23, 25–26, 50–55, 58–59, 61–64, 66–67, 69–72, 76–77, 79–87, 89–92, 97, 99–100, 104, 106, 114–15, 118, 120–24, 127, 136–40, 148, 152–53, 157, 160–61, 167–68
death drive, 12–13, 21–22, 25, 52, 80–82, 84, 89–90, 92, 118, 120, 123, 167
death penalty. *See* capital punishment
Debord, Guy, 23, 31, 34, 81, 84, 89. *See also* society of the spectacle; spectacle
decapitation, 6–7, 81, 101, 124, 129, 138
Delacour, Stephanie, 3, 6–8, 11, 35, 38–42, 53–55, 62–63, 66–67, 70–72, 75–77, 79, 81, 84–86, 90, 97, 100–1, 103–8, 120–21, 136, 138, 149, 151, 153
Deleuze, Gilles and Félix Guattari, 122, 145; *Anti-Oedipus*, 122
depression, 3, 8, 12, 35, 51–52, 79, 82, 99, 133, 136–38, 151–52, 156
Derrida, Jacques, 26, 149
desire, 7, 9, 12–13, 17, 20, 36–37, 47–48, 50, 59–60, 62, 69, 82–84, 87, 91–92, 99–100, 102, 109, 121, 123–24, 160–61, 164–65, 168–70, 172
Desire in Language, 27, 48, 119, 153
detective fiction, 1–2, 5–8, 10, 12, 14–18, 21–24, 26, 31–32, 35, 36–43, 53, 80–81, 86, 89–90, 95–103, 105–9, 113–14, 120–24, 130–31, 133–35, 137–39, 141, 149, 162, 169. *See also* crime fiction
Dostoyevsky, Fyodor, 129–30, 133, 137
Doyle, Sir Arthur Conan, 130, 141; *Sherlock Holmes*, 130, 141
Duras, Marguerite, 16, 119, 137, 140–41
Durkheim, Émile, 86

Eastern Europe, 9, 23, 51–52, 54, 87, 95–96, 99, 101–7
Eco, Umberto, 10, 16, 109, 127, 133–34, 143; *Baudolino*, 16; *The Name of the Rose*, 10, 133–34

ego, 3, 34–35, 38, 75, 82, 153–54, 169, 171, 173
Eisenstein, Sergei, 36
embodiment, 6, 18, 23, 32, 35–37, 40, 44, 51, 59–60, 63, 67, 69–70, 73–74, 89, 91–92, 148, 170
empathy, 72–73. *See also* agape; compassion
Enlightenment, 127, 146
Eros, 21, 92, 122
eroticism, 31, 39, 84, 92, 100, 104–6, 151, 163–64, 166
Eternal City, 8
ethics, 12, 13, 24, 33, 35, 46, 50–51, 54–55, 84, 119–20, 160, 169–70
Europe, 3, 8, 13, 19, 22, 26, 45–46, 48, 59, 87, 92, 102–3, 107, 144–45, 149, 151, 153. *See also* Eastern Europe; Western Europe

fantasy, 7–8, 12, 14–15, 34, 36–37, 46, 64, 80, 84, 90, 92, 98, 100, 104, 123, 125, 104–41, 144, 164, 170–71
father, 6, 13–14, 16, 26–27, 46, 48–50, 53–54, 62, 67, 71–72, 75–78, 86–89, 98–99, 101–7, 119, 122, 130–33, 135–37, 141, 151–53, 158–59; and language, 46, 49; Law of the Father, 16, 46, 49, 78, 136–37, 159; and mother as hybrid entities, 46, 50, 53; parricide, 6, 14–15, 98, 103, 120, 122, 135; paternal function, 13, 27, 78
fatherhood. *See* father
Female Genius, The, 104, 149, 161
feminine, 22–26, 40, 45, 51–53, 55, 95, 101–4, 149, 154, 156, 158–60, 163–67, 171–72
feminism, 9–10, 17, 24, 26–27, 95–96, 103–4, 122, 124, 152
fetish, 60, 158, 169
film. *See* cinema
flesh, 36, 74–75, 78–80, 84, 88, 90, 105, 150, 161, 166, 168, 170. *See also* body
foreign language, 14, 106
foreignness, 7–8, 40, 54–55, 62, 71, 79, 83, 95–96, 106–7, 149, 156, 163–64
forgiveness, 1, 3–4, 11–14, 17, 20, 24–25, 27, 123, 133, 173. *See also* pardon
Foucault, Michel, 26, 134
France, 3–5, 7–8, 26, 48, 54, 77, 95, 129, 144–46, 151, 153, 157, 169; French language, 2–4, 8–9, 38, 44, 52, 124, 145, 155–57; Kristeva's feelings about, 2–4, 19, 95–96, 141, 145, 153, 156–57
Fraser, Nancy, 12, 26, 177
French Revolution, 7
frescoes, 47, 52. *See also* painting
Freud, Sigmund, 5–6, 8, 10, 12, 14, 21, 36, 41–42, 48, 53, 68, 106, 109, 113–24, 127, 129–30, 134, 147, 161, 170, 172
future, 32, 39–40, 43–44, 72, 76, 79, 107–8, 117, 121, 126, 133–34, 151, 160, 163, 166
Future of Revolt, The, 44

gaze, 6–7, 81, 91–92, 132, 169–70
gender, 45, 61, 96, 99
genre, 5, 10, 14–17, 23–24, 41, 47, 80–81, 92, 96–101, 109, 114, 123, 126, 130–31, 134, 141, 148, 150, 156–57, 160–63
Giotto (Giotto di Bondone), 47, 51–52
"Giotto's Joy," 45, 47
Girard, René, 22, 46, 58–59, 61–63, 65–67, 69–71, 73, 76–77, 177–78, 186, 188
globalization, 32, 34, 80–81, 87, 96, 98–99, 106, 122, 150, 153
Godard, Jean-Luc, 36
Goethe, Johann Wolfgang von, 41
Gospels, 71, 77, 129
guillotine, 7. *See also* capital punishment; decapitation
Gulag, 12

Hatred and Forgiveness, 25, 40, 44, 85, 113, 161, 172, 182
Hegel, Georg Wilhelm Friedrich, 149
Heidegger, Martin, 83, 88, 147
heresy, 50, 100, 103, 105–6, 109. *See also* Bogomil heresy
heterogeneity, 21, 36, 50, 97, 108, 147, 157, 172

Highsmith, Patricia, 39
Hiroshima, 12
Hitchcock, Alfred, 36
Holbein, Hans, 91, 137
Holiday, Billie, 54–55
Holocaust, 12, 19
homosexuality, 104
hope, 8, 52, 73, 75–76, 87, 92, 123, 151, 160, 162
horror, 31, 69, 138, 140
horror films, 36. *See also* cinema
Hugo, Victor, 162
hybridity, 26, 46, 50–51, 53

icon, 22–23, 39, 48, 77, 79, 85, 87, 89–93, 95, 100, 102–3, 106–9, 131–33, 145, 153
In the Beginning was Love, 25, 104, 179
intersubjectivity, 107, 168. *See also* subjectivity
Intimate Revolt, 21, 25, 36, 44, 80, 92, 161–62; Kristeva's concept of, 78, 82, 87–88, 93
Ionesco, Eugène, 26, 53
Iraq, 8
Israeli-Palestinian conflict, 46
Italian language, 52, 54
Italy, 22, 45–46, 48–55, 146. *See also* Rome

jihad, 104
jouissance, 39, 99, 130, 159, 163

Kafka, Franz, 109
Kant, Immanuel, 108–9, 169, 173
Klein, Melanie, 149
Kristeva's fiction: autobiographical aspects of, 2, 9, 13, 15, 17, 23–26, 51, 53, 67, 86, 114–15, 134, 143–44, 151; in relation to psychoanalytic theory and practice, 2–3, 10–13, 16–18, 20–21, 23–24, 26–27, 43, 50–51, 53, 57, 73, 82, 100, 114–19, 122–23, 125, 129–32, 134, 139–41, 143–44, 148–49, 153, 155; reception of, 1, 4, 8–14, 16–18, 22, 95–96, 113, 155; sociopolitical aspects of, 2–4, 9–10, 13, 15, 17, 19, 21–22, 24–25, 32–33, 43, 65, 102–3, 121

Lacan, Jacques, 17, 26, 76, 78, 91–92, 97, 122, 125, 127–29, 132, 136, 141, 148
lack, 9, 14, 34–35, 43, 46, 59–60, 62, 75, 83, 86, 89, 91, 136, 161, 169, 173
language, 2–4, 6–7, 13–14, 17, 19, 21, 25, 31, 35, 40, 42, 46, 49–52, 54, 65, 70, 73–74, 80, 88, 92, 96–97, 101, 105–8, 114, 118–20, 122–23, 134–35, 137–38, 144, 146–47, 149–50, 157–60, 163–64, 168, 172
Language: The Unknown, 25
law, 16, 33, 49, 70, 78, 88, 96–101, 107, 121, 124, 136–37, 159–60, 170. *See also* father
Le Pen, Jean-Marie, 7
linguistics, 1–2, 5, 7, 13, 17, 46, 97, 106, 119, 147, 163
love, 5, 21–22, 25, 27, 38, 50–51, 54, 67, 69–72, 77, 84–85, 87, 101–2, 104–8, 126, 131, 136–37, 149, 152, 159–61, 163–64, 170–71. *See also* agape
Lukács, György, 10

McEwan, Ian, 26
madness, 100, 121, 128
Madonna, the. *See* Virgin Mary
masochism, 6, 45, 49, 82
maternal. *See* mother
malaise, 49, 57, 115–16, 118
Mallarmé, Stéphane, 118, 134–35, 146
Mann, Thomas, 148
Matisse, Henri, 48
matriarchy, 50
matricide. *See* mother
May 1968, 5, 157
melancholia, 2–3, 7, 12, 14, 26–27, 35, 105–6, 114, 133, 138, 164
Merleau-Ponty, Maurice, 74–75
metamorphosis, 34, 54, 58, 60–61, 63–65, 75, 77, 147–48
Mitterand, François, 5

modernism, 16, 24, 109
modernity, 10, 18–19, 23, 26, 31–32, 34–35, 37, 79, 84, 114–16, 118, 126–27, 153, 167, 173
mother, 3–4, 6–9, 13–16, 25, 39–40, 45–55, 62, 69, 81, 83, 86–87, 89, 96, 98–101, 103–9, 114–15, 117–20, 122–24, 136, 144, 149, 152, 156, 158–60, 163–66, 170–73; and father as hybrid entities, 46, 50, 53; matricide, 7, 14–16, 83, 87, 89, 96, 98–101, 104–8, 115, 120, 122, 124, 144, 149; mother tongue, 3–4, 6–8, 13–14, 46, 50, 114–15, 118, 120, 122–23, 136; phallic mother, 103, 156, 158–59, 172; pregnancy, 39, 83, 98–100, 105
mother tongue. *See* mother
motherhood. *See* mother
"Motherhood According to Bellini," 45, 48–49. *See also* Bellini, Vincenzo
movies. *See* cinema
multiculturalism, 122
murder, 6, 14, 16, 22, 26, 31, 33, 38–40, 53, 59, 62, 80–81, 83–85, 87–92, 96–101, 103–5, 108, 133–35, 148–49, 153, 157–58, 166
Murder in Byzantium, 1, 2, 4, 7–9, 21–23, 26, 31, 33, 35, 39, 79–82, 86–92, 95–96, 98, 100, 113, 122, 125, 130, 132, 134–36, 143, 149–51, 153, 155, 169–71
music, 50–51, 54–55, 58, 63–65, 68, 70–72, 84, 88, 90, 140–41, 157–58, 160, 163, 172
Mutafchieva, Vera, 24, 152–53; *I, Anna Comnena*, 152–53

Nancy, Jean-Luc, 135
negation, 106, 120
negativity, 1, 8–11, 14, 16, 18, 23, 26, 87, 113–14, 116–24, 149, 157, 159, 171
Nerval, Gérard de, 118
New Maladies of the Soul, 19, 32, 42, 173; Kristeva's concept of, 34, 37, 122, 139, 141
noir, 7–8, 23, 26, 113–14, 120–23
nomadism, 14, 40–41, 54–55
nonviolence, 64, 72
nouveau roman, 18, 26
"Novel as Polylogue, The," 145, 157, 159, 172

Oedipus, 36, 53, 61, 78, 97, 100–1, 108–9, 121–22, 136–37, 159
Old Man and the Wolves, The, 2, 5–6, 10, 21–22, 26, 31, 33–35, 38–39, 41, 45–47, 52–53, 57, 68, 70, 72, 75–76, 136
Oliver, Kelly, 1, 15, 26–27, 78, 123
Orpheus, 114–15
other, the, 4, 12, 25, 36, 38, 42–43, 58–61, 64, 68–70, 72–75, 87, 90, 93, 103, 108, 118, 129, 137, 140, 146, 157, 164, 166–67, 169, 171, 173
Ovid, 22, 53–55, 57–58, 61–66, 68–69, 72, 75–76; *Metamorphoses*, 22, 53–55, 57–58, 63–64, 66, 74, 76

painting, 5, 47–48, 58, 106–7, 128, 131, 137, 139–40
paranoia, 127–28, 141
pardon, 4, 27. *See also* forgiveness
parricide. *See* father
paternal. *See* father
patriarchy, 9, 10, 48, 104
peace, 46, 61, 71, 86, 161
perversion, 16, 31, 118, 120–23
phallic mother. *See* mother
pleasure principle, 21, 86, 169
Poe, Edgar Allan, 6, 26, 36, 97, 127, 130; "The Murders in the Rue Morgue," 6, 26, 130; "The Purloined Letter," 24, 26, 97, 127, 130, 132, 137
poetry, 12, 15, 17, 22–23, 49–50, 53–55, 57, 61, 65, 67–70, 72, 75, 99, 106, 114–19, 137, 144, 146–48, 150, 157–60, 163–65, 167, 170, 172
polylogue, 119, 156–60, 172
Possessions, 2, 6, 7–9, 13, 26, 31, 33, 38–40, 81, 124, 129, 139, 141
postmodernity, 16, 27, 96, 109, 124, 172
Poussin, Nicolas, 48

power, 14, 32–33, 35, 37–38, 44, 58, 61–70, 73, 76–77, 81, 85, 90, 104, 106–9, 117, 147, 150, 152, 167
Powers of Horror, 2, 25, 78, 97, 153
pregnancy. *See* mother
Proust, Marcel, 10, 76, 108, 120, 143–44, 168
psychoanalysis, 1–6, 8, 10–19, 21, 23–27, 34, 38, 41–43, 45–46, 48, 51, 53, 55, 57, 72–74, 78, 81, 83, 89–90, 92, 97, 108–9, 113–19, 121–25, 127, 130, 132–33, 135–36, 141, 147, 155, 161, 166–67, 169
psychosis, 23, 49, 87–88, 121, 128, 136

Raoul, Valerie, 13, 14, 25, 26
rationalism, 23, 49, 73, 96–99, 101, 105, 109
referent, 46, 97, 107, 132, 163
religion, 20, 22, 27, 33, 39, 61, 77, 102, 104–5, 107, 122, 150, 161–62; Catholicism, 47, 50–51, 54, 84–85, 130, 136; Christ, 47, 50, 52, 66, 70–72, 77, 85, 91–93, 105, 107, 129, 131–32, 136–37; Christianity, 47, 72, 77–78, 84, 93, 100, 102–4, 109, 130–31, 133; Crusades, 87, 98, 100, 102, 104, 131, 151–54; Hebrew Bible, 71, 77; Judaism, 59, 96, 102, 106, 127, 132–33; Orthodox Church, 3, 50, 77, 84–85, 87, 102–3, 109, 130, 132–33, 136, 145; Taoism, 102
Renaissance, 48, 91, 103
repression, 36, 87, 89, 99, 103, 106, 115–16, 120, 137, 147, 153
revolt, 5, 8, 21, 24, 33, 38, 41, 43–44, 78, 82–82, 87–88, 92–93, 96, 155–56, 160, 162, 167
Revolution in Poetic Language, 1, 96, 119, 146
Ricoeur, Paul, 168–69
Rimbaud, Arthur, 41
Robbe-Grillet, Alain, 16
Rodríguez, Richard, 27
roman à clef, 5, 10, 14–17, 26
roman noir, 7, 26, 121, 123
romance, 104–5
Romanticism, 117, 127
Rome, 22, 45, 52–55, 58, 63, 65, 68, 76, 103, 150, 162. *See also* Italy
Rose, Jacqueline, 45, 46
Roth, Philip, 9
Rothko, Mark, 48
Rousseau, Jean-Jacques, 41, 126, 134

sacrifice, 20, 22, 57–59, 61–62, 64–65, 67–78, 135
Sade, Marquis de, 158
sadism, 51
sadomasochism, 6, 82
Samurai, The, 1, 3–6, 9–11, 14–15, 17, 25–27, 45–46, 51, 54, 114, 118, 143, 146, 149, 151, 155
Sappho, 104, 106
Santa Varvara, 6, 8, 22, 31–35, 38–41, 53–55, 57–72, 76–77, 80–81, 84–85, 88, 90, 98, 105, 129–30, 139, 149–51, 153
Sartre, Jean-Paul, 132, 143
Saussure, Ferdinand de, 134
scapegoating, 22, 57–59, 61–65, 66–73, 77
self, 13–17, 19, 21, 25, 27, 31, 33, 38, 68, 83–84, 87, 113–15, 117–21, 123, 137, 166, 171, 173. *See also* subjectivity
Séméiotiké: Research Toward a Semanalysis, 2, 119, 145, 154
semiotic, 2, 13, 17, 22, 24–25, 35, 45–47, 49, 51–53, 101, 107, 114, 134–35, 137–38, 147, 149, 157–58
Sense and Non-Sense of Revolt, 32, 168
September 11, 2001 attacks, 8, 12
Severed Head, The: Capital Visions, 82, 86, 131, 138–39
severed heads, 19, 91. *See also* decapitation
Shakespeare, William, 146, 160; *Romeo and Juliet*, 160
Shoah, 19. *See also* Holocaust
Showalter, Elaine, 9, 26

signification, 8, 13, 17, 22, 24–25, 32, 35, 49, 86, 96, 107, 114, 117, 122, 128, 147–48, 157, 172
signified, 46, 107
signifier, 31, 35–36, 46, 49, 54, 97, 99, 107, 129, 138, 144–45, 148, 158
simulacrum, 128, 132, 137
skulls, 22, 79, 82, 91
socialism, 5
society of the icon, 22, 79, 87, 92. *See also* icon
society of the spectacle, 13, 21–24, 31–32, 34–37, 41, 80–81, 83–85, 87–90, 92, 98, 109, 132, 134, 137, 139–40, 144, 150, 169. *See also* Debord, Guy; spectacle
spectacle, 31–42, 69, 77, 80, 82–84, 89–92, 162, 172
Spivak, Gayatri Chakravorty, 145
Sollers, Philippe, 9, 26, 157–59, 163–64, 166; *H*, 157–58, 163–64, 171–72
specular, 36–37, 127, 148
St. Augustine, 84, 101–2, 109
St. Teresa, 149, 173
"Stabat Mater," 45, 49–51, 100, 109
stereotypes, 45, 53, 59, 61, 63, 71, 165
Stoyanov, Tzvetan, 143, 146
Strangers to Ourselves, 25
subjectivity, 12, 16, 19, 24–25, 33–38, 49, 55, 76, 78, 81–82, 87–89, 91–93, 97, 102, 107, 114, 117–20, 124, 127–28, 147, 149–50, 157–58, 162, 168–71, 173. *See also* intersubjectivity; self
sublimation, 39, 81, 89, 115–21, 123
Surrealism, 130, 141, 161. *See also* avant-garde; Dada
symbolic, 6, 13, 15, 24, 35, 37, 40, 44, 46–47, 49, 51, 53, 71–72, 84, 89, 96–101, 103–7, 119, 133, 135–38, 144, 147, 149, 157–59

Tales of Love, 25, 70–71, 160
Tel Quel, 113
Thanatos, 21, 92
Tibullus, Albius, 22, 53–54, 57–58, 64–65, 67–72, 75
time, 42, 44, 74, 80, 83, 99, 101, 108, 117, 160
Todorov, Tzvetan, 96–97, 101
Tolstoy, Leo, 129
transference, 3, 12, 74, 78, 118, 122–23, 170
translation, 8, 13–14, 26, 36, 70, 81, 101, 123, 126, 144–47, 172–73
trauma, 12–13, 74, 89, 133, 135, 159, 161

Ulysses, 107, 109
unconscious, 3–4, 8, 13, 15, 23, 38, 46, 80, 83, 114–15, 118, 120, 123–25, 158, 163, 168, 172
United States of America, 8, 13, 54, 169
utopia, 5, 117, 147, 151–53, 170

Venus, 48
violence, 6, 7, 13, 22–23, 31, 33–35, 40–42, 46, 54, 57–74, 76–77, 81, 98–99, 102, 105, 121, 125, 134–36, 139–40, 157, 159, 167–68
Virgin Mary, 47–52, 100, 109, 170
Voltaire, 51, 148

Western Europe, 9, 23, 50, 95, 101–3, 107, 130
wolves, 34, 38, 42, 52–55, 58–60, 62–67, 72
"Women's Time," 108
writing, 1–5, 7–8, 11–27, 39, 41–43, 45–49, 51–55, 61, 63, 67, 69–71, 81–82, 91, 95–96, 102–6, 109, 113–21, 123–28, 130, 136–40, 144–47, 149–53, 155–68, 171–73

Yeats, W. B., 90